CONTEMPORARY IRISH SOCIETY
An Introduction

1, 10, 11, 12, 15

Michel Peillon

———※———

CONTEMPORARY IRISH SOCIETY

An Introduction

GILL AND MACMILLAN

First published 1982 by
Gill and Macmillan Ltd
Goldenbridge
Dublin 8
with associated companies in
London, New York, Delhi, Hong Kong,
Johannesburg, Lagos, Melbourne,
Singapore, Tokyo

7171 1141 5

Origination by Healyset, Dublin
Printed in Great Britain by
Biddles Ltd, Guildford and King's Lynn

Contents

ACKNOWLEDGMENTS

Professors Georges Balandier and René Fréchet and Dr John Whyte all read the book and their encouragement was very welcome. Professor Conor Ward commented on an early version and his advice was most helpful.

The book was originally written in my native French and was translated by Malachy O'Higgins.

I am also grateful to Maureen Redmond who had the difficult task of deciphering the manuscript.

Finally, my thanks to Saint Patrick's College, Maynooth, for granting me the sabbatical leave that made this book possible.

A NOTE ON REFERENCES

References are indicated parenthetically in the text. *Italic* numbers refer to items in the bibliography. Where additional information, such as a page number, a table number, or — in the case of a newspaper or journal — a date of issue are felt to be necessary, it is given in roman type.

Introduction

Ireland occupies a singular place among the nations, and this singularity manifests itself in various ways. Demographic, economic and social statistics would seem to place Ireland somewhere between countries of the third world and the industrialised countries. The birth rate in Ireland, for example, is much lower than in most developing countries, but much greater than in industrialised countries. A poor relation within the European Economic Community, lagging behind its partners, Ireland enjoys a standard of living which is, however, incomparably better than that of third world countries. Half way between the developed countries and those which are striving, with increasing difficulty, to industrialise, Ireland tends to defy classification. At one time studies of Ireland focused upon how this former colonial society had succeeded, more or less, in raising itself into the ranks of the industrialised countries, having gained independence decades before the world-wide tide of decolonisation. However, it is futile to attempt to situate Ireland somewhere along a scale of modernisation, as if every society were obliged to pass through certain necessary stages and follow a predetermined line of development. Ireland is undoubtedly developing and changing at a rapid pace but this change and development should not be expected to conform to any given pattern. When Ireland takes its industrialised partners as a model of development it is manifesting a dependence on an example which may well have lost its relevance. In any event to catalogue social changes in Ireland under the single label of *modernisation* does not get us very far. The real question does not concern the transition from the traditional to the modern, but rather the model of modernity itself which Ireland assumes, and, more concretely, the identification of the forces and struggles through which each strives to direct and control the process of modernisation.

What one observes in Ireland is not so much transition as a profound mutation, and it is this that makes difficult the task of describing and giving an overall picture of Irish society. Industrialisation has radically changed the whole social structure of the country including that of rural society. The rapid urbanisation which has engulfed Dublin is almost of crisis proportions. Traditional attitudes and behaviour – such as obsequious obedience to the clergy and automatic allegiance to the Catholic Church – are being eroded. The near-unanimity with which the population of the Republic professes the Catholic faith might well, in fact, hide a delicate

1

state of coexistence between conflicting types of religious responses and a deep ambiguity at the heart of the Irish religious phenomenon. Traditional religious behaviour is nowadays in competition with other modes of religious observance. On the other hand, and in a more general way, numerous facets of traditional Irish society, far from being on the point of disappearance, are being given a new lease of life and are being mobilised to stem the tide of encroaching modernisation. Many complex currents indeed are to be discerned in the mutation of Irish society.

Neither must it be forgotten, as we strive to identify the most salient characteristics of social life in Ireland, that many Irish people refuse to identify the Republic as the Irish nation for as long as the six counties of Northern Ireland continue to remain part of the United Kingdom. After more than half a century of independence a majority of the Southern Irish still proclaim their ambition to see a united Ireland. At the same time they adjust remarkably well to the *de facto* division of the country, and many would regard with disquiet any actual unification of North and South. In the event, the partition of Ireland continues to play a preponderant role in the internal social and political life not only of Northern Ireland but of the Republic as well.

Ireland, then, is a society of contrasts and is defined by these contrasts. Most striking is that between rich and poor. A further contrast may be observed between a stable, developing Republic and a Northern Ireland convulsed by bitterness and violence. There is also a striking contrast not so much between tradition and novelty as between the pace and rhythm of change from one sector of Irish society to the other; as if each sector, developing at its own pace, followed a logic of its own and ignored all other sectors. These different rhythms of change, and the contrasts which they in turn engender, create numerous gaps and tensions within Irish society, such as that between ideology on the one hand and economic practice on the other, which we shall have occasion to examine. Ireland also seems to be simultaneously open and closed to outside influences. On one hand she exists within a wide-ranging network of economic exchange. Within range of the British mass media — British newspapers are circulated in Ireland and British television is received in many Irish homes — Ireland has adopted many models of behaviour from across the channel. A long tradition of emigration has created many close links between Ireland and countries like the United States, Britain and even Australia so that many Irish people feel that culturally they are part of the English-speaking world. On the other hand Ireland withdraws into itself, mistrusts and often censors influences from outside, and retires behind a cultural identity that it finds more and more difficult to define. Ireland is also a country of stark class contrasts, which reveal themselves not only in differences of status but also in differences of behaviour. Finally, and perhaps most strikingly, Ireland refuses to belong to any military alliance and professes a policy of neutrality in relation to all power blocs; in reality she is totally dependant on the western bloc and exists within a network of power relations which gives her very little control of her own destiny. Nevertheless, beyond these contrasts and oppositions and in spite of the turmoil which it is going through, Irish society preserves its calm. It continues to function regularly and despite everything appears as a model of parliamentary democracy. The institutions of the Republic are facing no serious threat; from the State to the family, via the Church and schools, the traditional pillars of Irish society are showing no signs of weakening – even though their significance might be undergoing a change. Not even the fragmentation of political life seems to affect the workings of State institutions – another aspect of Irish society that we shall later have occasion to study.

The Irish Republic is singular in other important respects, which, though stereotyped, are none the less real. Late marriage is very common and many Irish never marry at all. The Catholic Church still plays an influential role in Irish society, though the conclusions to be drawn from this phenomenon are often difficult to define. The dominant ideology expresses itself both in nationalist rhetoric and in a desire to preserve a highly idealised rural past. This looking backwards to an idealised past is very likely one expression of resistance to a modernisation imposed by outside constraints, and the search for an Irish identity in the past can be seen as a desperate attempt at national self-definition, and an effort to regain control of Irish destinies.

These are the themes that, in essence, will form the focus of this book. But the analysis undertaken by the book will not be content to describe. It will attempt to dig beneath the surface, to examine the foundations of Irish society as well as its dynamic. In doing so it sets itself a double task. In the first instance it will examine the statistics accumulated to date concerning the Republic of Ireland; it will look at the questions posed by numerous studies and the answers which they gave to them. Thus it touches upon economic, political and demographic as well as sociological issues. But as well as surveying these fields it will attempt to analyse, explain, interpret and put into perspective all those elements which have up to now remained disparate. The study is also a critical one in that it sets out to reveal what many would prefer to remain hidden, to challenge official interpretations of Irish society and to project an alternative one, to cast light on little known or hidden aspects of Irish life. While acknowledging the weight of those factors contending to determine the fate of Ireland, this study rejects the notion that they are irresistible. By setting out to show that Ireland is not at the mercy of the various influences to which she is exposed, the book sets itself the task of charting and even extending the field of possibilities open to Ireland; of showing that Ireland's future is not determined in advance, that she may choose between alternative models for the future.

Part one of the work attempts to sketch a portrait of Irish society, and

3

focusses on those of its characteristics which seem most persistent and most significant. This outline of the social framework is centred on the phenomenon of social differentiation and it attempts to discern the lines along which Irish society is divided. These lines of social different-iation reveal contrasts in behaviour and attitudes, and demarcate different groups of individuals from each other. They do not necessarily designate inequality as between groups although social differentiation is undoubted-ly underwritten by hierarchies of all sorts. The picture of social different-iation presented in part one is in fact severely limited in that it considers only the socio-professional categories. This is simply because of the pre-dominance of this line of differentiation over all the others, though this would doubtless have to be proved empirically. Such a demonstration would be inappropriate in this context: suffice it to say that it would involve measuring the relative importance of diverse lines of social dif-ferentiation.

The social framework thus outlined gives a static summary of Irish society and constitutes a point of departure for studying the line-up of forces which fashion this society. The social particularisms which we have noted often lead to degrees of solidarity within groups, but they are not sufficient to designate social class. Part two of the work seeks to discern the major social forces at work in the Republic and to reconstruct their dynamic, that is to say, the logic of their actions. The index of the exist-ence of such forces is to be found not only in their capacity for collective action but more importantly in the influence they have in the shaping of Ireland's future. Such capacity reveals itself in collective actions which derive from what I choose to call a social project.

The passage from social category to collective force is not automatic. Diverse factors hinder or encourage this transition. The so-called conservat-ism of the Irish working class has often been remarked upon, to be explained in terms of a profound attachment to rural life, or the pre-dominance of the national question on the political scene to the exclusion of the social one, the influence of religion in exalting universal solidarity and an abstract consensus, the safety-valve of emigration, or the weakness of capitalism itself in Ireland. But all these explanations miss the mark, since it is necessary to distinguish between the factors which impede or encourage the development of a group reality — what is traditionally called class-consciousness — and the factors which determine the orientation which collective action takes — its radical or moderate character, for example. The two sets of factors could not coincide unless one held that the working class only became a group capable of action by adopting a revolutionary line. To assimilate the different factors in this way would fly in the face of the facts, since the Irish working class displays a remark-able capacity for collective action without ever embracing a radical orient-ation. If one thing is sure, it is the ability of the working class to make its presence felt in the Republic of Ireland.

4

Neither can one ignore the Irish entrepreneurial class, an important pivot in the Irish social structure. It is generally supposed that the bourgeoisie is characterised by a high level of cohesion, and that this cohesion arises from the fear of opposing social forces, since only fear could persuade the bourgeoisie to transcend its competing interests. Others suppose, equally erroneously, that the bourgeoisie has no need to organise itself since the State emanates from it. In any event it is assumed that the bourgeoisie speaks with one voice. A social class which succeeds in uniting its members in a collective show of force increases the power of the group and puts it in a position of strength. The unity of the bourgeoisie as a class thus raises an important question, which has not received sufficient attention, at least in Ireland. Does the bourgeoisie propose to uphold a social project? Is it capable of coherent collective action?

It has often been said that the farmers hardly constitute a social force, that their way of life isolates them culturally and politically, that distance and lack of social interaction between them hinder the emergence of class-consciousness. Local and regional allegiances, it is held, also work against widespread feelings of solidarity. In brief, the conventional view is that farmers can never act as a class except when they are organised and led by social categories from outside the rural environment. But in recent years these factors have lost much of their relevance, and farmers in Ireland have on many occasions asserted their collective will as a social class well capable of looking after itself. In contrast, professional groups such as office-workers, the petite-bourgeoisie and the liberal professions have failed to emerge as collective forces, though the reason why is not clear. But no matter. The fact remains that certain social classes emerge and act collectively to achieve certain ends. They participate in the shaping of society and stake their claim in Ireland's future.

Lastly, the social classes are not the only forces capable of shaping the destiny of Ireland, or the only groups capable of acting collectively in the furtherance of a social project. One must ask whether the Catholic Church and the nationalist gaelic movement constitute such forces, and whether they contribute significantly to the shaping of Irish society. Part two of the book endeavours to point to the major social forces in Ireland and to understand their dynamic, that is to say, the logic of their collective actions.

Part three focusses on the relations and interactions between the different social forces mentioned, and the different levels of activity on which they operate. The analysis of political life and of economic and ideological activity involves us deeply in the internal workings of Irish society. Part three also pays close attention to the presence of the State in Irish society, to the manner in which the State, a special form of collective action, links up with the main social forces. Besides the very specific roles undertaken by the State in Ireland, it also fulfils universal functions. But it is less important to establish a classification of the functions performed by the State than to examine the manner in which the State performs these functions. Only this will enable us to trace the complicated and unstable network of links between the State and society. The nature of the State's presence in society is connected with the manner in which it presents itself in the functional dialectics of conflict and integration, of coherence and incoherence, of unity and diversity, of continuity and change, and above all how it copes with these. This third part, I believe, clarifies the relationship between the State and society: it is partly by 'managing' society, in working on it and on itself that the State simultaneously inserts itself in society and dominates it, manifesting its unity and intensifying its tensions. Irish society shapes itself through the State. In the process it is sometimes subject to determining social constraints, at other times it transcends them, but more often than either it takes them in hand and manipulates them towards its own ends. How does society in Ireland 'make' itself? How does it shape its future? These are the questions that this study sets out to answer.

PART ONE

THE SOCIAL FRAMEWORK

1

The Farmers

In the nineteenth century land in Ireland was owned by a small group of landlords, army officers, and wealthy notables. In the 1870s a thousand or so of these held estates, some of them of fabulous extent. The Marquis of Donegal owned an estate of 162,961 acres, while that of the Marquis of Conyngham measured 156,976 acres (*44*). These landlords rarely became involved in the running of their estates, preferring to spend their time in England. They rented out their land to middlemen, themselves landed gentry or wealthy merchants, whose only interest was in gathering rents. Gradually these middlemen were replaced by more docile estate agents, who belonged to the minor gentry or to the officer or merchant classes, and were not slow to assume the trappings of landlord status. Their responsibilities did not go beyond the drafting of leases, the calling in of rents, and those decisions involving investments and improvements in the estate. The tenants for their part entered into agreements with agricultural labourers, whose labour they assured by sub-leasing to them small cottages and strips of land for the cultivation of potatoes. Finally, numbers of agricultural labourers, attached to no farm, undertook piece work on an irregular and seasonal basis. Hired from day to day they often tilled conacre land from year to year or tended small herds of milch cows, with little hope of any but the most precarious existence (*46*).

No aspect of local life escaped the influence of the landlords, who closely supervised the workings of the local county council, and whose responsibility it was to raise taxes, and appoint administrators of hospitals and workhouses. Those who got themselves elected as members of parliament at Westminster were invariably recruited from among this ascendancy class, as it came to be known. It was these same people who set the tone and fixed the canons of good taste at social gatherings in Dublin Castle and elsewhere. (For an amusing description of the life-style of the gentry see Somerville & Ross: *Experience of an Irish R.M.*) But towards the end of the century the Land War had already undermined their hegemony, and embittered relations between the ascendancy and tenant classes had begun to poison their lives. Many sold off parcels of their already mortgaged lands to finance their lives of idleness across the channel. Several acts of parliament, passed under pressure of the agrarian unrest, had further curtailed their power, since the new legislation protected tenants against arbitrary eviction. During this period the landed gentry also lost their hold over local government in Ireland and even though they were still entitled to seats on the county councils, they wielded much less influence than before. The rebirth of Irish separatism and the Gaelic revival completed the alienation of the landlords, whose loyalty to the British crown remained firm: it was in the nature of things that they should take their stand against the independence movement, and against all attempts to drive a wedge between Ireland and Britain (*138*).

In this way the Anglo-Irish ascendancy gradually lost its economic and political supremacy in the country. It held aloof from the War of Independence and continued to a great extent to ignore the existence of the Free State after 1922. Those who remained in the country withdrew into a closed introverted world. Shorn of economic and political power they nevertheless re-emerged as a status group, with a strongly felt sense of their own superiority and determined to cling to their distinctive life-style and code of behaviour. Life carried on for these internal emigrés, interrupted only by golf and bridge, sustained by a strongly-felt affinity for the old country. British regimental flags continued to hang in Protestant churches, Sunday services included prayers for the royal family, children were often sent to English preparatory and public schools. Appearances continued to be kept up, though their substance was rapidly evaporating, 'Politically the Anglo-Irish had indeed effaced themselves but they had retained their predominance and much of their arrogance', according to one of their more lucid members (*92*, 146). They clung to vanished glories as their numbers continued to decline. With the passage of time, however, many of the Anglo-Irish came to terms with the new society, entering the professions and playing an important role in the business world. Their formerly exclusive class opened its doors to the more 'acceptable' Catholics of the new rising middle class. In this way the old ascendancy class became reconciled to the new order and rubbed shoulders, in their golf and sailing clubs, with the new middle and professional native Irish class.

The Anglo-Irish ascendancy has not entirely disappeared, but its size is difficult to gauge. Many country parishes have their 'gentleman' living in his remote mansion. Some control fishing rights on rivers and lakes, and often possess a title or British army rank of some sort — the British army was a traditional refuge for the younger sons of the ascendancy family (*115*).

Many examples are to be found in nineteenth-century novels of the spendthrift extravagance of the landed gentry and the way in which they dissipated prodigious fortunes in the midst of the destitution prevailing around them. The novels bring back to life 'hard-riding country gentle-men' (Yeats' phrase) whose wealth conferred power and independence to behave as they wished. A more attractive landlord occasionally appears in these novels but even then his immersion in hobbies such as archaeology or botany, while attesting to his independence, also suggests a lack of contact with the world around him. Nevertheless the changing role of the landlord in Irish society is often reflected in these same books. A note of sadness creeps in at the spectacle of the landlord in his remote run-down estate, struggling to keep his house in order, to hold on to his trusted servants, to keep his head up in a sea of debt and to preserve his birthright against all the odds. Nostalgia becomes the dominant note in the Anglo-Irish temper as their world crumbles and vanishes, through old age, child-lessness, lack of vitality or faith in the future. All the more so when, like undeparted ghosts, they witness the arrival of caricatures of themselves to take their place, successful entrepreneurs only too eager to ape the life-style of the gentry.

The Farmers

The land question, which nourished and exalted the nationalist struggle, dominated the whole second half of the nineteenth century. It took incessant agitation, relentless pressure from the Land League, the ferocity of the Land War, a serious threat to British sovereignty in Ireland, and numerous acts of parliament before tenants were enabled to buy out their land, so that Irish land at last passed from the hands of the landlords into the hands of those who worked it. But the transformation, when it came, was a radical one. In 1870 only 3 per cent of those who worked the land owned it, whereas in 1921 the figure reached 64 per cent. By 1923 the agrarian revolution was complete and the new farming class was to be the backbone of the newly established Free State.

By the turn of the century, then, the violent peasants had been trans-formed into a community of small farmers, clinging to their newly acquired lands and property rights. But the period also marks the begin-ning of their decline (56). From then on the number of farmers in Ireland began to fall — at both ends of the scale: a sharp decrease is registered in the number of farms of thirty acres or less, as well as in the number of large farms. The increase in the number of medium-sized farms, however, failed to redress the balance. The progressive elimination of small farms is the natural result of developments in agriculture and the raising of the commercial viability threshold from thirty acres in 1920 to fifty acres at the present time — varying according to the fertility of the land and the type of cultivation. The consolidation of farms, a necessary condition of economic viability, thus places small farmers in a precarious position. Many of them seek employment in the locality to supplement their income from the farm, which they continue to work: in 1976 22 per cent of Irish farmers were working part-time on their farms (43). In the poorer parts small farmers and relatives receive unemployment benefits during the winter months (42, 135). Moreover, the number of dependents (brothers, sisters, sons, daughters) who might help with the running of the farm dropped sharply from 264,094 in 1926 to 52,921 in 1971, thus

11

contributing to a massive rural exodus (235).

Agriculture is often referred to as Ireland's principal national resource, still offering many possibilities for growth. But this growth, though hailed for a long time, has so far failed to materialise. Many farmers, reluctant to modernise their farms, continue to cling to traditional techniques and indeed have been offered little incentive to do otherwise. Modernisation would undoubtedly require land reform, always a difficult, delicate business, since increased agricultural productivity can only be achieved on large farms. Mechanisation, crop specialisation, flexibility of response to a fluctuating market – in short, everything that is meant by viability and development potential – cannot easily be achieved by small-scale farming. The characteristics of the most successful farmers are rarely found among small farmers: willingness to borrow, high educational level, involvement in agricultural organisations, and so on (66). The policy of modernisation backed by successive governments is aimed at increased agricultural productivity and at the same time at guaranteeing a decent standard of living for farmers; it encourages land reorganisation, facilitates productive investment, promotes innovation as well as education in up-to-date farming methods. But this policy is a costly one in social terms, involving as it does the elimination of small farmers and a significant overall drop in the number of farms, while the possibility of reabsorption remains severely limited.

The Irish co-operative movement offers other possibilities for development but the small farmers have not availed of it to any significant degree. The co-operatives – of which there are many – only intervene at the post-production stage (the creameries, for example, which treat, condition, and distribute milk), or in the purchasing of equipment (12). They fail whenever they seem to pose a threat to the independence of the farmer, or seem to interfere in the running of the farm. Curiously, those most in favour of the efforts of the co-operatives appear to be those already involved in farming organisations, and the better educated farmers – in other words those who in all probability have the least need of them (118). This resistance among small farmers to what they see as a threat to their independence blocks the way to what for many of them offers the only possibility for development.

The Traditional View of Rural Ireland

Arensberg and Kimball, in the 1930s, painted a picture of a tradition-based Irish society composed of parish communities and small family farms (3). Each farm reflected a uniform way of life and of organising the daily routine. The father, the head of the household, worked in the fields, repaired the farm buildings and took care of all transactions on the local cattle market. But, though feared and respected, he kept aloof from the more intimate aspects of family life. He often spent his evenings out in the company of his friends. He had little contact with his daughters but worked side by side with his sons on the farm, passing on to them his knowledge of the land. In times of urgency his wife would be called upon to help in the fields; she also milked the cows, fed the animals and sold the produce of the farmyard or the garden. But, most importantly, she kept house, cooking, washing, cleaning, sowing, darning. Important decisions were not taken by her but she exerted preponderant influence in everything concerning the upbringing of the children, marriages, and so on. Her closeness to her daughters, who helped her with the housework, and to her sons, to whom she was profoundly attached, forged emotional links which made her indirect influence in rural Ireland decisive. On the other hand, the sons, who remained 'lads' as long as they lived on the farm subordinate to their fathers, played no part whatever in decisions affecting the farm. Occasionally they hired themselves out as farm labourers in the locality to supplement the family income. In any event, marrying, as they did, very late, the 'lads' led lives unencumbered by responsibility.

The rural community at this stage is also depicted as forming a closely knit network of families, linked by numerous kinship ties as well as by ties of neighbourly obligation. Mutual help, which acted as a stimulus to solidarity, was to be seen at work – in harnessing ploughs, the lending of equipment, saving hay or cutting turf – as well as in social life, family gatherings, and the general obligation to keep one's door permanently open to visitors. This high degree of social integration fostered intense parish rivalries, which exploded from time to time on occasions of inter-parish hurling or football matches. This account probably exaggerates the integration of the Irish countryside. Patrick Kavanagh, who grew up on a small farm in Monaghan more or less during the same period, paints a different picture in *The Green Fool* when he speaks of the virtues of 'an amount of vicious neighbourly hatred to keep us awake'. According to Kavanagh, neighbourly help was very much a matter of close reciprocal dependence and obligations which time and again led to inter-family feuding.

Since the Great Famine (1845–9) farmers no longer divide the land among their sons, and only one son inherits on the death of the father. This practice, which arose from the strict necessity to avoid further subdivision of already diminished farms, has had a profound effect on the demographic pattern of rural Ireland. A farm could usually support only one family, sons and daughters leaving as soon as they married. In other words, the sons and daughters faced the choice of either leaving the farm or remaining single. Only one son could inherit: he usually took over the farm at a relatively mature age, since the father rarely stepped down before dying or at least reaching an advanced age. The new farmer, fixed in his bachelor ways, was unlikely to find many marriageable girls in the vicinity, since they had long since emigrated. These factors explain why the average marriage age for men was almost 36 in 1946 and was still as

13

high as 31−2 in 1969. Moreover, marriage was traditionally regarded as a business arrangement between families, in which the integrity of the farm and the family's social status were at stake. Cultural norms reinforced the tendency to late marriage; the 'normal' age for marriage for 'boys' being 35, for 'girls' 25−30. Marriage, when it came, was greeted with resignation rather than joy by the men, marking as it did an end to bachelor carousing (from which women were strictly excluded). Further, not only late marriages but permanent bachelorhood have profoundly influenced the demographic pattern of Irish rural life, and even today 40 per cent of farmers never marry (119, 222). Late marriages, permanent bachelorhood, and emigration of the young contributed to the creation of a serious imbalance in the population structure of rural Ireland, with a preponderance of old people. In 1961 more than a quarter of farmers were over 65, a state of affairs which fostered inertia, blind adherence to traditional values and stubborn resistance to change (14, 146d). On the other hand the conjunction of late marriages and bachelorhood meant that many farmers did not produce heirs. The farm disappeared on the death of the owner; it was sold and divided up by neighbours wishing to increase their holdings.

Those farmers who did marry produced large families − the average family size in this category was six children, a fertility rate only equalled by the urban working class (222, table 4). Everything encouraged large families in the country: a traditional desire to perpetuate the family line, a desire on the part of parents to secure their old age, an insistence on the procreative role of the woman, who in turn exerted her influence on the community through her children, particularly her sons. The emphasis on female fertility curiously went hand in hand with a rigid puritan morality which proclaimed sexual relations, forbidden outside marriage, to have a strictly procreative function. Only one son could hope to take over the farm, and one daughter was likely to marry locally; the others emigrated to different places such as the United States or Australia, or else to join the Irish community in Britain (81). Daughters thus tended to leave the family home younger, but tended not to travel as far, often no further than the nearest town, or Dublin, or took the boat to England. The extreme subordination of girls and women in the countryside and the lack of appeal of farm life were an added incentive to them to seek out a new life in the cities and towns. Only family obligations held them back, just as the same obligations often brought them home: looking after a widowed father, or aged parents, or even a bachelor brother. In any event emigrants invariably kept in contact with their families, and were on hand in times of difficulty (82, 208). But the flight from the land, often intensified when technological changes (such as were caused by the switch from tillage to grazing) led to alterations in demands for farm labour (119). The progressive elimination of small farms also added to emigration. On the other hand, emigration paradoxically helped to prop up small farms since emigrants sent home regular remittances to supplement income from the farm.

One final characteristic completes this picture of life on a small Irish farm. John Messenger, in studying a particularly remote rural community, detected an element of magic in the Catholic religious practices and attitudes of the people (150). According to Messenger, ritual obligations were seen as affording direct access to salvation, and the saints were invoked on account of powers attributed to them on earth. Superstitious traditions, of pre-Christian derivation, enshrined certain 'holy places', claimed to foretell the future, promoted fear of spirits and ghosts and even certain attenuated forms of witchcraft. It is not certain whether such beliefs and practices were widespread but in any event religion in rural Ireland is permeated by a strong tendency to evoke its direct intervention in the affairs of this world. Moreover, rural Catholicism is characterised by rigid puritanism in sexual matters, whose origins have often been the subject of debate. Does it originate in the clergy, who, formed in Maynooth with its allegedly strong jansenist tradition, pass on its influence to their docile flocks? Other researchers, more conscious of social and historical forces, see in rural puritanism a reaction to the new conditions in Ireland after the Famine. According to this view, insistence on sexual morality helped people to regulate their behaviour and give stability to life in a community where a large proportion of members were not married either because they were waiting to emigrate or because circumstances made it impossible to marry for the time being. In this way the puritanism of Irish Catholicism was a response to a *de facto* situation in which the clergy were actually obliged to interpret in a rigid fashion the existing norms of sexual morality (34, 119).

An Updated Picture of Rural Ireland

Recent sociological studies have set out to update the traditional, stereotyped view of rural Ireland. It is by no means certain that rural life in Ireland ever resembled the above portrait and, whatever the case, it is true that the situation has changed radically since Arensberg and Kimball carried out their research.

In *The Green Fool*, Patrick Kavanagh, no doubt recalling his youth, has one of his characters say: 'I despised learning. What good is grammar to a man who has to work with spade and shovel?' This distrust of farmers for education has disappeared and they now willingly send their children to school. Many of those who are not destined for work on the farm go to secondary school. Until recently, the vocational schools did not attract many of these, which suggests that farmers regard manual labour as a socially inferior activity. Or, more simply, perhaps this merely reflects the fact that there are few vocational schools in the countryside. In any event, country parents nowadays try to equip their children (especially their daughters) for the future, whether this is to be in Ireland or as emigrants (*243c*). But these favourable attitudes towards education must not be exaggerated, and even within the one family, a diversity of educational standards is often to be found, where certain children drop out of school after primary level, and others carry on (*80*). But statistics nevertheless show that farmers are favourably disposed towards school since in the mid-60s this category was well represented in secondary schools and, during the same period, one farmer's son or daughter out of twenty-seven attended university (*160, 243c*).

The modern Irish rural family differs greatly from that painted by Arensberg and Kimball — which was patriarchal, authoritarian, and organised according to a precise division of labour. In fact, recent research has shown that rural Ireland contains a great diversity of family types, from the traditional type to more democratic families in which parents share the housework, both participating in decision-making, and avoiding stereotyped sexual roles (*84*). The view of an integrated, harmonious rural community where neighbours are often cousins no longer holds true either. The extended family no longer ensures close day-to-day co-operation and only exceptional family events, such as christenings, marriages and funerals, bring families together. Not that ties have loosened, since more efficient transport, and particularly the spread of the car, greatly facilitates contact. Family obligations still impose their constraints and parents still count on their children to look after them in their old age. The neighbourhood, in which daily co-operation ensured reciprocity of interests, has also changed character. The mechanisation of agriculture has probably destroyed the balance of mutual dependence. The introduction of tractors decreased the need for outside help and introduced very marked differentiations of status within the community between those who own tractors and those who do not. Radio, television, and rapid access to nearby towns have also had their effect on local community life, and families visit each other less regularly. Leisure has become more individualised, and relations between neighbours less intense. Finally, the different responses to modernity and to the technology and status symbols deriving from it have divided the rural community along clearly visible social and cultural lines (*82*).

One study of village life in the West of Ireland illustrates dramatically the rupture of traditional rural communities (*14*) Brody observes the elimination of help among neighbours, the preponderance of old people, the departure of the young, in particular the young women who do not intend to marry in the village; he reveals the isolation of many farmers, and the demoralisation to which they succumb, which is reflected by their high level of mental ill-health and alcoholism. The villagers are divided into those who, content with traditional ways, do not envisage leaving, and all the others who are impatient to get away. Many farmers, under-employed on their small farms, only manage thanks to remittances sent regularly by relations abroad. This dependence on the outside world, which does nothing to stimulate co-operation and gives no incentive for close contacts, adds to the depression of this group.

Emigration in the past was regarded as a sad necessity, an uprooting and a painful family separation. The departure was celebrated in wake fashion: the family would stay up all night, the neighbours would pay a visit, and would be offered food and drink. Today young people do not leave home out of necessity and a departure is not regarded like a bereavement. The isolation and boredom of life in remote areas competes poorly with the attractions of urban life, which promises more freedom and unlimited possibilities for social life. The erosion of self-confidence among country people and their lack of conviction concerning the advantages of country life have modified attitudes towards emigration.

But perhaps these considerations only apply to the remotest country areas of Ireland. A study carried out at the same time in Co. Cavan showed that many of those young people who envisaged emigrating would have preferred not to (*81*). It is also true that in the 1970s a new dynamism has been injected into the countryside, and an unexpected prosperity has given a new lease of life to rural communities, with the benefits accruing from Ireland's accession to the European Economic Community (EEC). However, we should be guarded in our optimism, since this prosperity may well turn out to be a temporary reprieve for many Irish farmers, all of whom have not benefited from the EEC to the same degree. Perhaps the new vigour of Irish rural life will even serve to deepen already existing divisions and intensify the dualism which characterises agriculture in Ireland (*272*).

Two Farmer Classes?

Arensberg and Kimball in their classic study of a rural community in Co. Clare specify two classes of farmers, distinguishable in many different ways. Their notion has not, however, been followed up, and even though research suggests the existence of certain very marked characteristics for large and small farmers, no systematic analysis has been undertaken along these lines. Nevertheless, the gap between the two types of farmers has widened. The large farms, more productive and better adapted to the market, are run on small business lines. These farmers organise their work, are ready to borrow, have ready recourse to expert advice and easily adapt to new techniques (*11, 66*). Small farmers, on the other hand, stick to traditional ways and conceive of agriculture as a way of life rather than as an activity producing for the market. Moreover, these small farms barely subsist, and often only survive with outside help, such as wages from temporary work, social welfare payments, and remittances from emigrant relations. These two types of farmers differ in many other ways. Better educated, younger, more inclined to join farmers' organisations, the viable farmer looks to the urban middle classes, whose tastes and manners he

17

tends to adopt. All this would strongly suggest the existence of two groups of farmers, differentiated by their life-style and their mode of social existence.

Other factors strengthen the hypothesis for two types of farmers. In the first place, emigration takes place mainly from the poorest counties, those where small farms predominate (*119*). One might risk the affirmation that rural emigration comes exclusively from the small farms. The high rate of permanent celibacy increases considerably as farms decrease in size. In 1966 42 per cent of very small farmers (with less than fifteen acres) were celibate whereas the figure was a mere 18 per cent for those farmers with more than 200 acres (*119*, 162). Political attitudes also follow similar lines of demarcation. The largest farmers, apart from the fact that up to recently they tended to vote Fine Gael, organise themselves more easily into pressure groups and are increasing their influence in society as a whole (*65, 66*). On the other hand, small farmers vote more for Fianna Fail, but show no capacity for organisation or for exerting pressure on a national level. Even the type of information farmers receive, the newspapers they read, varies: they all read provincial and Sunday newspapers, but only the largest farmers buy national dailies, in particular the *Irish Independent* (*24*).

All this points to social division among Irish farmers but does it prove conclusively the existence of a definite cleavage between two groups? It could be that a fundamental cultural homogeneity spans these diversities, that compared to the urban middle classes they have more in common with each other than otherwise. Farms are evolving towards a single type, neither small nor large, but medium-sized or in the process of becoming so. It is possible that these divisions will disappear with the small farm. However, certain observers of Irish rural life express alarm at the effect of the modernisation policies of the EEC. They denounce the dislocation of rural communities, the ever-increasing dualism between an expanding sector, capable of seizing opportunities for development, and another, stagnant sector, propped up and badly served, whose future is uncertain and whose demographic structure is seriously imbalanced (*272*). To establish whether or not a social cleavage exists within the farming community would necessitate further research, and in fact the problem, raised a long time ago, has never been adequately investigated and is still awaiting an attempt at solutions. One might wonder at this neglect, given that the farmers have attracted more study than any other category in Ireland. It is arguable that a strong ideological attachment to the vision of a well-integrated rural community, by a society glorifying its past and anxious at this critical moment of transition to preserve certain aspects of it, has prevented Irish society from seeing itself as it really is.

2

Bourgeoisie and Petite Bourgeoisie

The separation between property and control of capital, a general phenomenon of advanced capitalism, coincides at the outset with two distinct elements within the Irish bourgeoisie and enables us to define its somewhat loose boundaries. In effect, side by side with the owners of industrial and commercial enterprises, a new group of salaried managers has recently sprung up, who direct their main business efforts towards profit and expansion. In defining bourgeoisie we are including in this category only those executive managers who effectively contribute to policy-making and to the running of the firm and excluding all other levels of the administrative hierarchy of which executives are the summit. Official statistics, which distinguish a category of *managers*, exaggerate its extent because they fail to distinguish executive from non-executive managers and include in a single category several levels of the administrative hierarchy.

Moreover, all owners of private businesses are not bourgeois. A further distinction has to be made between large and small businesses. Small businessmen, such as independent artisans, shopkeepers, small employers, retailers, mechanics, publicans, small hoteliers, and small construction businesses fall into the category of petite bourgeoisie. While it is agreed that small businesses employ five persons or less, the actual size of a business is not decisive when it comes to categorising it. The difference is more fundamental than a merely quantitative one, being based more on the attitude in each case towards profit and the potential for expansion. The bourgeoisie anticipate, and go beyond the given situation by transforming it. The petite bourgeoisie, in adapting to circumstances, behave in exact contrast to the bourgeoisie, who constantly strive to fashion attitudes, in order to enlarge the horizons of the market. Finally the owner or manager of a bourgeois enterprise supervises the work of his employees, and does not work side by side with them.

The Bourgeoisie

Rents raised by landowners from their tenants constituted a primary source of wealth in Ireland from the sixteenth century on. Nevertheless Irish capitalism did not originate from this wealth although it was occasionally invested in commerce and industry. The Irish bourgeoisie owes its origin and development to income from the import-export trade, and at a

19

later date Dublin merchants furnished the initial capital for the textile industry in Ulster (*41, 220*). Capital also came from England, attracted by higher interest rates and by investment incentives held out by Grattan's Parliament. Despite the rise of banking towards the end of the eighteenth century – financed, moreover, from England – Ireland never succeeded in shaking off its dependence on the London money market, with the result that a financial bourgeoisie failed to develop. Especially since, with the Act of Union of 1801, the attractiveness of Ireland to investors disappeared, and the flow of English capital into Ireland dried up as Irish investors began to look to the mainland. The first Irish industries, such as textiles, brewing, distilling, and ship-building, depended on energy generated by watermills; accordingly they were usually found outside the towns, or in the middle of the countryside. These industries prospered as late as 1850-60. But, being in general small-scale and dependent upon traditional methods of production, Irish industry could not hope to compete with English manufactured goods which now flowed unimpeded into the Irish market, helped by the development of the railways. These goods spelt ruin for Irish industry and brought industrial development in Ireland to a halt. Added to this was the fact that savings tended more and more to be invested in profitable colonial enterprises or on the British mainland.

Following on independence the new Irish Free State was quickly obliged to offset the shortcomings of the private sector. From 1927 on it established a number of publicly financed semi-state enterprises, introduced tariff barriers to protect Irish industry (hard pressed by competition from English manufacturers) and to stimulate the development of new Irish industries. But existing industries, operating in a restricted and protected market, were given little encouragement to expand. Under the Control of Manufacturers Act 1934 the State also sought to ensure national control of industry and very reluctantly tolerated foreign investment in Ireland. However, after a long period of stagnation a radical change in the mood of the nation occurred in the late 1950s, leading to an about-turn in national economic policy. The government, under Sean Lemass, undertook an intensive programme of industrial development, set up new semi-state enterprises, but above all set about attracting foreign capital, by encouraging the setting up of multinational enterprises on Irish soil. The campaign was largely successful, and foreign companies today form the backbone of the Irish economy.

This brief account is merely an attempt to sketch the historical background of the contemporary Irish bourgeoisie. It pinpoints the fact that the industrial bourgeoisie of Ireland developed and achieved dominance within a capitalist class whose wealth derived from trade. It also explains why a financial bourgeoisie is largely lacking in Ireland as well as underlining a permanent paradox of Irish capitalism. Irish investors have invariably preferred to invest abroad rather than risk their capital in local

20

industry, yet they do not hesitate to seek the protection of the State when they feel it is necessary. Here also lies the explanation of the fact that most of the larger enterprises in Ireland today are subsidiaries of foreign companies: local industries who owed their survival to a protected market failed to expand and remained for the most part small-scale.

The Irish bourgeoisie is small in number. There are about 3,000 industrial enterprises in the country (*123*). But since it is extremely difficult to ascertain the degree of concentration and the network of affiliations between them, the actual number might be very different. It has also been estimated that there are 5,000 construction companies, as well as 6,000 businesses in the services sector (*233*). These approximate figures include a majority of small businesses, whose owners could not be said to belong to the bourgeoisie proper. As for the financial bourgeoisie, it is estimated that the number of financial operations (including banks, credit companies, and insurance companies) is not much in excess of a hundred (*189*). Nevertheless, in spite of its smallness, the Irish bourgeoisie as a social group has increased both in importance and in numbers, and one can estimate that it accounts for from 2–3 per cent of the active population (*234*).

In affirming the existence of an Irish bourgeoisie it is necessary to distinguish it from other closely related social categories. The effort to define its particularities encounters certain obstacles, not least the fact that it has received insufficient recognition as a separate social category, possibly on account of its smallness. The Irish bourgeoisie as defined above is often regarded as a sub-category within a much larger middle class whose attitudes, aspirations and life-style it is assumed to share. Nevertheless, research and statistics from diverse sources suggest that we can attribute a specific identity and a distinct social role to this bourgeoisie. Population studies show that family size in this category (3–4 children in the average Catholic family, two in others) is considerably smaller than in the working-class and rural community and somewhat larger than in other sections of the urban middle class who, from office workers to professionals, have considerably reduced the sizes of their families (*222*). The bourgeoisie can be distinguished from the larger middle class by their lower rate of geographic mobility. Between 1875 and 1926 very few emigrants to the United States came from the bourgeoisie. More recently it has been established that their members migrate very little within Ireland whereas white-collar workers and professionals were significantly more mobile (*70*). The picture changes somewhat when we distinguish between owners as such and managers: many of the latter have gained their professional experience either in Britain or the United States. Before the outbreak of the present strife in Northern Ireland, emigration between Dublin and Belfast was much greater among senior management than among any other category.

The role of the bourgeoisie in Irish political life also distinguishes them from the middle class as such. They take little interest in local politics, and indifferently support Fianna Fail or Fine Gael. In the words of one prominent Irish industrialist: 'I find it hard to distinguish any difference in principles when one studies the economic planks of their platforms' (*103*, April 1968). Their political indifference might be explained by the commitment of both main parties to the ideals of private enterprise. Naturally, businessmen often contribute to the finances of a party of their choice, and the bourgeoisie undoubtedly seek to influence government policy. But as a group they tend to keep their distance from party politics, and to exercise their collective power through other channels.

A further characteristic of the Irish bourgeoisie is the relative social mobility to be found within their ranks. In effect, employers tend to come from highly diversified backgrounds, including white-collar office workers and even certain categories of the working class (routine non-manuals). This may be explained by the fact that, unlike the professions, the bourgeoisie have up to recently had no selection mechanisms of a kind that might bar entry to all but a privileged few. Which is not to suggest that inheritance counts for nothing since 'family businesses' account for 25 per cent of the total number (*89*). But access to the bourgeoisie is gradually becoming more professionalised: in other words, management positions more and more require possession of a university qualification of some kind. In 1974, 28 per cent of Irish managers had a university degree (*76*), and this no doubt explains their increasing anxiety that their children receive the best possible education. Curiously, they encourage their sons and daughters in the direction of the professions, and many of these are to be found in the medical and law, rather than the engineering or business, faculties of the universities. Marriage patterns suggest another characteristic of the bourgeoisie, for whom marriage is paradoxically both an open and closed institution. Closed, since one tends to marry within one's social class – the level of endogamy is higher among the bourgeoisie than in any other social category except the professional and working classes (*91*). Nevertheless, when the sons of the bourgeoisie marry outside their own class they tend to choose a wife from fairly low down on the social scale, among office workers. The same liberty is not granted to the daughters of the bourgeoisie who are expected, in marrying, to maintain their social status. Finally the sons of the bourgeoisie marry later than those of the other middle-class categories, and in greater numbers (*222, 225*).

All this points to the existence of a very definite, clearly distinguishable social category. The fertility of the bourgeoisie, their geographical and social mobility, and the nature of their involvement in political life all give a specificity to this social group within the larger middle class. However, as well as being distinguishable from other middle-class categories certain distinctions exist within the bourgeoisie itself. We have already noted the distinction between the commercial and industrial bourgeoisie, though it is more difficult to assess whether this distinction manifests itself as a social one. It would appear, nonetheless, that the commercial bourgeoisie are more cautious, more anxious to maintain the status quo, whereas the industrial bourgeoisie tend to be attracted by change and possibilities of modernisation.

As a social group the Irish bourgeoisie present a much greater religious heterogeneity than the rest of the population. Whereas non-Catholics represent a mere 5 per cent of the total population of the country, research shows that 27 per cent of Irish entrepreneurs fall into this category (*Irish Times*, 31-7-73). This over-representation of Protestants in the bourgeoisie has its roots in the past. Since the seventeenth century Catholics have undoubtedly made a significant contribution to Irish business. Incapacitated by law from buying land, many sons of the minor Catholic nobility set up as merchants. On their side the Anglo-Irish nobility despised commerce and preferred industry. However those Anglo-Irish who remained in Ireland after independence often turned to business and thus joined the ranks of the bourgeoisie. But in any event religious differences within the bourgeoisie do not necessarily manifest themselves socially — as different ways of being bourgeois.

Two different groups — owners and managers — have already been distinguished within the bourgeoisie, though obviously the two categories often overlap. The distinction is often merely a legal one: many managers own the firm they manage, or control a majority of its shares. In any case enough research has been carried out in this area to enable us to sketch a fairly precise portrait of the Irish executive, even if it is not totally representative (76). In the first place it is an interesting fact that the vast majority are of Irish nationality, even though the proportion of nationals declines as we climb the ladder of responsibility. Many of them have had a university or other third-level education, evidence of the tendency towards ever increasing professionalisation among this sector of the bourgeoisie, so much so that formal education and adequate training are recognised as essential to fill such positions.

Irish executives exhibit a high spirit of competitiveness and they 'are not satisfied to be no better than other people'. They enjoy responsibility, decision-making, administration. They accept that they be judged on results, are in no doubt that they are succeeding at their task, and that they deserve the positions of power which they occupy (64). In evaluating the factors contributing to social success they place education and hard work on top of the list and refuse to accept that luck or personal contact are sufficient to achieve success (89). They consider that executives ought to be able to generate confidence, and adhere to a business ethic that puts great emphasis on honesty, hard work, realism, and reliability. Great importance is attached to the necessity of striking a balance between the demands of family, social and business life: Irish executives are possibly unique in this respect and seem to be successful in ensuring that the pressures and involvements of business do not interfere with personal and family life (*64*). The authoritarian strain which is said to characterise Irish society has often been commented upon. One study of a group of Irish executives came to the conclusion that 'it may be that the more authoritarian style has been more effective in Irish culture'. This authoritarianism takes the form of personal domination and lack of consultation in the day-to-day running of business (*5*). Those in positions of responsibility tend to assert their personalities and to display a lack of sensitivity to the problems of their subordinates. This traditional, authoritarian style is a throwback to a time when employers had no need of collaboration from their employees, never thought of delegating responsibility, had no confidence in the competence of their employees, placed great importance on the hierarchical factor, relied on their intuition rather than on rational planning and displayed a distrust of innovation of any kind as a threat to the status quo. However, a new style of management may be discerned in Ireland today which stresses co-operation among personnel, and the need to create a collective sense of the enterprise which will generate participation and initiative. This style is to be found mainly in the larger, more dynamic companies where, we are told, management morale is higher than elsewhere.

Finally, it is necessary to refer to a further distinction within this new bourgeoisie: that generated by competition between foreign and national capital. There is, however, no evidence that the dominant presence of foreign companies in Irish capitalism has given rise to a new and distinct social category within the Irish bourgeoisie, especially as the majority of managers of subsidiaries of overseas companies in Ireland are Irish. This does not necessarily mean that the relations between national and foreign capital does not raise important issues, merely that the presence of foreign capital to date has not manifested itself in social terms.

The Petite Bourgeoisie

The Irish petite bourgeoisie, which accounts for 3—4 per cent of the active population, continued to consolidate itself during the long period of economic protectionism. But from the late 1940s on, its position began to erode; small businesses, in particular, have declined in numbers. Many small traders have carried on at a subsistence level, though their businesses are no longer going concerns (*235*). More attention has been given to these traders than to other sectors of the petite bourgeoisie, so that consideration of them may be constructive in examining the petite bourgeoisie as a whole. The trend is clear and figures show that between 1956 and 1966 the number of small businesses fell from 38,260 to 34,230 (*233*). But this decline is particularly observable in certain types of business – such as small grocers – while others such as licensed premises have held their own and others still, such as filling stations, have prospered. Furthermore, small businesses tend to prosper in Dublin and the towns where there is a concentration of population and a higher standard of living, while declining elsewhere (*201*). Despite the odds the small grocer's shop continues to survive as a feature of the social and economic landscape of Ireland.

The grocer occupies a particular niche in Irish society and has even been credited with playing a focal role in the social structure of Ireland. At country crossroads and villages numerous grocer and hardware stores cater for the daily needs of the rural population. These shops are often tended by women — widows, or wives of local craftsmen — and their clientele is made up of local families, friends, and not too distant relatives. However, a new type of business has gradually appeared alongside these traditional grocer shops. In his study, *Inishkillane* (a fictional name for a village in the West of Ireland), Brody discerns a clear demarcation line between the traditional, declining, grocer's shop and pubs and the prosperous enterprise which has adopted a progressive, dynamic style (*14*). This business, simultaneously a grocer and a hardware store, is geared towards high turnover and profit. Although it serves as a gathering point for local youth, the owner does nothing to encourage this tendency. He runs a guesthouse on the side for the tourist season and receives paying guests in his own house. He owns two small boats which he hires out to a local fisherman. He has inherited a small farm, which he has since enlarged and on which he grazes cattle — an activity which takes up little of his time. A new 'gombeen man', quick to take advantage of the isolation of the rural community, he becomes an agent of urban culture in the countryside. And since many of these new grocers come from the towns, they are not tied to the local community by the traditional rural network of family bonds and obligations.

Within the towns themselves shopkeepers present a different profile, and Arensberg and Kimball, in their well-known study of Ennis in Co. Clare, saw them as the link between urban and rural Ireland (*2*). Each shop drew its clientele from the local farming community. Its owner, marrying a farmer's daughter, would automatically become a member of an extended family, with all the obligations thus involved, while at the same time enlarging his clientele. He would also recruit assistants from among the sons of local farmers, establishing yet further family connections. Moreover, this arrangement suited the farmer perfectly, allowing him to launch his son as an apprentice in the grocery trade, which was a respected one in the rural community. This process of mobility went even further: the grocer went out of his way to provide the best possible education for his children, encouraging them in the direction of non-manual white-collar jobs or even towards the professions, thereby opening up a channel between the farming community and the urban middle classes. This explains why businesses rarely remained long in the same family (rarely more than three generations) and why only half of Ennis' shopkeepers had inherited their businesses. With their good education and their aspirations to another life-style, the children of the grocer lost all interest in the family business.

The theme of this study, carried out some forty years ago, reappears in a more recent study of the shopkeeping community in Skibbereen, Co. Cork. (110). In Skibbereen many shops and bars remain in the traditional mould. Tended by elderly people, or by women, these shops are merely a supplementary source of family income. The clientele is drawn from a circle of friends, neighbours and relatives who regard the shop as a meeting place as much as a place of commerce. The shop itself produces little profit but does confer a certain status on the family within the community. Certain characteristics of the grocers of Ennis are to be discerned in their counterparts in Skibbereen: their ties with local farming families; the importance of family divisions among the clientele; the group's instability, rooted in the desire to give their children the good education which will enable them to escape their small shopkeeping background. But a new breed of shopkeeper has arisen, better educated and more profit-conscious. They employ salaried assistants and, in the case of the supermarket owner, girls awaiting marriage to operate the check-outs.

These small traders invariably show a marked tendency to conform, and an eagerness not to infringe social norms. Success in business depends on acceptance by the community, and indeed social and religious conformity even become commercial virtues. The emphasis put on respectability goes hand-in-hand with a marked sensitivity to status symbols, as is illustrated in numerous Irish novels and short stories.

The grocer and the publican are often involved in local politics, where their positions as focuses of social interactions give them a certain influence, the shop or pub being obvious centres of local news and gossip. These same tradesmen tend to be active in voluntary associations, which increases their authority. They are well represented in politics at county council and even parliamentary level. Few of them, however, are to be found at the top of the political tree or at ministerial level. Their disproportionately large representation in local and national politics spans the whole political spectrum, including even the Labour Party (24).

All these considerations concerning the Irish small town retailer, and in particular the grocer, do not necessarily indicate the existence of a united homogeneous group conscious of its collective interests. But nevertheless, as a social category, they occupy a special position in Irish society. One is slow, nevertheless, to generalise from the above data, or to apply them to the petite bourgeoisie as a whole. Attention has, for example, been drawn to the rather privileged link between the farming community and small traders; but the farming community produces few small businessmen. Moreover, the position of the self-employed artisans is difficult to determine in Ireland. The hypothesis that independent artisans differ in their attitudes and behaviour from wage-earners does not seem unreasonable. In many countries wage-earners aspire to independence and dream of setting up businesses on their own. Some try, though few enough persevere. Is there mobility between the working class and the petite bourgeoisie in Ireland? Do wage-earners change their attitudes when they become self-employed. No information is available here, but in any case the frontier between the working class and petite bourgeoisie in Ireland is fairly rigid, and few wage-earners succeed in crossing it. However, it may be concluded that the Irish petite bourgeoisie is a fairly mixed social category, including as it does independent artisans, small traders, and small-scale industrial enterprises.

3
Clerical Workers and the Liberal Professions

Irish society is usually seen as being divided into three clearly distinguishable categories: the farmers, the working class and the middle class. Doubtless these three divisions exist and play an important structuring role in the country as a whole. But to regard bourgeoisie, petite bourgeoisie, white-collar workers, and professionals as belonging to a single social class is to simplify a far more complex reality. There is strictly no Irish middle class as such, though to assume its existence has some usefulness insofar as it enables us to distinguish between its various sections on the one hand and the working and farmer classes on the other. It is true also that the term middle class may be used to designate a certain ensemble of characteristics, a certain way of life in which diverse social categories participate with greater or lesser intensity: late marriage (*225*, table 2) a very low level of permanent celibacy (*223*, table 3), relatively small families (*223*, table 8), a desire to educate one's children up to and beyond university level (*160*, table 4), a tendency to join voluntary organisations, strict supervision of children, a relatively democratic family organisation where sexual roles are not rigidly defined, a social life revolving around dinner-parties etc (*88*). However, beyond these shared characteristics, significant differences may be discerned which point to further categories within the 'middle class', arising as much from actual social position as from what might be called life-style. In other words, it is not possible to reduce to a single social category — the middle class — the several categories usually referred to by that name. In spite of what they share in common, the bourgeoisie must be distinguished from the petite bourgeoisie, office workers from professionals — as well as the latter from the bourgeoisie.

The Liberal Professions

The term liberal professions usually designates very precise occupations (such as doctors, solicitors, barristers, architects) to be distinguished from salaried workers. However, in Ireland, the term has developed a somewhat wider range of reference, to include teachers and nurses, who might otherwise be considered as not belonging to the 'professional classes'. Nevertheless the inclusion is justified on the basis of the long period of training required, and the highly personalised nature of the services involved both considered as distinguishing marks of the professions. This has led to a further sub-classification which distinguishes between *higher professionals* (the traditional liberal professions) and *lower professionals* (such as teachers and nurses). Originally the liberal (higher) professionals were distinguished by the fact that they practised their professions independently. But nowadays many architects are employed by firms, doctors work in hospitals, and many lawyers are employed by large companies, so that 80 per cent of them are in fact salaried, while the 6—7 per cent who do practise independently are classified as employers; these figures have moreover remained stable over the last fifty years (*235*).

The liberal professions have considerably expanded, from 4 per cent in 1926 to 9 per cent of the active population in 1971 (*235*). Its intake of women has risen dramatically especially at the lower levels. This expansion, by creating numerous openings at the top of the social ladder, has greatly increased social mobility. The opening up of the (lower) liberal professions has particularly benefited the children of the petite bourgeoisie and of office workers, but those of the working class hardly at all (*89*). Primary school teachers continue to come from farming or small shopkeeping backgrounds, while entrance to the higher liberal professions remains relatively more difficult and exclusive. But the children of both higher and lower categories are likely to maintain their social position. Access to the professions is the result of long formal education, which operates as an effective channel of transmission, since the children of professionals (1 out of 3/4) have a high probability of entering university (*160*, table 4). The relatively intense concentration of this category in third-level education is not merely a result of their privileged material situation, though this is obviously a contributory factor. It results from their positive attitude towards education of which it is also a product. Education is seen as a factor of social status, as well as a guarantee of a good job. Moreover, professional parents are familiar with the labyrinth of higher education, and are thus in a position to guide their children through the appropriate channels towards the most prestigious courses of study. In any event, it is a fact that the professionals succeed in handing on their social status to their children (*89*). This exclusiveness, measured in terms of social mobility, reappears in marriage statistics: the children marry within their group or at any event not into the working class (*91*) — a further index of the closed nature of this social category, a feature which is much more marked among higher than lower professionals.

Socially exclusive as they might be, they are nevertheless geographically extremely mobile. In 1961 68.2 per cent of women and 53.3 per cent of men among higher professionals resided in a county other than their county of birth. This figure is higher than for any other category (*70*), and does not include overseas emigration, which is also high among higher professionals. A secondary education already produces a movement from the countryside to the towns, which is accentuated by university education, especially since the possibilities of professional job outlets are

29

limited in the country and small towns. In Co. Cavan, research has shown that young people with professional aspirations do not envisage living in the locality and in fact do not stay once they qualify (*81*).

In a sense the liberal professions may be considered a model for the middle class since they offer the sharpest contrast with the farmer and working classes. They share many demographic features with office workers (small families, late marriage, low rate of permanent celibacy) but they exemplify them in a purer form. Their tendency to form a distinctive pole of social behaviour, which is found among office workers in a somewhat attenuated form, is also to be seen in their high degree of involvement in voluntary organisations, their religious conformity, and their liberal but vigilant attitudes towards their children. They differ from the bourgeoisie in their lower rate of fertility and by a marked tendency to emigrate, as well as by their more positive attitude towards formal education and their greater social exclusiveness. This exclusiveness, and the nature of their involvement in politics, are the principal features distinguishing the professionals from both the bourgeoisie and white collar office workers; more than anything else, they are the source of the professionals' specificity.

Members of the liberal professions show little interest in local or county council, as opposed to national politics. Since the foundation of the State 25 per cent of Dáil deputies and 60 per cent of ministers have come from this group (*24*, 95-6). Their lack of interest in the local scene may also be discerned in their tendency to ignore local newspapers and to read the more prestigious national dailies (*24*, 131-2). There are no doubt many reasons for the success of the professional classes in political life. Their social contacts, their social ease, their ability to marshall ideas, their prestige, are all contributory factors. It would be worth studying the rather paradoxical role played by the liberal professions in Irish political life: a social category with no collective project to advance but which nevertheless exhibits a definite desire for political power.

The image projected by the higher professionals is one of great independence in the exercise of their skills. The highly specialised nature of their training and the highly personalised nature of their work prevents over-rigid control as well as the reduction of their activities to a routine. This virtual atonomy and the security of their position encourages individualism and a relative freedom of social behaviour, leaving them free to conform more casually to social norms. This individual and self-confident image is reflected in numerous works of fiction, where it often emerges in the form of eccentricity.

Clerical Workers

This category embraces the entire administrative hierarchy, from secretaries to higher administrators, stopping short only of executives (in the classifications used for official statistics the category is broken into *Salaried Employees* and *Intermediate Non-manual Workers*). Though a mixed category, office workers exhibit special characteristics which, while distinguishing them from the working class also mark them apart from both the petite bourgeoisie and the liberal professions, and which place them in a transitional position between two poles of social differentiation. Office workers have considerably increased in number over the last fifty years from 5 per cent of the active population in 1926 to 12 per cent in 1971. This expansion is due in part to the influx of women who made up 53 per cent of the category in 1971, compared to 26 per cent in 1926 (*235*). The increase is not surprising, and is accompanied by a rationalisation in which routine has a levelling effect. This levelling tends to draw office workers towards the working class, a tendency that they resist, while their social behaviour and their way of life sharply distinguish them from the working class. Everything in fact attaches them to the middle-class model; their positive attitude towards education, their religious practices, their ways of bringing up their children, the division of labour within the family, their dinner-parties, even if their participation in the model is less intense, less pure than that of the professionals (*88*).

The intermediate position of office workers between two clearly defined poles of Irish society is visible from demographic trends. They marry earlier and less than the professionals. They rear much smaller families than the working class, but slightly larger than the professional classes (*223*, table 8). Their eagerness to adopt a middle-class life-style and its status symbols, their determination to give their children the best possible start in life – and thereby the best education – with limited material resources partly explains the low birth rate within this group. Their intermediate position is further illustrated (though less clearly) in migratory patterns both within and outside Ireland. Many women from this category are attracted to Dublin and more than a third of office workers reside in counties other than those where they were born (*70*, 29). Fewer migrants, then, than among professionals but considerably more than among skilled industrial workers, the stable element in the cities.

However, office workers contrast greatly with professionals in two clearly defined areas. The first is that of social mobility; if the professional class, as has been suggested, is the most closed social group in Ireland, the office workers constitute, on the contrary, the most open. At the beginning of the 1970s a third of office workers had a working-class background, though being born into this category is not a guarantee that one will pursue a non-manual career, since a third of the sons of office workers chose manual careers (*89*, tables 19, 20, 21). It is also noteworthy that sons of office workers often marry working-class girls, whereas their daughters prefer to marry above themselves on the social scale (*91*, 18-19). Furthermore, and in further contrast to professionals, office workers seldom involve themselves in politics. The proportion of local represent-

31

atives, Dáil deputies or ministers from this category is negligible. Are they uninterested in political affairs or do they lack a collective identity to express (*24*, 95)?

The office worker category embraces an administrative hierarchy within which a career may be pursued, with a system of grades through which one may rise more or less rapidly or automatically. This phenomenon once again stresses the transitional position of this category between the two extreme social poles, and enables us to define it. In any case, at the bottom of the scale but naturally even more so at the top, office workers refuse to allow themselves to be assimilated into the working class, and when they become involved in collective action it is to affirm their difference from the working class and to preserve those advantages which depend upon a recognition of this difference. For example, office workers of one of Ireland's largest employers, the Electricity Supply Board, have for a long time enjoyed a special status compared to that of the manual working staff, many of whom are highly qualified. A higher salary and social security advantages, such as pensions and sickness benefits, constitute so many indexes of their privileged position. As soon as salary scales alter to their disadvantage they undertake collective action to re-establish the differential (*255*). The problem arises partly because these office workers – and the same is true of most civil servants – are recruited at an educational level which does not correspond with the routine nature of their tasks, so that their salary hopes are based much more on their educational level than on the work they perform. This does not, however, eliminate the frustration they feel at the gap between their capacities and their actual responsibilities. On their side the manual workers and technicians resent certain practices which daily bring home to them their inferior status, such as separate entrances and separate canteens, and are quick to denounce as unjustifiable the material advantages enjoyed by the white-collar staff.

Bank officials offer an even better illustration of the determination of white-collar workers to distinguish themselves from the working class and to protect hard-won advantages. Bank officials have traditionally enjoyed a special status in Ireland, even within the white-collar category. They were recruited on the recommendation of worthy, reliable citizens such as parish priests, businessmen, or higher officials within the bank. Banks looked to their employees for the virtues of discretion and reliability and the advantages accruing to bank officials meant the acceptance by them of a certain paternalism, and certain social constraints, such as the implicit obligation not to get involved in political or religious controversy. The reserve demanded of bank officials has contributed to the image of conformity and boredom often associated with their position. Nevertheless recruitment to the banks has greatly changed in recent times, since candidates are now obliged to have passed the Leaving Certificate with a high mark in mathematics and to submit to strict selection procedures, so that the importance of personal contact has diminished. Nowadays many recruits come from working-class backgrounds. The keenness of the competition for the limited number of places in the banks is a measure of the prestige and material advantages that go with them: good salary, pleasant working environment, security, a clearly defined career, guaranteed pension, generous holidays, and numerous other advantages (256).

Bank employees are represented by the Irish Bank Officials Association — a very militant association when it comes to defending the relative advantages of its members. The expansion in the banking sector has led to large-scale rationalisation of banking structures and to an influx of young officials, mainly women. This has produced a change in mood among bank officials and encouraged a militant stance among their representatives: the younger women resented the new monotony of their jobs, the failure to tap their capacities and their extremely limited chances of promotion. The IBOA has been effective in defending the interests of its members but refuses to commit itself or pronounce on broader issues, fearing no doubt that to do so would run the risk of endangering their own claims in the name of more general issues. It does not, for example, lend its signature to national wage agreements, preferring to fight its own battles, and justifies its claims by evoking the unique character of the banking profession. The IBOA rejects all comparisons of bank employees with other white-collar categories, in their determination to ensure the legitimacy of their privileges (94).

Many office workers belong to unions which restrict their membership to this category. Several of them were for a time affiliated to the formerly influential Irish Conference of Professional and Service Associations, which has always been careful to keep its distance from the Irish Congress of Trade Unions, while pursuing its particular claims. Other categories of office workers have affiliated themselves to the general trade union movement; some of them have actually joined unions which recruit members among both working-class and white-collar categories. Moreover the capacity to organise and effectively defend their interests does not extend to the whole of the white-collar category. Many, especially in the smaller firms, are badly paid and belong to no union or association. It would thus appear, that despite some points of contact, office workers may be clearly distinguished from the working class as such. The latter in fact do not recognise the former as 'class allies' and withhold their support from them. Workers always refuse to pass another worker's picket in any circumstances, but do not scruple to pass a picket mounted by a union or association of office staff: a clear proof that office workers and manual workers do not perceive each other as belonging to the same social class.

4

The Working Class

Manufacturing did not make its appearance in Ireland before the middle of the eighteenth century and, even later, there was no clear distinction between industrial and agricultural work, between town and country. The mass of the labour force was composed of 'cottiers', landless labourers hired out by the farmers, who cultivated a potato patch attached to their cottage. Some of them attempted to supplement their meagre income by hiring themselves out for occasional work, while their wives often set up domestic cottage industries such as spinning and weaving (40). Industrial workers, a small group of artisans in the towns and villages, organised themselves in guilds according to trade (15). Neither an industrial bourgeoisie nor a proletariat had yet emerged from this group and in fact the small number of workers employed in manufacturing quickly levelled off, and remained stable up to the middle of the nineteenth century.

The economic crisis which preceded the Famine of 1845–9 and the new policy of the landlords (who opposed the endless division of land and switched from tillage to grazing) had swollen the ranks of the agricultural proletariat. The Famine itself increased the dependence of the cottiers on occasional work to earn a pittance that was becoming more and more uncertain. The evictions which followed accelerated the rural exodus. Many farm labourers joined the ranks of the labour force or the urban destitute. The Irish working class, the same one we encounter several decades later, was born at the end of the nineteenth century when manufacturing industry established itself in Ireland and employed unskilled labourers, with no job security, who often eked out a pitiful existence in the slums of Dublin. Further, independent tradesmen unable to compete with products manufactured both in England and in Ireland, declined in number and joined the ranks of an unstable working class. In 1901 the industrial workforce in Dublin was made up of 10,000 workers skilled in various trades and 30,000 unskilled labourers such as dockers and carters (126, 278).

The successive transformations of this working class may be traced in population censuses, a rich mine of information. Those of 1881–1911 do not distinguish between labourers, tradesmen, small businessmen and even small shopkeepers, but refer simply to an 'industrial class'. Nevertheless these statistics clearly reveal the rise of industry, since, while the number of both domestic employees and female labourers declined rapidly, the number of manual labourers rose all the time. A more precise picture emerges after 1926, although even here successive changes in the statistical categories employed make the task of analysis a difficult one.

Before proceeeding it might be as well to offer a definition of working class. Despite what is often said the working class is not composed solely of manual workers, even though these are obviously in the majority. One must also include certain 'non-manuals', workers in the transport and service sectors. This definition raises technical difficulties since it does not correspond exactly to any of the socio-professional groups recognised by official statistics, or even any particular combination of these. In census terms working class includes all manual labourers, other non-manual labourers and certain 'non-manual intermediaries', such as supermarket cashiers, bartenders, and so on.

Despite these difficulties certain tendencies may be discerned. In the first place the working class as a whole has increased in numbers, with ups and downs, between 1926 and 1971: the increase has been steeper since 1961. Secondly the internal composition of the working class has also changed. The active participation of women in the workforce has remained at 25 per cent. The latter tend to be employed in domestic occupations, or manual occupations demanding little skill. The male working class, in contrast, remains principally manual and the proportion of skilled workers increases with each census. In any event, down through the years the working class has become the largest social category. If one takes into account the dependents of all those workers either working or unemployed, approximately 41–2 per cent of the Irish population belongs to the working class – and this figure does not even include agricultural labourers. So that, if only for reasons of its size, the characteristics of this class weigh heavily in any study of Irish society as a whole.

The Working Class: A Pole of Social Differentiation

The subject of the working class has attracted the attention of not a few researchers and a great deal of information, even though somewhat dispersed, has accumulated around it. This information derives from diverse studies which do not centre on the working class itself, and no systematic, coherent effort has been undertaken to date to define in a rigorous fashion this particular social category. However, the particularity of the working class appears from whatever aspect one studies it, and it asserts itself as a pole of social differentiation in Irish society: in the working class may be defined specific modes of behaviour and a specific life-style. A very large social category, it contains social cleavages within itself. It has, moreover, become common practice in sociological studies to invoke certain classifications, according to which the working class is divided into four strata: three of these relating to degrees of manual skill, and a fourth containing non-manual workers whom, from the point of view of social behaviour, we

35

are entitled to regard as belonging to the working class.

The aspect of the working class which has generated the most information relates to education. Here, unsurprisingly, we learn that the categories
of unskilled and semi-skilled labourers have received no post-primary
education, and in certain cases never finished in primary school. Skilled
workers have either passed through vocational school or served a long
apprenticeship (*140*). A more interesting question from our point of view,
because expressive of attitude and a useful index of social behaviour is:
what education does the working class tend to give its children? At the
beginning of the 1960s working-class children were less involved in post-
primary education than children from any other social category. Those
who continued on after the minimum school-leaving age – and many
working-class children left school as early as possible – entered a vocational
school, or to a lesser degree (except for girls) a secondary school. The
number of working-class children in secondary education was, and
probably remains, low and in this respect they resemble the children of
small farmers. Many working-class children who entered a secondary
school left before completing a secondary education. Subsequently, the
working class disappeared almost completely from the educational system.
The educational scene has changed considerably since the early sixties,
however; the authorities have encouraged more and more children to
avail of secondary education with the result that many working-class
children have succeeded in passing through secondary school and even
into third level. But these measures, favouring those who knew how
or wished to seize the opportunity offered to them, hardly affected
the lowest levels of the working class.

The affirmation of a low level of working-class participation in the
schools and universities must be qualified and account must be taken of
some highly significant variations. Children who abandon school after the
primary certificate invariably come from the least skilled sections of the
working class. Their family backgrounds are often very precarious – very
poor, from very large families where the father is unemployed or an
invalid, and totally dependent on the social welfare system. By contrast
non-manual and skilled workers, better disposed towards school, are often
prepared to make sacrifices. Within the working class the category of
skilled workers has most successfully made use of the available opportunities and has to some degree increased its participation in the
educational system – though it is difficult to gauge how much. As for the
universities, the position of children of skilled and non-manual working-
class background has improved to some small degree, but the children
from the lowest working-class categories are scarcely represented at all in
the universities (*26*).

One might be surprised at the still low level of working-class participation in the schools, given the availability of free education, though it
could be explained by the necessity for children to supplement the meagre

family income. One might also explain it in terms of parental aspirations, and a negative attitude towards education as such. Nevertheless the working class realises as much as any other social group the importance of education for success in life. But other factors intervene besides parental attitudes, which are often in any case ambiguous. Might it be said that working-class parents fail to motivate their children sufficiently, or to help them in their studies? Is it possible that the gulf between working-class culture and the formal culture of the school system is too wide? It is a fact that the working class are not impressed by the notion of 'hard work' as a pre-requisite to success – and that this attitude derives from their own experience of daily drudgery with little hope of anything better. Personal contact, and among the lowest working-class categories, luck, are perceived as being much more important factors for success. The notion of social and material success as being dependent on 'who you know' and luck rather than on hard work – in the last analysis a magical conception of success – is unlikely to promote a positive attitude towards education (89, table 11). But again it must be decided whether these attitudes perpetuate the social condition of the lowest categories of the working class, and determine their lack of interest in education, or whether these attitudes are a rationalisation of their own everyday experience, that is to say of their alienation from the educational system as it stands.

The under-representation of the working class in the schools directly relates to the question of social mobility, where the position of the working class is rather special. The sons of workers tend to follow in their father's footsteps, and in this they are surpassed only by the liberal professional class. It would appear, therefore, to be difficult for the sons and daughters of workers to cross the frontier from working to middle class and for this reason this particular frontier is a very divisive one in Irish society. Only a skilled working-class background makes it possible for some to make this leap. This is not to conclude that there is little social mobility within the working class (or even mobility between higher working-class categories and office workers, the possibilities of which we have already noted). Within each stratum of the working class the majority of its members come from the higher or lower stratum. Mobility, then, but over very short social distances (89, tables 20–24).

The social polarity here attributed to the working class may be discerned in numerous other areas. It presents a sharp contrast with the middle class by its marriage rate – lower than the middle class's, much higher than the farmers' (222, table 3) – and by a tendency, rare in Ireland, to settle down at a young age. Curiously, male unskilled workers often marry slightly above themselves on the social scale, which is not true of non-manual and skilled manuals who marry within their own group (91, table 3). The high working-class fertility rate contrasts with that of the middle class, and is higher even than that of farmers (119, 19), even though working-class attitudes towards contraception tend to be positive. This difference of attitude between the working class and the farmers does not, however, find expression in behavioural patterns (232). Religious practices are also less intensively adhered to in the working class than in any other group (139, 162). The majority of working-class people vote Fianna Fail even though the electoral support of the Labour Party is drawn almost exclusively from the working class (148). Moreover, very few working-class people are elected to positions of political power either locally or nationally (24, 95). The working class more than any other is exposed to unemployment, which often assumes catastrophic proportions for semi-skilled and unskilled labourers (226). It can easily be imagined that job insecurity, until recently a feature of working-class life, has a profound effect on working-class attitudes and sentiments. It once again underlines the gap between working-class and white-collar workers, who until recently enjoyed great job security.

A.J. Humphreys has attempted to give an account of working-class life in Dublin with particular reference to a skilled working-class family background (88). He traces the daily family routine, underlining the clear division of labour within the family. The husband works outside the home and rarely participates in domestic chores except for the occasional odd job of repair. In the evening he joins his friends at the pub or from time to time attends a union meeting. The pattern repeats itself among the sons, so that housework falls squarely on the shoulders of the mothers and daughters who help them. The latter, anxious to get married, regard marriage as a means of improving their social position. The sons are less anxious to get married and are expected to fulfill their parents' ambitions for them. This pattern has modified itself considerably since the 1950s when this study was carried out, and the division of family labour according to sex has become less rigid. Nevertheless sexual roles are more stereo-typed in working-class than in middle-class families and the habit of the working-class husband of going alone to the pub persists.

These statistics confirm the identity of the working-class as a pole of social differentiation in Ireland, but the above characteristics exhibit nuances along a certain hierarchy, starting at the highest point — skilled workers — and working down the scale through non-manuals to semi-skilled workers, and finally to a sort of marginal and unstable lumpen proletariat. The tendency to marry young, for example, has already been remarked; this tendency is much more pronounced among semi- and unskilled workers than among others. The same may be said for the other tendencies already mentioned, which would suggest that the real pole of social differentiation is to be found at the bottom of the working-class scale, since other strata present only imperfect and less intense realisations of the behavioural and attitudinal patterns associated with this pole. The internal differentiation within the working class, then, may be considered in terms of the hierarchy suggested above, or in terms of a hiatus between,

38

on the one hand, semi- and unskilled workers and, on the other, skilled and non-manual workers. This latter division exemplifies an internal polarisation which the statistics reveal when it is sought to define general types within this social category.

A similar division is to be seen in the treatment by Irish fiction writers of the working class. They show little interest in the stable section of the working class, and preoccupy themselves with a sort of sub-proletariat, the insecurity of their lives, urban poverty against the background of Dublin slums, and they appear to delight in the pathos of working-class destitution. The novels have no monopoly in this respect and many academic works focus on the same class, building up a statistical and socio-logical picture which completes the one to be found in literature (72, 194). The social group in question live in the present, taking no account of the future, spending their money as they earn it, and make no effort during the rare stable periods to put money aside for future emergencies. They are also permanently crippled by endless hire-purchase repayments. Their children have virtually no chance of escaping from their background and so follow in the same pattern. The parents, who consider school a waste of time, are not prepared to make sacrifices to educate their children, and parents and children alike look forward to the day when the child can leave school and earn some money. Even at school, the children are irregular attenders, and prefer to find occasional employment. Their social ambitions are limited, or unrealistic; moreover, to continue at school would mean cutting themselves off from their friends and provoking the hostility of their peers. The parents exercise little control over their children who, even at a young age, are allowed to roam the streets, or hang around the local shop, until late at night. Juvenile delinquency is endemic in such social conditions, and young people, left to themselves, become sexually active early on. Teenage marriages in turn lead yet again to frequent pregnancies, large families in overcrowded living conditions, in already densely populated urban areas where seem to be concentrated all the poverty and all the problems of the country. This is the world brought to life by Sean O'Casey more than fifty years ago. It would require few changes to bring O'Casey's portrait up to date: this social group still exists almost unchanged, and perhaps its persistence explains in part the fascin-ation it continues to exert. But it exists very much on the periphery of Irish society and remains marginal in every sense of the word, situated on the edge of a stable society, and a constant source of embarrassment. Nevertheless Irish society continues to spawn this sub-proletariat, and there are no signs that it will cease to do so, or that there is any danger of social revolution from this particular source.

In only one respect can a clear hiatus rather than a hierarchical grad-ation within a single social class be discerned within the category under consideration. This relates to migratory patterns. The contrast is illus-trated by a study carried out in Co. Cavan (81), which shows that unskilled workers envisaged emigrating and did so to a much greater degree than anticipated, while skilled workers, though expressing the intention to emigrate, tended to do so much less. This is obviously due in part to the fact that the latter found work locally much more easily than the former. Unskilled and semi-skilled workers emigrated in large numbers to Great Britain, whereas skilled workers migrated less than any other social group in Ireland. This contrast is somewhat obscured when it is pointed out that 80 per cent of skilled and non-manual workers reside in their county of birth and that the figure increases to 88 per cent in the case of unskilled workers (70, 29). This would seem to mean that the working class as a whole constitutes a stable element in the towns while almost all other urban categories are caught up in a vast migratory movement. But in fact this high figure (88 per cent) hides the fact that unskilled workers, when they moved, did not do so within Ireland, but migrated overseas.

A Rural Working Class

Up to now we have insisted upon an internal differentiation within the working class, either in hierarchical terms or in terms of a cleavage between skilled and unskilled workers. But another distinction might be drawn: that between the urban and rural working class. An industrial working class exists in the villages and towns, since not all factories are to be found in the cities. The somewhat special character of the rural proletariat emerges from a study of the work force in two county-based factories, one in Scariff, Co. Clare, the other in Tobercurry, Co. Sligo (125). Here the workers have retained their close links not only with the countryside but also with farming activity. Generally young and relatively unskilled they continued to live on the family farm. Certain among them still worked there occasionally, others worked a little farm of their own. Similar characteristics may be seen among workers on the Shannon industrial complex, which recruits its labour force from the surrounding countryside of Shannon and Limerick. There is even a possibility that rural communities may divide into two categories — farmers and a new rural working class, and that this division might lead to tensions or even produce an unbridgeable chasm within the farming community (161). More significant in terms of size are the farm labourers who work on farms and possess no land of their own. In 1926 they formed 10 per cent of the active population of the country but by 1971 their number had fallen to 50,000, a mere 4.7 per cent. They resemble in many respects the unskilled workers of the towns, and like these rarely have gone beyond primary school, and are almost totally unrepresented in third-level education (143). However, this should be qualified by the fact that, in contrast to the urban working class, agricultural workers have relatively higher educational aspirations for their children even if they fail to realise them. They would like to place their children in non-manual or skilled occupations

40

but the latter tend to settle for semi-skilled jobs in the factories. Another characteristic which they share with the urban working class as well as the farmers is their high rate of migration (*119*). In general their salaries and standard of living compare unfavourably with those of their urban counterparts.

On the other hand agricultural labourers differ from urban workers and resemble the farmers in their tendency to marry late or not at all. So much so that it becomes difficult to place them squarely within the working class, with whom they exhibit increasing affinity. However, the hostility between farmers and farm labourers makes assimilation of the two groups impossible. This occasionally bitter hostility was less in evidence in the nineteenth century on account of their common opposition to the landlords. But the antagonism became manifest as soon as tenants became freeholders. They proved none too generous, paying their labourers low wages, obliging them to work long hours and offering them often uncomfortable living quarters (*46*). Everything, in fact, separates the two categories in a rural world where ownership of land counts for everything. The conflict has received expression in the short stories of, for example, Mary Lavin. In one story of hers a farmer says, apropos farm labourers: 'these people crowding around us were not of our kind.' And farmers fear that a daughter might marry an agricultural worker, in which case she would, in the eyes of the community, be marrying beneath herself.

5

Status in Ireland

Instead of the table of social differentiation invoked in previous chapters, Irish sociologists usually prefer to see social structure in terms of a hierarchy of status or prestige. According to this preference, individuals and groups are ranged along a scale of social status which does not necessarily coincide with the scale of material inequalities. Such an approach seeks not to establish the existence of different social categories but rather to attribute to them positions in the social hierarchy; it decides that certain groups belong to higher or lower strata than others, and judges them to be inferior or superior. The establishment of a scale of status runs into many difficulties, since it presupposes a convergence of judgments among individuals concerning their own position as well as that of others on the scale, that they more or less agree on the hierarchy of prestige – a prestige, let it be noted in passing, that still remains satisfactorily to be defined. It is not necessary to enter into the conceptual and technical objections arising out of the elaboration of such scales, since the classifications used in studies of Ireland have been borrowed from elsewhere. Neither should one use such difficulties as a pretext for dismissing out of hand any consideration of the notion of status: people do judge themselves socially, do assign a social status to others, and this is a well-known fact. Moreover, these scales more or less coincide with the groupings which we have already discerned, even if they occasionally put together in a single stratum groups which we have assigned to different categories. This simply means that the social hierarchies in question rest on a perception of social difference: but, further, they attempt to organise these differences, to establish an order among them. They are not content merely to observe poles of differentiation, to point out that certain groups manifest certain characteristics or specific social behaviour patterns; they seek to know which types of behaviour are, in the judgment of those societies under study, inferior or superior. Does a vision of Irish society in terms of status stratification advance, deepen, or sharpen our analysis? Does it add to or complete the picture we are seeking to establish of those aspects of Irish society which are both essential and stable? In other words, is there in fact a hierarchy of status in Ireland about which most people are in agreement?

Office workers cherish their social identity and keep their distance from manual workers. Their affirmation of a status apart, of their superiority to the working class, is most clearly seen in their collective activity. Employees with the Electricity Supply Board are organised into unions along very subtle lines, being divided into two technicians' unions, one union for clerical workers and the lower administrative grades, and another for the upper end of the administration scale (255). We have already seen how many office workers' associations refuse to affiliate with the official trade union movement in Ireland (the ICTU). The claim of office workers to a special social status was accepted in Ireland as being a matter of course and for a long time gave rise to no resentment or sense of injustice. However, from the 1960s onwards successive modifications of salary differentials between different social categories have provoked numerous industrial disputes; and beyond these salary differentials lay the question of the relative social status of the categories concerned. Workers and technicians came to resent as unjust and inequitable the privileges accorded to office workers, as well as the material advantages accruing to their position, which were legitimised by their status. They set about reducing the salary gap between themselves and office workers, but were successfully resisted by the latter. For a long time 'the salaried man saw himself as being different in kind from the wage earner — more responsible, owning his own house, more prudent in his expenditure and committed to expenses not experienced by a wage earner such as sending his children to secondary school and if possible to university' (132, 102). The wage claims of office workers, their efforts to protect their relative advantages over skilled workers, rest thus on a conception of a certain social status which they demand but which is being accorded them with more and more reluctance. To quote again from Charles McCarthy: 'The virtual disappearance of the status security of a highly structured society, the great social tensions as the categories of employment were more and more put in question — categories such as skilled and unskilled, clerical and manual, salary earner and wage earner, with all the implications for a class structure . . .' (132, 99–100), all these factors worked towards the erosion of well-established positions. Social groups no longer agree on their relative social positions — on their status — or on the material advantages which derive from these. The partial collapse of the hierarchy upsets society as a whole, certain categories strain to catch up on others, who in turn hasten to recreate the gap. This agitation results from incessant comparison between categories, and the criteria of comparison are what are seen to be at stake in the ensuing struggle.

The existence of conflicts for the recognition of hierarchical positions does not necessarily invalidate the relevance of general scales of status, since the conflict concerns the existence of such scales — publicly recognised, agreed or tolerated by society at large. However, the intensity of the conflicts reveals the profound disagreement on the subject, each group seeking to impose its own view of its place on the scale. And in fact it is impossible to say who actually possesses the authority to nominate a definitive hierarchy which could succeed in convincing all social groups of its validity. The existence of a quasi-official scale of 'established relativities' was attacked by industrial actions in the 1960s and has been under attack ever since. Efforts to establish an objective scale, based on the content of qualifications, responsibility and even seniority, have failed to stabilise the situation. In any event, to quote M. P. Fogarty again: 'the clerical worker who expects today to be conceded by others a clear margin over the craftsman is liable to be in for a rude awakening' (256). However, the situation is changing very rapidly and clerical workers are no longer as anxious to conform to the way of life of the better-off sections of the middle class. In the past bank officials liked to be identified with these, and their aspirations were taken seriously in the countryside where they enjoyed the same status as accountants and agricultural advisers (83). It seems that clerical workers have abandoned their former ambitions without, however, ceasing to belong to the middle classes, albeit at a lower level. A few clerical workers will work their way up to top executive positions on the administrative scale. But the social ambitions of this group are today projected onto their children, who are encouraged to succeed at school, to work towards one or other of the professions, or at the very least to maintain their status as non-manuals – which in their case is not guaranteed. Clerical workers, with the exception of certain entrenched groups, insist less than formerly on their superiority over manual workers – a superiority which they think ought to be expressed in terms of material advantages, and which is conceded to them more and more reluctantly. Even the emergence of white-collar trade unionism has not absorbed clerical workers into the working class, and in any event trade unionism is far from being a working-class monopoly.

The Working Class

The distinction between clerical workers and manual workers is paralleled within the trade union movement itself by a clearly discernible gap between skilled and unskilled workers. Without doubt, skilled workers enjoy greater prestige but their relative advantages are not so clearly established as to avoid any tension. Again within the ESB a pay rise at the lower end of the scale led to a strike among skilled workers anxious to re-establish the differential, whereas a widening in the gap is resented by the unskilled workers and in turn provokes them into strike action (255). A similar logic underlies a series of disputes in the maintenance sector which affected the whole country. The unions representing this sector demanded pay rises for their members, on the grounds that the increasing complexity of their work required greater technical skills. When these were successful in their claims and gained substantial salary increases the unskilled workers set about narrowing the gap once again. This recreated the original situation and led to a further spiral of claims. All this indicates that the gap between the two categories is not fixed, not so much because of differences in the technical content of skilled and unskilled jobs but because their respective status are at stake: what ought to be the legitimate social status gap between skilled and unskilled workers, and how should this gap be reflected in differences of salary? In effect, status is that which an industrial dispute — whether through strike or negotiation — seeks to establish.

In a study carried out in Drogheda seeking to measure workforce potential, in order to predict its size and characteristics, a section of young people were asked to rate a list of occupations according to their preference (227). They tended to identify a good job with high wages and, to a lesser extent, with security, pleasant working conditions, and with interesting work. Judging occupations as good or bad involves considerations other than prestige. Nevertheless the vast majority of those interviewed were of working-class background, and the results were remarkably clear. Non-manual occupations and skilled manual occupations were almost all positively evaluated by the boys. Girls on the other hand exhibited no attraction towards manual occupations, preferring non-manual occupations of a stereotyped female nature (such as typists, secretaries, hairdressers, as well as teachers). These judgments suggest a view of Irish society; an implicit hierarchy rising from unskilled manual workers to the liberal professions, in which social prestige corresponds with the distribution of material advantages. Such considerations would seem to suggest that, for these young people at least, prestige accrues from material and other advantages, more or less corresponding with those cleavages, resulting in inequality which marks Irish society as a whole.

Alexander Humphreys had already underlined the ambivalence of status in the lower social prestige groups. To define a category other than one's own as superior is often accompanied by resentment and even hostility (88). The fact that members of the 'inferior' categories should interiorise their 'inferior' status — and many instances might be cited of young people ashamed to reveal 'give-away' addresses, and of girls associating with boys from a higher social group — does not, however, mean that they accept or resign themselves to the position of inferiority to which society assigns them.

The Bourgeoisie and the Liberal Professions

In the eighteenth century the Anglo-Irish nobility despised commerce and industry. Even today the theme of the anxiety of the rising middle class, especially of the commercial bourgeoisie, to associate with the aristocracy and, in spite of the latter's disdain, to ape their manners, finds expression in many Irish writers. The concern of this bourgeoisie with their social status can be discerned in their relation to the professions. It is universally recognised that the latter enjoy much higher prestige in Ireland than entrepreneurs and business executives. The very high esteem attached to academic achievement is a source of profound irritation to industrialists, who place great importance on the practical spirit. 'Doctors, lawyers, architects, these guys are the top' (*64*, 102). But the ensuing hostility often expresses itself as attraction. The aura surrounding professionals impresses businessmen to such a degree that they often present themselves as being professionals in their own right, in the special sense that 'professional' is beginning to acquire. And they invariably encourage their children to enter the most prestigious university faculties. In other words, they are eager to translate their economic superiority into a social one. The Irish bourgeoisie are well aware of their relatively inferior status and are slow to accept it. It is not surprising that individuals in this category regard themselves as being middle rather than upper class. But a more significant fact is that an appreciable proportion of this group do not succeed in placing themselves on the social scale at all, even though their material position and their influence might seem to justify their regarding themselves as belonging to the top categories in society (*89*, table 15). This hesitation doubtless reflects their unease about the divergence between their own vision of their social position and that assigned to them by society. Another index of the relatively low prestige of the business community: almost thirty-three deputies elected to the Dáil in 1973 might have described themselves as businessmen, while only six of them did (*103*, 1973).

The higher professionals themselves refuse to be regarded as upper class, no doubt for historical reasons, and prefer the more neutral label of middle class. Reference has been made to 'the unwillingness of the Catholic *nouveaux riches* to be considered as aping the old Ascendancy families while at the same time they are desperate to live up to the image of the style which the Ascendancy represented' (*111*, 215). This remark could be applied to the liberal professions as a group. The Anglo-Irish ascendancy class, which dominated the whole colonial period, answers best to the description 'upper class'. As well as its political and economic supremacy, it possessed a culture, a set of manners, a life-style, which constituted the measure of social status. In short, even the expression 'upper class' has associations with a bygone epoch. In any event the nationalist, Catholic, gaelic ethos of modern Ireland could not permit itself to glorify an elite colonial establishment from whom it had wrested political power, and which was supposed to symbolise centuries of oppression. It might be asked, nevertheless, whether this ascendancy class does not still, in spite of everything, represent the focus of prestige in Ireland. Their symbolic persistence in many areas of Irish life would suggest that this is in some degree so. British peers and army officers officially retain their titles in Ireland, and are referred to by those titles in everyday life, in the media, and even in official political discourse. The most prestigious institutions in the country retain their title of 'Royal' (Royal Dublin Society, Royal Irish Academy, Royal College of Surgeons, etc.). In spite of de Valera's efforts, top hats and tails are *de rigueur* at many social occasions. The titles, the symbols, the costumes, and the ceremonies of certain public functions copy the traditions of the British aristocracy. Horse riding and fox-hunting, favourite sports of the landed gentry, still remain in favour. Moreover, the *nouveaux riches*, often from abroad, buy up country houses and set themselves up as gentlemen-farmers. A British accent is still a mark of distinction, and rugby, the traditional game of British public schools, is played in the more exclusive Irish schools.

The prestige attaching to the liberal professions reflects perhaps certain similarities they share with the ascendancy, whose 'superiority' was often justified in terms of 'family', and a natural ease of manner which was the result of generations of breeding. The process of education to the liberal professions, slow and long as it is, suggests certain comparisons with the above assimilation of a distinctive culture and life-style. The professions also project an attractive façade, and give the impression of having lots of leisure time — always associated with the aristocracy. Their wealth is not based on business, nor on the search for profit, which recalls the contempt of the aristocracy for trade. For them the ability to accumulate wealth was never a criterion of social prestige. The liberal professions, which offer a very personalised service, encourage self-confidence and ease of manner in moving in the social world. Could it be said that the prestige of the liberal professions in Ireland derives from the fact that they embody, albeit approximately and inadequately, the aristocratic ideal?

Prestige in the Country

Numerous anthropological works allude to social status in villages and show that the rural community confers a very personalised esteem on certain individuals on account of their talents as singers, dancers or storytellers, or on account of their strength and courage. However, over and beyond such considerations, prestige is also granted according to such general criteria as ownership of property, education, or the success of children or relatives who have emigrated abroad. In Ireland a rather uniform scale of social status may be discerned in the countryside and villages. Arensberg and Kimball divided their rural community into four principal categories (*3*). The liberal professions enjoyed high prestige. These naturally included doctors, priests, vets, teachers, but also local county council employees. However, these individuals did not fully participate in the local community and only mixed on a superficial level in local society. After them came the farmers, according to the size of their holdings and who, in the villages studied in Co. Clare, were distinguished into two groups: large and small farmers. It would appear that the prestige enjoyed by small shopkeepers more or

47

less equalled that of the farmers – we have already seen how traders choose their wives among farmers' daughters, which would suggest equality of status. Then came the artisans, themselves graded according to their skills, physical prowess, or the routine nature of their respective tasks. In Kavanagh's *The Green Fool,* when a shoemaker, whose trade carried little prestige, became a small farmer, a neighbour remarked to his (the shoe-maker's) son: 'yer as good as any one of us, yer a farmer's son now'. But artisans have all but disappeared from the rural scene. At the bottom of the scale come the workers and labourers in the co-operatives, and the farm labourers. The above hierarchy dates from a time when the city and town were two worlds apart, and each had its own scale of prestige. Today town and country are much closer, but can one, for example, define the status of the farmer in Ireland as a whole? The liberal professions enjoy high prestige in both worlds: farmers will readily concur in this, and are invariably proud when one of their children enters one of the professions. They have a healthy respect also (especially where their daughters are con-cerned) for the secure and often prestigious jobs in the civil service and banks. Manual work in factories is regarded as inferior and generally despised (*111, 143*). Nevertheless such conclusions, valid as they are, must be qualified. In the first place rural Ireland has recently undergone a profound internal transformation and the perception of which occupations carry prestige varies according to the category of farmer. The occupational aspirations of young people from small farms bears this out (*48*). Although girls tend to shy away from manual occupations, a majority of boys express no aspiration at all or else hope to obtain a qualified manual skill, which they regard as leading to a desirable occupation.

The farmers, although not a homogeneous category, since they are spread over a somewhat extended scale of prestige, tend to see themselves as belonging to the middle class and exhibit common characteristics with the petite bourgeoisie and clerical workers. Nevertheless the more far-sighted and enterprising shopkeepers tend to regard the farmers with some disdain and the daughters of small shopkeepers rarely marry farmers. This perhaps proves no more than that country life is less attractive than city life, and that more prestige attaches to the latter. Country people often regard city people as being cynical, pushy, even immoral, while city people regard country people as being old-fashioned, slow, and narrow-minded. On balance, however, city life enjoys greater prestige than country life in modern Ireland, even though most Irish families have close links with some part of the countryside. And the fact that the activity of the farmer is limited to the country probably diminishes his status considerably.

The above might seem less than conclusive and it remains difficult to situate Irish farmers in a general scale of status. But our attempt to do so reveals other ambivalences relating to the petite-bourgeoisie and clerical workers. The fact that many children of small shopkeepers become clerical workers suggests an approximate equivalence of each on the social scale. But on the other hand the anxiety of these to leave their shopkeeping background for clerical jobs — a desire to escape from one to the other — might indicate that a change of social status is involved. The uncertainty of the farmers' position — an uncertainty which only exists relative to the city — did not lead to problems in the past. Nevertheless the profound interpenetration between town and city, the permanent contact and the resultant continuous comparisons between the two, lifts the farmer out of his rural context and raises the question of his status in the country as a whole. Here we must content ourselves with affirming the difficulty in so placing him, as well as the relative uncertainty regarding the position of clerical workers and the petite bourgeoisie.

Conclusion

The above considerations assume the existence of a hierarchy of prestige between social categories. However, other dimensions reveal further differences such as that discerned between town and country. Different degrees of prestige attach to the generations in the urban and the rural context. In the traditional rural world the old occupied a place of dignity in the community, even when they relinquished control over their farms. At family gatherings they were accorded a privileged position around the hearth (3). Nowadays this respect is often tinged with antagonism. Their knowledge of traditional skills no longer confers prestige in a world in a state of constant technological and social change. Here the scale of prestige is reversed, and prestige is monopolised by the young who symbolise the future and the capacity to adapt to an ever-changing environment. But we must not digress: in attempting to establish a coherent picture of Irish society, our focus must be on the relative prestige of the diverse social groupings.

The very notion of prestige, blurred as it is, raises questions that have not yet received satisfactory answers. On the one hand, one ignores the reality of prestige factors at one's cost (where by prestige is meant the way in which people tend to judge themselves as being 'superior' or 'inferior' to those around them). But for a scale of prestige to exist it demands, as a minimal condition, a certain consensus, and this is where difficulties arise. Can one describe Irish society as a hierarchy governed by a scale of prestige, when the most bitter conflicts in Ireland arise in the last analysis from disagreements over the relative prestige of opposing groups: between skilled and unskilled salaried workers, where the latter demand parity to prestige with the former, who in turn desperately demand parity of status with office workers, who refuse it, and so on? We have also observed the uneasiness and the irritation felt by the bourgeoisie in relation to the liberal professions. Finally, the farmers cannot be placed in any definite fashion in a national hierarchy of prestige, and the ambiguity of their position in turn reinforces uncertainty as to the relative positions of the petite bourgeoisie and the office workers. These difficulties, ambiguities and uncertainties must not be forgotten, since the majority of social studies are implicitly based on a vision of Irish society in terms of status, and these studies have as often as not borrowed scales drawn up for other societies.

But the analysis of status/prestige does help to investigate in depth the relations between social categories, as well as those areas of uncertainty where conflicts of status tend to arise; as if each social category were struggling to define a precise notion of its place in society, to justify it and consequently impose it on society as a whole. In the event, the status of the various categories is continually in dispute, under negotiation, only to be disputed again. This signifies once more that each category has its own particular way of determining its own position, and that considerations of prestige, far from ordering the structure of social differentiation into a clear-cut hierarchy, serve on the contrary to highlight social differences. Judgments of prestige based on a sense of social structure constitute at the same time a perception of the distribution of material and social privileges and a recognition of the different life-styles which underline these inequalities; further the designation of a social hierarchy demands a sense of social differentiation, and, in the last analysis, actually embodies and realises it.

PART TWO

THE SOCIAL FORCES

6

The Project of the Irish Bourgeoisie

Once a year Irish managers gather in Killarney for the conference of the Irish Management Institute (IMI), to reflect on the role of businessmen in Ireland and the contribution they make to Irish society. They discuss the future of private enterprise and discourse on the vision of the society which it is their ambition to achieve. In fact the project of the Irish bourgeoisie could be summed up simply as a commitment to economic development and the creation of more and more material wealth. 'Progress relates to more food, more houses, more of the things that go into houses', we are told (*103*, 1966). And again, we are asked: 'Do we want orderly economic progress at the highest possible level?' It goes without saying that the desire for such development is regarded as being universal, and that the horizons are unlimited. 'There is no limit to what modern free society may achieve' (*103*, 1971). Optimum economic development demands free enterprise and the profit motive, on which conditions alone a healthy economy may thrive. Entrepreneurs have no doubts as to the legitimacy of profit, which is the measure of a business's success.

The Irish bourgeoisie is dedicated to a revised philosophy of laissez faire, according to which the unrestrained drive for maximum profit by everybody leads automatically to progress and social harmony. Profit rewards both investors and managers, it produces a high standard of living, and attracts talent to industry and commerce. As well as motivating entrepreneurs, profit determines whether a firm can reinvest and hence expand. Every firm is in competition with other firms, but the bourgeoisie as a class seeks to establish favourable conditions in society at large for the successful accumulation of profits. This casts a completely different light on the orientation of the bourgeoisie, whose real commitment is to profit and for whom economic progress is declared to be either the instrument of the profit drive or its result. Economic progress then remains nevertheless the sole justification of profit, and the credibility of the bourgeoisie as leader of the economy and promoter of progress resides entirely in its ability to develop the economy.

If social progress relies upon the activity of the entrepreneurs, and their ability to generate profits, the demands of the bourgeoisie in this area are justified. This explains the reforming zeal of Irish entrepreneurs, since Ireland's industrial climate is not favourable to development. The public do not hide their hostility towards them and suspect their motives.

According to the entrepreneurs, schools stifle the creative, innovative impulse, and play down the value of material achievement. The political structure, obsessed with the past, as well as the residue of authoritarianism, does not contribute to the fashioning of a climate in which the economy is likely to prosper. Finally the lack of prestige attached to manual work does not help economic development, since most young people prefer white-collar office jobs as a result. In a word, the bourgeoisie wishes to mould a society which will suit itself – in its own image.

Profit, it is alleged, guarantees economic development, and expansion creates new opportunities for profit. But this cannot really legitimise the indefinite economic progress envisaged by the bourgeoisie and does not confer upon it the status of a universal class in whose hands the future must lie. Development, but for what? The answer of course is evident, and the captains of industry never tire of repeating it: wealth must be created before it can be shared; the high standard of living demanded by everyone, the improved social services that the same people are begging for will not be realised until wealth is increased. But the project of the bourgeoisie hides the fact that the demand for development is always given priority and that the ends purportedly served by development are often relegated to the background. Further, their satisfaction is continually deferred, thrust aside in the name of indefinite progress. Also, the bourgeoisie claims that the creation of wealth through the profit drive is the surest means of economic development. It naturally never questions this claim. And what if the drive for increased economic development undermines the ends of general welfare which it supposedly serves? What if it engenders inequalities instead of reducing them?

In fact, appeals for a greater sense of social responsibility on the part of the bourgeoisie, even from within the bourgeoisie itself, are increasingly heard. One entrepreneur has even declared, in reply to an appeal to the social conscience of businessmen, that business could not take upon itself such responsibilities and that a decision to contribute money to charitable organisations was purely a personal matter. For him, social responsibility would appear to be equated with charitable alms-giving. Voices have been raised among businessmen concerning their contribution to society. 'Those of us who share responsibility for the direction of management centres find ourselves under increasing questioning about what our values are – business does need a new ethic, it does need a new relationship with society' (*103*, 1974, 63–4). The Irish bourgeoisie presents itself as the group most capable of leading the country forward, of solving social problems, and in doing so hopes to prosper and perpetuate itself. But do its accomplishments justify this claim; do they live up to their promises? In 1966 the possibility of bringing together all associations representing the Irish business sector under one umbrella organisation, to be called The Nationwide Irish Business Organisation, was seriously envisaged. The project did not materialise. This attempt and its failure raise several important questions. Why did the bourgeoisie wait so long before attempting to unify itself? Why was the effort not taken more seriously? Today the bourgeoisie speaks with a myriad of tongues and twenty-two organisations are licensed to negotiate salaries with the employees of their respective sectors. One must not of course paint too black a picture. It has to be recognised that a certain unity exists: the Federated Union of Employers (FUE) dominates the salary negotiating scene and the Confederation of Irish Industry (CII) concerns itself with the needs of businessmen outside questions of salary.

The FUE watches over the interests of employers in all questions concerning industrial relations and during salary negotiations with employees. In this context it defends short-term interests and the immediate conditions of profitability. These interests derive from the project of development, but the FUE never invokes or promotes this project as such. The CII serves a more diversified function and tries to strike a balance between the incantations to develop and the daily defence of particular interests. It helps its members in many ways, furnishing them with all sorts of information, and even promoting certain industrial sectors abroad. It liaises between industry and government departments, putting pressure on them in fiscal and legislative matters. In its weekly bulletin, *Newsletter*, the CII unambiguously sets out how it sees the situation in Ireland and repeats as a leitmotiv the measures which it sees as necessary (*32*). The creation of new jobs, a national priority, will only be accomplished by expansion of the industrial sector; but the restricted national market does not allow this expansion, which depends almost entirely upon the success of exports. It is necessary therefore to create an environment favourable to exportable products, and to protect their competitiveness. It demands travel grants for exporting industries, as well as subsidies to enable small industries to invest in equipment, and to borrow. It demands tax exemptions and opposes all proposals to introduce capital gains and wealth taxes. It demands both cuts in public expenditure and a more adequate allocation of this expenditure to the industrial infrastructure. It presses for protective measures in favour of vulnerable sections of industry, such as textile, clothing and shoe industries. It expresses impatience at price-control mechanisms, considering competition as the most effective way of controlling prices. It participates actively in the Buy Irish Campaign, and is committed to the anti-pollution drive. It resists all efforts to index salaries to prices and in difficult periods asks wage-earners to accept a provisional drop in their standard of living.

The associations which represent the bourgeoisie only get involved in very down-to-earth activities, going no further than invoking the need for industrial development. As pressure groups, they do not aspire to embody a social movement or to invoke directly a vision of society in the future. In fact the bourgeoisie has no need of a special organisation to back up a project which is to a large extent underwritten by the State.

55

Economic development through private initiative is the economic philosophy of the State, which thus overlaps the project of the bourgeoisie. This is not to say that its interests always correspond with those of the State or that the State only takes into account the interests of the bourgeoisie. The bourgeoisie has to defend its interests, even and especially against the State. The bourgeoisie in Ireland then is not obliged to propagandise for a project which has, in any case, become the predominant one, but it continues to watch over those interests which derive from it: this is precisely the function of the representative organisations of the captains of industry and commerce.

The Bourgeoisie and The Working Class

The confidence which the bourgeoisie exhibits in its role as the leader of Irish society is to be seen in the degree to which it ignores other social classes. It ignores them precisely because they concur in its project, or are irrelevant to it. Nevertheless the bourgeoisie cannot but know the working class and wage-earners with whom it is in daily contact and whose labour it organises. An ex-president of the CII has formulated the attitude of employers towards employees: 'there is open conflict between employers and employees, but not antagonism' (*103*, 1972). The employers, though they recognise these evident conflicts of interest, never refer to the unions as enemies. All parties no doubt hold to their position but learn to live together, maintaining dialogue and neutralising the destructive potential of divergent interests. Employers desire disciplined industrial relations and regard favourably the emergence of strong, representative unions, capable of working out coherent policies and of applying them to contain spontaneous actions. They welcome a responsible organisation that they can get on with, negotiate with, and with whom they can lay the foundations of peaceful coexistence. In one of its brochures the CII foretells the coming demise of the authoritarian employer of tradition, and hopes for the development of 'human relations' within the firm (*33*). Moreover, the employers' associations readily claim to have excellent relations with the unions, saying that they work in harmony, not against one another. All the more so in that beyond immediate clashes of interest, they are partners sharing fundamental interests. Increases in salaries depend upon the success of the enterprise and only industrial expansion can absorb the unemployed. Wage earners have therefore a direct interest in economic growth and expansion. Starting from the affirmation of conflicts of interest the circle is closed by the conclusion that beneath these conflicts there is a profound identity of interests. Appearances only hide a paradox. 'We must continuously strive to reconcile the apparently conflicting interests of management and workers' (*103*, 1966). Relations between the two groups, from the perspective of the bourgeoisie, undergo a three-fold transformation, or rather are seen in different guises. Day-to-day conflicts are contained by strong and responsible unions (conflictual relations); employees and employers share the same desire for industrial expansion and thus become partners (relations of co-operation); finally the satisfaction of the workers' aspirations depends upon the prosperity of the bourgeoisie, that is to say on the success of its profitable enterprise. The workers are invited to follow the lead of the bourgeoisie, thus establishing relations of dependence and subordination. Accordingly, even in relation to the working class, which is so important for it, the bourgeoisie presents itself as a universal class, the class of progress. All groups in Irish society stand to gain from its leadership – or so it would have us believe: such is the promise it holds out.

The State and the Bourgeoisie

The bourgeoisie in nineteenth-century Britain advocated economic liberalism and complained at any interference from the State, whose presence in the economy it denounced as socialism. The Irish bourgeoisie as a whole still clings to the philosophy of laissez faire but has learnt how to prosper in the shadow of the State. It does not relish being abandoned in its task of creating material wealth but constantly involves the State in its activity. It has found in the State a partner which does not hide its intention of bringing about an environment favourable to economic development, by furnishing aids, creating a more efficient infrastructure and setting out fiscal and budgetary policies to this end. The State involves itself directly in industrial activity and has set up numerous semi-state bodies. The Irish bourgeoisie does not protest against this encroachment of the State into the territory of private enterprise; if the State undertakes risky investments, it has no objection to working side by side with the bourgeoisie. Tension between the private and public sectors has faded into the background, but more aggressive advances by the public sector could well reanimate them. A State capitalism based on publicly controlled enterprises, and operating according to a logic of economic viability and profitability, does not sound like an unrealistic alternative in Ireland. In the meantime, thanks to the convergence of the two projects, relations between factory managers and higher civil servants appear to satisfy everyone. Reciprocal and almost continual consultations, the informality and the openness of contact as well as social affinity all contribute to the satisfaction of the two groups. The Irish bourgeoisie does not hide its satisfaction with the State bureaucracy and one of them sums up the situation in the following terms: if you study bureaucracy and accept that it is there, you can handle it (64).

National and International Capitalism

The Irish bourgeoisie often proclaims its will and ability to lead Ireland

57

to industrial success. In spite of this the majority of recent industrial developments has been carried out by foreign rather than national companies. 'By the end of 1972 over a half of the fixed assets of all Irish registered industrial and service companies were in fact owned by foreign companies. But the proportion controlled by foreign firms is higher' (*212*, 277). The majority of companies availing of grants from the Industrial Development Authority are foreign, which between 1960 and 1970 constituted 70 per cent of new industrial projects. Not only is the foreign sector growing, but, made up of large firms, and directed towards exports (see Table 1), it possesses a much greater capacity for growth. This raises serious questions for the future of an Irish bourgeoisie.

Number of Employees	1964	1973
500 and Over	28%	35%
100–499	10%	27%
25–99	9%	14%

Table 1. Proportion of foreign companies according to size in the industrial and service sector (L. Gorman *et al, Managers in Ireland*, Dublin, IMI 1974, 23).

The necessity of attracting new investments from abroad is accepted by the bourgeoisie. Foreign companies have even been praised for bringing capital to Ireland, for transmitting technical and managerial skills to Irish workers and managers and for employing Irish labour. The CII unreservedly welcomes these newcomers, even though this welcome has not always been unanimous, and even though tensions emerge from time to time. Aid granted to new, especially foreign, enterprises in the form of tax exemptions have often been denounced as unjust in a competitive market. Liam Connellan, director-general of the CII, has taken up the theme of the different treatments accorded to foreign and national enterprises in regard to income tax (*103*, 1974). The CII has argued that Wealth Tax (introduced by the National Coalition government but abolished by Fianna Fail after 1977) benefits the subsidiaries of foreign companies and encourages the sale of Irish companies to foreign capital. Was it expressing its profound convictions or was it playing the nationalist card to combat a wealth tax towards which it felt a natural revulsion? It would not appear, however, that relations between the two sectors, national and international, lead to serious difficulties in the business world; after all, foreign companies belong to the same employers' associations as the others and are represented by them under the same conditions. But the nature of relations between them should become more apparent in the future, because economic development continually raises the question whether foreign and national companies operate side by side in their respective areas, ignoring each other, or whether they operate in a context of latent tension which could erupt from one moment to the next. Or have the national bourgeoisie been in fact subordinated to the foreign sector, and obliged to follow its lead?

Dilemmas for the Future

The project of the bourgeoisie, focused on economic growth, has become the major aim of Irish society as a whole, backed up not only by the State but also by the farmers and the trade unions. The dominance of the bourgeoisie will continue unquestioned as long as it is able to ensure expansion at a more or less regular pace. But can it? The question has been posed by the managers themselves: 'The rights of private enterprise to be entrusted with the task of creating the nation's wealth rests firmly on its ability to do so more efficiently than any other economic system' (*103*, 1967). 'Private enterprise does not always live up to its promises and the spirit of enterprise is not always in evidence' (*103*, 1973). The demands of economic expansion often force the bourgeoisie to make delicate choices. It can have recourse to a larger and larger State presence in the economy, which would furnish the capital and the basic infrastructure, would give its support to enterprises and involve itself directly in profitable industrial activities. But in placing the State at the centre of industrial activity the Irish bourgeoisie would risk the emergence of a strong State, and even of a dominant State capitalism. It could, on the other hand, appeal to foreign capitalism, which might sustain the present rate of growth for a time. But in associating itself thus with foreign capitalism the bourgeoisie would subordinate itself to a much more powerful partner at the risk even of being absorbed by it, and of losing its identity and its interests as a national bourgeoisie. Or is it possible that the Irish bourgeoisie can fulfil its own destiny and, keeping other rival projects in the background, succeed in spite of everything in carrying on its shoulders the weight of national economic growth? One thing remains certain: no collective social force has yet arisen which could seriously threaten the bourgeoisie, or usurp its dominant role. The foreseeable future for Ireland is a capitalist one, and the presence of other social projects has so far presented no challenge to the hegemony of the bourgeoisie.

7

The Collective Action of the Farmers

The ability of peasants to engage in a common course of action is indisputable; history is not lacking in examples of agrarian revolt. The land war in the second half of the nineteenth century transformed the whole social landscape of Ireland and gave birth to a new class of farmers (*46, 121*). Irish tenants did not hesitate to resort to the whole gamut of tactics in their struggle, including violence. They resisted eviction by throwing rocks and boiling water against the forces of the law. They blocked access paths to their cottages, and, after eviction retook possession of the land by force. They avenged themselves ferociously on unscrupulous landlords, mutilated their cattle, set fire to their houses and threatened them with death. Physical assault, ambush, assassination even, and other activities of Moonlighters, are well documented. By judicious use of the boycott the Land League exercised tremendous pressure on its opponents in the countryside, making their lives intolerable. More than that, the tenants gathered at disciplined mass rallies and refused en bloc to pay rent to landlords. This is typical of the type of radical action that is associated with almost all agrarian agitation. But it would be a mistake to assume from the radicalism of its tactics that the Land League was a revolutionary movement.

What did the Land League hope to achieve; what were its aims? A relative improvement in the state of the Irish rural economy after the Famine lasted until the agricultural depression of the 1870s. But then a succession of bad harvests made the payment of rent difficult and revived that sense of insecurity that was seldom far beneath the surface with Irish tenants. The agrarian movement grew out of this feeling of insecurity, which fuelled resentment towards landlords. The three demands of the Land League – fixity of tenure, free sale, and fair rents – were effectively granted in the Land Act of 1881, which fatally compromised the existing system of land tenure in the countryside.

The Land League, which organised the struggles of the tenants, attracted 'a class of respectable and sturdy tenants who were possessed of competent means' (*121*, 40). The movement was not recruited among the more destitute elements of the rural population and in fact it was the farmers who rented land, rather than the cottiers and agricultural labourers, who were stirred by the demand for the appropriation of the land by the farmers. Michael Davitt lost much of his support and credibility when, deviating from the aims of the movement, he demanded the nationalisation of the land. The tenant revolt set itself the target of liquidating the power of the landlords: in this it succeeded, but went no further. Three further Land Acts were passed to finalise the purchase by the farmers of the lands which they worked. They thus accomplished what they had set out to do but their victory had nothing to offer other groups in the countryside. What the land war accomplished was the birth of a farmer class anxious above all to affirm its newly won property rights.

However, the land war did contribute to the campaign for national independence. Presiding over the League, Parnell embodied the convergence of rural agitation and nationalist struggle. Moreover, the Irish National League — Parnell's constituency organisation — subsumed the Land League from 1882 onwards. This fusion of two movements was facilitated by the fact that so many landlords were of English origin: hostility towards the gentry nourished anti-English sentiments and vice versa. National independence alone, it was often affirmed, would lead to a solution of the land question. The Fenians, at the centre of the separatist movement, suspected this formulation and tried to keep the two currents apart, so as not to subordinate one to the other; in their view the satisfaction of the claim of the Land League would not necessarily lead to national independence. The majority of Fenian leaders welcomed the dispossession of the landlords in favour of the tenants, but at the same time feared that agrarian agitation would lose sight of the essential goal of national independence. In other words, whilst recognising in the land struggle a powerful element in the national struggle, they feared that it would stop short of their hopes and that a premature settlement of the land question would weaken their position. In fact the farmers did settle their quarrel long before any solution to the national question was to be glimpsed on the horizon. Nevertheless the land movement profoundly marked the nationalist movement. It crystallised the national temper by feeding resentment against foreign or absentee landlords and exalted the national consciousness. The tide of national feeling so created long survived the metamorphosis of the tenantry into small farmers and it finds expression today in republicanism, that fusion of nationalism and social radicalism.

This land movement, the most significant in the history of Ireland, affords proof of the capacity of Irish farmers for collective action. It is not distinguished chiefly by its violence, which plays a part in all large-scale agrarian agitation, but on the contrary by its capacity for disciplined organisation, by its willingness to negotiate as a class with the landlords. Have farmers in more recent times given evidence of the same aptitude for collective action?

The Collective Action of Farmers and its Orientation

Several organisations claim to speak in the name of Irish farmers, but nevertheless one voice prevails. The Irish Farmers Association (IFA) brings together the vast majority of farmers and is recognised as the official negotiator on behalf of Irish farmers. The principles on which the general orientation of farmer policy is based are clearly enunciated in the Association's programme and in its claims for farmers (99).

Agricultural development, the realisation of the full potential of the soil could be said to summarise the IFA's philosophy: produce more milk, butter, cheese, and so on. Only an increase in agricultural production will improve the standard of living of the farmers and keep them on the land. Increased production requires modernisation of farms, which means buying equipment, adjusting to the demands of the market, innovation, and the application of constantly changing skills. To this end the IFA demands improved advisory services to farmers, public funds for land development, and for drainage and afforestation schemes. It agitates for a greater effort to provide agricultural education and for the setting-up of market-survey agencies.

The modernisation of farms requires money, which raises the question of the availability of capital. The IFA negotiates with the government on behalf of the farmers for special low-interest loans. The farmers justify their resistance to capital and wealth taxes, as well as their reluctance to be caught in the income tax net, by their need for capital. Taxes, they say, would take away from them that part of their income necessary for re-investment and modernisation. The most controversial aspect, however, of agricultural modernisation, concerns land reform. The IFA endorses the idea of the viable farm and usually follows those EEC programmes which distinguish between *developing farmers* (capable of reaching the viability threshold with the aid of financial grants) and *commercial farmers,* whose farms are already viable. The size of many small farms presents a great obstacle to viability. But a farm can only expand by adding land to it from somewhere else, and for this reason, programmes have been developed to free non-productive lands and to transfer them to young farmers receptive to new ideas and qualified in the latest agricultural techniques. Retirement plans for elderly farmers have been set up with the aim of renewing traditional farms and eliminating farmers who are not capable of, or who have no intention of, modernising their farms. The IFA adheres implicitly to these programmes, while insisting that the hand of no farmer ought to be forced. The Land Commission is continually being criticised for its inability to transform the structure of farming in Ireland; but an over-vigorous policy of reform would doubtless draw upon it the wrath of the farmers.

An acceptable standard of living also depends on the ability to obtain a good price for agricultural products. Farmers have succeeded in sustaining prices on certain products by State subsidies on food and in the past have demanded grants for exports; they resist imports, which reduce price levels. The IFA welcomed Irish accession to the European Community, which substituted a policy of artificially sustained prices for dependence on Great Britain, which had been able to import cheap supplies from Ireland. The organisation concedes, however, that the maintenance of high prices for agricultural produces will not by itself solve any fundamental problems, and will not contribute to the long-term metamorphosis of Irish agriculture.

The IFA envisages therefore a situation in which farmers, having become efficient, will be capable of developing to the full the wealth of the land and will enjoy a well deserved prosperity. Such a vision does not necessarily involve any antagonism towards other classes and limits itself to rural Ireland as such. True, farmers entertain their suspicions of civil servants, whose powers of decision, on which all subsidies and loans depend, are deeply resented. Neither do they hide their opposition to capitalist efforts to control the outlets and the transformation of agricultural products. The co-operative movement was founded precisely to protect farmers and to preserve their control in this domain. But these fears only concern well defined groups and do not involve entire social categories. In a sense, farmers may be compared to small business or independent tradesmen, as the farm becomes more and more a small business enterprise, managed for profit. But in fact, and over and beyond such attitudes, the collective voice of Irish farmers in the IFA is silent with regard to the non-farming categories in the community. It is committed to a vision of a community of small property owners and condemns both socialism and monopolies.

The dominant perspective for the future of the Irish rural community does not, however, go unchallenged by small farmers. The Irish Creamery Milk Suppliers' Association, which brings together small farmers from the Munster region, proposes an entirely different perspective (99). It takes literally the principle, enunciated in the constitution, of keeping as many people as possible on the land. The traditional rural family is praised as the pillar of Irish society and the defence of the small farmer is accompanied by an idealisation of country life; simple and laborious, happy though frugal. The ICMSA thus strives to strengthen the economic position of the small farmers, almost all of whom are milk producers, and to protect them from elimination. For it, economic development should not mean the conversion of small farms into ranches: on the contrary they hold that it is the family on the small farm which is most capable of extracting maximum wealth from the land. The ICMSA thus believes in intensification of agricultural production and demands that the State place at the disposal of small farmers the means of modernising. It demands priority for small farmers when it comes to loans, sustaining of prices, protection of the market, and so on. It wants nothing to do with land reform and does not hide its hostility towards European programmes for modernisation and the retirement of elderly farmers. Far from wishing to see the elimination of small farmers the ICMSA hopes to see their number increase and this hope indeed forms the cornerstone of its philosophy. The Associ-

63

ation invokes rural Irish tradition, playing on the strong nationalist sympathies often found in small farmers and occasionally gives expression to the peasant radicalism of the land wars of the nineteenth century. It also gives vent to the prejudices of small farmers in regard to the towns in general, and in regard to the civil service in particular, as well as towards the trade unions, which are associated in their mind with nationalisation. Irish small farmers are most sensitive to any supposed threat to their property.

The National Land League shares to a large extent the perspective of the ICMSA but expresses itself in more violent and more political terms. The survival and consolidation of small farmers and the division of large farms into smaller units form the leitmotiv of their pronouncements. Bitterly opposed to the ranchers it would like to ally itself with the trade union movement. But the League only represents a small and marginal section of the small farmer counter-project. In fact such a perspective offers quite a realistic alternative to that of the dominant project. A number of economists have argued that the move to replace a labour-intensive by a capital-intensive agriculture contains grave dangers. Not only does such an agriculture drive farmers from the land, but neither does it allow for maximum exploitation of the riches of the soil: a commercially based agriculture is not geared towards maximum production but towards maximum return on capital invested. For this reason, it is argued, the interests of small farmers do not correspond to those of the commercial farmers, who dominate the agricultural associations, subordinating and submerging the interests of the former (*29, 98*).

Two projects, therefore, may be discerned within the farmer class. The first envisages the creation of an efficient agricultural economy, based on modernised, medium-sized farms, small profit-making enterprises geared towards the market and procuring for farmers a standard of living comparable to that of the urban middle classes. The second resists all efforts at modernisation which involves structural land reform – and ultimately the elimination of the smallest farmers. It looks to intensive agricultural production, which, it claims, is alone capable of preserving in the countryside a socially desirable way of life, especially when the alternative involves swelling the least skilled ranks of the urban proletariat.

Rural Social Movements

Side by side with those representative organisations through which the collective voice of the Irish farmers finds expression, other forms of collective action exist. They testify to a desire to regenerate the countryside and correspond by their size to what we shall call rural social movements.

Macra na Feirme brings together young farmers and was the moving force behind the foundation of the IFA, the principal voice of the farmers, with which it has kept in close contact (*146*). An advocate of structural land reform, it also seeks to reduce the age of farmers and to replace elderly farmers by young farmers familiar with modern agricultural techniques. It proposes the introduction of long-term leases, the simplification of succession laws in order to do so, thus facilitating modernisation. Furthermore, Macra na Feirme takes an interest in the quality of rural life, and encourages initiatives which contribute to the development of social life for young farmers. It organises amateur drama festivals, debating societies, evening entertainments and even adult education classes. Its aim is to train in every rural community leaders who are capable of expressing its needs, of mobilising it, and encouraging it to take charge of its own future, so as to bring life back to the country in a changing world.

The aims of Muintir na Tire are somewhat similar: the social, economic and cultural rebirth of the Irish countryside – a rebirth which only the rural population is capable of bringing about (*154*). Lack of confidence in the future, and in the prospect of improving standards of living, rural exodus, demographic imbalance: all have an undermining effect on rural life. Solutions to the problems of country life will only be found when everybody involves himself or herself in the task of renewal and mobilisation – when the villages, by helping themselves, overcome the general demoralisation. The efforts of Muintir na Tire have focused on tangible economic improvements (afforestation, jobs for the unemployed, irrigation and draining schemes, etc.) as likely to act as a catalyst for the release of other energies. But it has also sponsored activities aimed at the improvement of social life: the tidying up of towns, sewage systems, libraries, and so on. Finally, it contributes to social life by organising sports meetings, encouraging the formation of amateur orchestras and theatrical groups. It has even ventured into the area of social services, which it regards as charitable work.

The movement concerns itself with the rural community, but its actual roots are elsewhere. Founded and for a long time controlled by the Catholic clergy, it embodies a clearly defined Catholic morality: 'a Catholic plan for the reconstruction of the social order' was how Muintir na Tire first defined its purpose. Its basic themes – independence, solidarity, personal responsibility, involvement, social peace – all echo Catholic moral teaching (*216*). It encouraged people to go beyond the individualism which dominated rural Ireland, and which discouraged all initiative, trying to stimulate the development within the community of leaders who would help to disperse the apathy of the majority, take charge of their own lives and thereby restore life to the countryside. Nevertheless, its programme shows that Muintir na Tire, which seeks to be a focus of activity in the rural community, is not so much representative of the latter, as an outside force acting on it from above. The leaders of Muintir na Tire leaned heavily on the major ideological props of Catholic, nationalist Ireland between the 1920s and the '50s: loyalty to the Church, attachment to the land and to rural life, and a profound sense of Irish nationality. The idealisation of rural life implicit in its original programme created an affinity between it and the survival struggle of the small farmers. The rebirth of the country-side demands among other things that people do not emigrate, that the highest possible number of people remain on the land. Muintir na Tire casts a cold eye on all programmes for structural land reform and makes no reference to the predominance of small farms in the West of Ireland. In appealing to the good will of farmers, it seeks to change farmers' attitudes without going to the heart of the reasons for rural decline. It has, more-over, deviated from its original programme and now, with an interest in regional development, has turned an eye towards Brussels. In the event, high agricultural prices within the EEC have done more than anything else to bring back life to Irish villages.

The co-operative movement has also profoundly marked rural Ireland (12), and continues to offer its own solutions to the problems of the small farmer. The idea was that farmers would join forces, buy equipment to-gether and pool their resources. However, this type of co-operation did not materialise and instead farmers came together to finance the distribution and transportation of their products. The creameries afford a good illustra-tion of this type of co-operation: they produce stable outlets for milk pro-ducts and guarantee them reasonable prices. The co-operatives protect the farmers from commercial and industrial exploitation and back them up in different ways: finding group purchasers for their products, advising them and guiding them in their efforts at modernisation. However, these co-operative ventures take place outside the farm, and operate with a certain type of land structure without modifying it in any way.

The co-operative movement has influenced rural Ireland, albeit in an indirect way. The co-operative firms create employment in the countryside: certain small farmers draw wages from them on a part-time basis, without ceasing to work their farms. The co-operatives have stimulated a general demand in the commercial and service sectors. They bring skilled and clerical workers to the small towns and villages, and in so attracting young men and women they rectify demographic imbalance to some degree and encourage participation in the social life of the community. Thus they halt decline and demoralisation, forcing farmers out of traditional moulds of thought and giving them renewed self-confidence for the future. But despite its importance, the achievements of the co-operative movement are limited. It has not taken root in the West and the North West, which, because of their relative underdevelopment and their large number of small farms, might be thought to have needed the movement most. The success and sometimes even the survival of the co-operatives often depend on the commitment and leadership of people from outside the farming community, such as agricul-tural advisers and co-op managers. Their economic success undermines the co-operative spirit since, once they have become large-scale enterprises themselves, they exclude farmers from their control and management. The additional capital which their expansion requires now comes from the banks.

The rural social movements, then, focus on the two projects which we have outlined. Macra na Feirme concentrates its efforts on the modern-isation of Irish agriculture and a change in land structure, and thus coin-cides with the dominant project of the farmers. Muintir na Tire envisaged a renewal in rural life by keeping the greatest possible number of people on the land and in encouraging villagers to participate in the social life of the community; but the movement has lost a great deal of its vigour and could not claim to constitute a collective action of farmers. The co-operative movement occupies an ambivalent position between the two projects. On the one hand co-operation acts as a substitute for structural land reform: small farmers co-ordinate their activities to overcome the handicap of their small holdings. On the other hand the co-operatives campaign for agricul-tural modernisation geared towards the commercial world. The prestige of the co-operative movement in Ireland probably results from its ambivalent involvement in both contradictory projects (even though in each case co-operation signifies different things).

An Overview

The two projects to be discerned in the farming category are legitimised in terms of development of agricultural production, revealing the strength of the ideology of development in Ireland. But this insistence on development has driven a serious wedge down the middle of the farming community, according to the different ways in which the larger and small farmers see the future. The former envisage a community of efficient medium-sized farmers engaged in commercial agriculture and enjoying a standard of living comparable to that of the towns. The latter look forward to an Irish countryside regenerated by the presence of numerous small farmers inten-sively cultivating their land.

The farmers see potential dangers and threats from several sources. Let us recall them. Civil servants, agents of a remote impersonal centre of power, are often seen as irresponsible and incompetent and are the object of much of the fear and hostility of the farmers. Farmers also resist any capitalist attempts to control the outlets for the agricultural produce, as well as speculative investment in land. They resent the ability of the trade unions to bring effective pressure to bear so as to gain material advantages for their members, and to succeed in claims which they often regard as excessive. But these hostilities are really marginal to the farmers' project, and do not always result from it. Preoccupied exclusively by rural Ireland they do not envisage a transformation of society at large, which society hardly impinges on their horizon, and whose organisation hardly matters to them as long as it does not threaten their right to private property and their independence. Their hostility towards socialist ideas is related to the suspicion that these would undermine the independent operation of their farms. In fact farmers tend as a rule towards inflexibility, and there is a strong conservative element in their midst, though this is perhaps more a reflection of a certain temper than of their actual project. Both these projects exist within a particular social reality, in which certain needs are sought to be satisfed. The determination of the small farmers to survive obviously finds support among those of them least likely to attain the commercial viability threshold, while the desire for modernisation and development finds support among farmers who have already passed this threshold, or are likely to. Nevertheless several apparently conflicting projects may be found within any one category. It is easy to understand why better-off farmers might support small farmers in their efforts to survive, since the survival of the latter means high prices and high profit margins for the farmer. Moreover, most Irish farmers belong to the middle range and might hope to prosper either in one direction or another: either by intensifying their production or by expanding and adopting agricultural methods geared towards the market.

Each project spans a particular field of interests. The dominant project presses for radical land reform, more systematic exploration of markets, easier access to capital, and sustained agricultural prices. On the other hand the campaign to regenerate the countryside and for the survival of small farms goes hand in hand with demands for high prices, State subsidies and so on. The respective interests of both projects diverge and occasionally clash, as for example in the implicit acceptance of a necessity to reduce the number of small farms by the first group and the commitment to keeping people on the land by the second. Other interests are shared, however, by both groups, such as the demand for high farming prices — where both find themselves sharing the platform, even though the demand does not have the same significance for both — and in their sympathy with the co-operative movement.

8

The Trade Union Movement

The various associations affiliated to the Irish Congress of Trade Unions (ICTU) range over the different categories of the working class, clerical workers and even members of the liberal professions. Nevertheless, the manual working class dominates the trade union movement, which can be characterised without too much exaggeration as the most important form of organisation and collective action of the working class. At the very source of the movement, it remains its inspiration and gives it its weight. The unions sprung up in the first instance as trade associations, whose aim was to regulate the practice of the craftsman and protect him from the abuses of exploitation. It encouraged co-operation between workers, controlled entry and apprenticeship to a trade, and negotiated wages and working conditions (15). The craft unions were reluctant to be absorbed by the larger movement which came after them and thus risk their independence. Even today they look askance at national wage agreements and fiercely resist all attempts to limit particular claims in the name of more general considerations. Their desire to preserve this autonomy is a stumbling block in the way of trade union reorganisation. Though a number of the new craft unions admit semi-skilled workers to their ranks, the latter tend more often to join the more recently formed general unions. These attract principally labourers and unskilled workers, non-manuals and even clerical workers. They also welcome qualified workers who have been apprenticed to trades which were not traditionally controlled.

The ICTU forms a federation of clearly separated associations and each one of the ninety unions which compose it organises itself independently, defines its own interests and pursues its own policies. Such a union structure casts light on the nature of the working class and the logic of its actions. It allows for a purely 'sectional' definition of interests while simultaneously organising the whole workforce and attempting to formulate a simple coherent policy. In its manner of organising and identifying itself it oscillates between two poles of a dialectic of particular and general interests, a unity without fusion. The organisation of the ICTU into sections, complicated by added distinctions between branches of unions based in Britain and Irish unions with no external connections, has created many problems. But unification is only coming about slowly and often runs up against the sensitivity of various unions jealous of their independence of action. Congress encourages amalgamation between small unions, but its advice is rarely followed and amalgamations seldom occur. The division of members into different unions often raises thorny questions as to delimitation between socio-professional activities. Moreover, numerous strikes are directed not against employers but against other unions, and scrupulous respect for strike pickets can go so far as to paralyse whole sectors of the economy. In May—July 1974 a bus strike in Dublin, whose sole reason was a disagreement between rival bus-driver unions, lasted for several weeks. However, the structure of the trade union movement reflects its own self-image: the rationalisation of union structures does not only involve considerations of efficiency (93, 87). Something deeper is involved, the very nature of the trade union movement in Ireland.

The federal organisation of the trade union movement does not contribute to a reduction of internal tensions. However, far from producing sectional divisions, it expresses them, administers them and, of course, to some extent fossilises them. Solidarity has never existed between manual and non-manual workers. According to Charles McCarthy tension between skilled and unskilled workers increased throughout the decade 1960—70 and reached such a pitch that during the maintenance dispute the general unions mounted strike pickets as a form of reprisal against the craft unions (132). Skilled workers have always striven to maintain a clear salary gap between themselves and unskilled workers. Every salary increase which favoured the less well paid provoked a claim by the skilled workers ⸱⸱ this in spite of efforts by Congress officials to narrow salary gaps and even more in spite of the declared intention to seek special treatment for the lower paid in national wage agreements. The craft unions who represent well-organised categories of workers refused to get involved in general salary policies and use their often strategic positions to press for substantial pay rises for themselves. They are regularly accused of acting without consideration for the weaker sections of the workforce, and Congress often complains about indiscriminate wage claims which, though they might satisfy the short-term interests of particular categories, do not promote the more general interests of the union movement as a whole. The movement was polarised on this point every year when negotiations on a national wage agreement came round.

The ICTU is aware of the conflicting currents which it harbours, and obviously takes account of the preferences of its members, whatever this might cost it. It will defend the interests of affiliated members first and foremost, and only then the interests of the working class as such (if such exist!). For example the ICTU has never spoken out for a minimum wage, despite its declared aim of coming to the assistance of the least paid categories. It has refused to endorse such a demand on the grounds that it would detonate another cycle of rises, so that the most favoured categories would reproduce the original pay differentials. A committee set up to take a closer look at the question concluded that a minimum salary would solve nothing, and that only a broader union participation

70

and more dynamic union activity would be of help to the lower paid workers (*96*, Summer 1974). In fact the intensity of union participation does not directly determine the efficacy of collective action, since the least skilled categories belong to unions in greater number than in any other categories. Table 2 indicates the proportion of union membership according to very general social categories and reveals a progressive increase in the number of union members in their 'lower' categories. It proves at the same time that members of the working class, already much larger than other categories, join unions in much greater numbers than these.

	Men	Women
Liberal Professions	49%	
		30%
Clerical Workers	58%	
Skilled Workers	63%	
		39%
Unskilled Workers	72%	

Table 2. Union members according to socio-professional category (ICTU, *Trade Union Information*, Dublin, October-November 1974).

Orientation of Union Activity

The stated aim of the trade union movement is the raising of the standard of living of its members — in other words, in raising wages and salaries. Moreover this aim covers the major part of trade union activity in Ireland, and is behind strikes as well as negotiations. The demand for a large share of the national wealth for workers takes many forms: salary increases, pensions, social welfare, fewer taxes, price controls, food subsidies and so on. It involves itself in that other major Irish problem: unemployment. Here one can discern the basic principle underlying all trade union activity: to strive to the maximum to contribute to and to accelerate economic growth which alone creates employment as well as making possible higher salaries. Everything that slows down economic activity provokes the hostility of the unions and everything that contributes to it is finally tolerated or even endorsed. This principle is at the basis of all Congress policies. The ICTU has always insisted upon planned economic development in order to efficiently utilise all available resources and to direct energies to the same end. It has pleaded for the setting up of growth centres and has demanded more active and more direct intervention by the State in the creation of new industries and in the expansion of the public industrial sector. It presses the State to boost expansion by an adequate policy in relation to borrowing. It criticises the commercial and nationalised banks for not 'harnessing their means to the needs of the Irish nation'. It regards semi-State bodies as the spearhead of economic development and sees in State exploitation of oil and mineral resources the only way in which Ireland can fully profit from its natural wealth. The ICTU worries about the concentration of property in industry and fears monopolies but it does not object to company takeovers, as long as jobs are protected. In a similar spirit the unions have adopted a prudent attitude towards productivity improvement plans (which link salary increases with improved productivity), recognising such efforts as being necessary for Irish economic development even though endangering jobs. Finally the unions opposed Ireland's entry to the Common Market, fearing that it would lead to increased unemployment.

The priority given by the trade union movement to the need of the Irish working class for economic development underlines the ambiguity of its attitude towards the capitalist nature of the Irish economy. The unions are not unaware of the weakness of the Irish bourgeoisie and a document debated during a recent national conference accused the Irish entrepreneur of lacking in enterprise: 'The true spirit of enterprise is a rare quality', lamented the document, referring to the incapacity of the private sector to carry out its role (96, July 1972). The anti-capitalist feelings of the trade union movement are focused on the multinationals and the enemy becomes 'international finance', to whom must not be entrusted national economic development. The unions are continually demanding stricter control over foreign companies and 'national' development of the country's wealth.

Anti-capitalist denunciations are aimed at the rich farmers, speculators and tax evaders. The unions complain about property speculation, the absence of wealth tax and the exemption of the farmers from the tax net which weighs heavily on wage-earners. But these denunciations are rarely aimed at the industrial bourgeoisie for fear of slowing up industrial development. The unions support the bourgeoisie when they fight for the protection of the Irish car assembly industry, or rub shoulders with the employers in the Buy Irish Campaign. At its annual conference in June 1974 the Irish Transport and General Workers Union declared itself ready to help the government solve the problem of inflation and unemployment. It even suggested subsidising ailing companies with State funds (95). The same union joined forces with the Federation of Irish Textiles which represents employers in the textile sector, and made representations to the government calling for the erection of customs barriers. Similar delegations have been conducted on behalf of the clothing and shoe industries. Generally speaking the unions have always claimed State aid for private companies in difficulty, customs protection for industries suffering competition from abroad, and for subsidies for export industries. The trade union movement is not sworn to the destruction of capitalism and perceives the bourgeoisie not as an enemy but simply an opponent. Capitalism is defended on the grounds that 'there is nothing to replace private enterprise'. In fact, Congress has pointed to alternatives to private enterprise such as nationalisation or co-operative effort – though it makes no gesture of commitment in this direction itself.

72

The unions present themselves as the protectors of the weak and the oppressed. They articulate the needs of the old and the deprived and demand improved social services on their behalf. They oppose high indirect taxation on the grounds that they fall most heavily on the poorest sectors. They denounce the widespread poverty in Ireland and see in the annual budget a corrective mechanism for redistributing the national income. They propose a minimum income for every family, to be guaranteed by the social welfare system. All this forms part of the programme of the ICTU, though relating only tenuously to trade union activity, which concerns itself almost exclusively with improving the standards of living of workers, defending jobs, and protecting working conditions.

The influence of trade unions is exerted more and more in regular consultations and negotiations. Union leaders spend a great part of their time on committees, conferring with civil servants and representatives of other interests; they even participate in the management of certain organisms. The list of committees and boards which include national trade union leaders — whether as a result of nomination or in a personal capacity — is impressive. (The list of union representatives participating in various official bodies is given in *Trade Union Information*, July-August 1970. It lists ninety such bodies, and is not exhaustive.) This participation represents a deliberate ICTU policy and corresponds to its notion of the trade union movement as a social partner. This notion has been institutionalised in the National Economic Council, a sort of forum where the principal economic interests meet. In the same way the ICTU called for State intervention to control prices, and the result was the setting up of the National Prices Commission made up of representatives of the different economic interests. The unions, very attached to a quasi-corporatist decision-making process, favour meetings between organised interests and the direct search for compromise.

Other problems occupy the unions, other claims are formulated. But whether they fail to get priority, or fail to be translated into deeds, commitment to them rarely goes beyond ritual gestures of concern. Thus, for example, the question of industrial democracy has received little attention from the unions until recently. The defence of democratic rights, denunciations of repressive legislation and discrimination of all sorts issue regularly from the unions, without having much effect. ICTU avoids direct reference to partition (and let us not forget that the ICTU is one of the rare associations in Ireland which extends to the island as a whole, affiliating workers from Northern Ireland as well as from the Republic). It regularly appeals for peace after every outbreak of sectarian violence, even though many of its members, especially in the Republic, profess deep sympathy for an Irish republicanism that seeks the unification of Ireland. But these purely ritual gestures have little influence on day-to-day union activity. It has moreover been demonstrated (*87*) that union leaders judge the success of unions by their efficiency in industrial relations and their ability to negotiate high salaries and better working conditions for their members. The relevance of the trade unions in Ireland might be said to be limited to this domain.

Rival Tendencies

The preceding considerations took into account the official face of the trade union movement. But the formal coherence of Congress policy should not hide the fact of conflicting tendencies within. The controversy repeated year after year concerning the National Wage Agreement adequately illustrates the conflicts and their nature. During the 1970s the ninety unions affiliated to the ICTU came together to negotiate binding collective wage agreements, and the meeting produced profound agitation within the ranks of Congress. The defenders of the agreements pointed out the great advantages they offered to the weakest categories of workers and emphasised the reduction in wage gaps while benefiting the lesser paid workers. Such agreements also obliged unions to put aside their preoccupation with narrow sectional interests, and helped them surmount their rivalries and work towards greater solidarity among wage earners. They also guaranteed industrial peace, within which the economy could consolidate itself and develop. The national wage agreements projected the image of a responsible trade unionism confronting in a realistic fashion the most pressing social problems (inflation, unemployment, urban development, excessive inequality) – in short the image of the unions as social partners.

Those who oppose the agreements denounce the restraint they impose on the actions of individual unions. Far from reducing salary gaps they actually fossilise them and depress the average wage. They penalise the best organised workers, whose salary increases cause no harm to other workers. In any event, they say, the introduction of a minimum wage would solve the problem of low salaries. The national wage agreements inhibit the independent actions of each union, which is obliged to bow to collective decisions, and they put a stumbling block in the way of legitimate claims. Centralised negotiations bind in advance, and destroy the democratic base of the ICTU by removing members from the centres of decision, only involving them in negotiations from a distance and indirectly. Those trade unionists who oppose the agreements cherish the autonomy of each union, press for the satisfaction of sectional interests and adopt a more intransigent attitude towards employers. The two conceptions of trade unionism in Ireland result in a paradoxical confrontation. The defence of social justice leads to a kind of domesticated trade unionism while a greater militancy in industrial relations, often with an anti-capitalist flavour, leads to the promotion of more exclusively sectional interests.

The trade union movement operates, in the name of wage earners, as a pressure group and has recourse to a whole range of strategies, even though, as has been noted, Congress increasingly participates in official commissions where the interests of wage earners are set off against those of other social forces. It enjoys a somewhat special and complex relationship with the bourgeoisie. It fights on behalf of workers for a greater share of the national wealth, but it lends support to the capitalistic project for economic growth. It daily pits itself against a bourgeoisie whose leadership it accepts. It opposes the employer but follows the entrepreneur. It praises the entrepreneur while attacking the speculator and the tax evader. Committed to being a collective pressure group, the trade union movement does not demand a leadership role in society for the working class. It makes no attempt to attract other social groups and the occasional wink in the direction of small farmers convinces no one. The trade unions, defensive associations operating within capitalism by and large accept the industrial project of the bourgeoisie. They offer no serious alternative to the capitalist future of Irish society.

The Projects of the Working Class

The orientation of working-class action can be more easily grasped if we regard it under three aspects, or three principles which underlie it. In the first place, the principle of identity underlines the way in which the working class perceives itself, and the structure of trade union organisation bears this out. The Irish working class is subdivided into numerous groups, each aware of its own specificity. The federal organisation of the ICTU, its obsession with wage agreements and the priority of defending the interests of all categories of workers, illustrates well the principle of identity and reveals the dialectic of the workers' movement, caught between a desire to unite all categories of workers and the conflict of particular interests within its own ranks.

The principle of opposition indicates that a social force can only exist in opposition to other social forces, that collective action is by its nature directed against others. The Irish trade union movement defines its enemies as speculators, tax evaders, and international capitalism. It accepts the Irish bourgeoisie as a force capable of promoting industrial development, but it perceives it as an exploiting group, an obstacle to the complete liberation of the workers. The principle of opposition of the project of the working class is therefore split, fragmented.

Finally, the principle of totality implies a definition of the global goal towards which a social force is reaching, a vision of the desired society of the future. The dream of an 'unalienated' society has been the mainspring of workers' movements in many countries. But in Ireland the socialist project only manifests itself in tenuous form or is relegated to the background by the trade union movement. The latter supports anything that facilitates and accelerates industrial expansion, but it exhibits no urge to propose, never mind achieve, any alternative to the capitalist organisation of Irish society. The unions offer no challenge to bourgeois claims to social hegemony. They do not present their programme as a solution to the major problems of Irish society or as containing principles whereby a new society might be differently organised. Without any claim to universality they do not invite other social groups to join them in strategic alliances. Their totality of reference remains capitalist society: the workers' movement advances no rationality as an alternative to the irrationalities of capitalism.

Here we have put our finger on the dominant project of the working class. Focused on industrial development it accords priority to the amelioration of the incomes and working conditions of wage-earners. It proposes a vision of working-class solidarity, watching over the interests of the most vulnerable and weakest categories of workers. It offers a moderate trade unionism, anxious about salaries and working conditions, but not prepared to challenge the authority of the employers in their factories. It daily combats the bourgeoisie, while in fact recognising its dependence on it for the management of the economy, a recognition which occasionally obliges it to enter into alliances with it. Through this project the trade union movement strives to reform capitalist society, to modify it in the direction of greater social justice and equality. But it does not contemplate social upheaval. On the other hand, a radical transformation of society is hoped for by another section of the working class, a secondary project which is proposed by many small organisations on the leftist fringe which do not have as wide a support, but which matter all the same. The anti-capitalist orientation here is stronger and more distinct, and although priority is still given to industrial expansion, private enterprise and the drive for profit are not regarded as efficient or even acceptable means of achieving it. State intervention, nationalisation and planning are regarded as more likely to succeed in this task, and more likely to harmonise economic development and social justice, which are the declared aims of this project.

The nature of these projects is not reflected in the more or less militant stances of the trade union movement. The strongest unions are those which represent workers in the best bargaining position — in other words the skilled workers. But vigorous defence of particular and sectional interests is not socialism by itself even if it expresses itself in socialist phraseology. The division of the working-class project into two tendencies does not necessarily reflect the division within the working class between skilled and unskilled workers. Moreover the secondary project tends to express itself more politically than through trade union action.

A final remark by way of conclusion: the dominant project of the working class overlaps that of the bourgeoisie without, however, becoming identified with it. They both emphasise economic and especially industrial development and profess, admittedly with differing degrees of enthusiasm, a belief that private enterprise is capable of achieving this task. Nevertheless, the partial overlap of the projects does not eliminate the fundamental conflicts of interests between the two groups. The interests arising in those areas which do not overlap outnumber interests shared in common. In any event, it has been seen that the relative compatibility of the two projects does not involve a corresponding compatibility of interests.

9

Social Categories with no Project

Not all categories to be discerned within the framework of Irish society undertake collective actions and even when they define common interests and defend them, their collective actions are not necessarily in pursuit of a particular project. This chapter focuses on the special forms of collective action undertaken by certain social categories, such as clerical workers, the liberal professions and the petite bourgeoisie, who affirm no vision for the future and thus fail to stamp their particular mark on the face of modern Irish society.

Clerical Workers

The collective actions undertaken by clerical workers strike us in the first place by their diversity. Many clerical workers are not members of the unions which represent them, though the level of membership varies according to the type of work involved. Moreover, an exact calculation of the figures involved cannot be drawn from statistics, since these classify all non-manual workers, without distinction, under the heading 'white collar'. But the fact that many clerical workers – a majority of them even – do not belong to trade unions would not necessarily mean that they were uninterested in or incapable of collective action. Many clerical workers are, in any case, affiliated to general unions such as the Workers' Union of Ireland, the Amalgamated Transport and General Workers' Union or to mixed unions such as the Irish Union of Distributive Workers and Clerks. They thus partake of a network of unions which brings together a wide range of wage-earners. The groups of clerical workers within the mixed unions enjoy great independence in pursuing their own particular claims. Their involvement in the trade union movement does not prevent them from endorsing the established salary scales, which have institutionalised their superior status and their relative material advantages. Their autonomy of action is subordinate, however, to union policy and it is difficult to gauge their capacity to influence the latter.

Other branches of clerical workers have formed their own unions, which are, however, affiliated to the ICTU. One of these is the Local Government and Public Services Union which has on many occasions shown its commitment to the trade union movement, whose policies it publicises in its journal *Forum*. But it nevertheless advances its own claims and insists on legitimate salary differences for different categories of employees. We should not be too quick to generalise from one organisation which represents a wide range of administrative and technical wage-earners, including even some representatives of the liberal professions, all under the aegis of local authorities. Nevertheless the one example strongly suggests certain tendencies among unions of clerical workers which set them apart from workers. The fact that certain associations of clerical workers already affiliated to Congress came together in the now defunct Irish Conference of Professional and Service Associations strengthens this suggestion. The clerical workers' unions find themselves caught between two necessities – on the one hand that of pressing wage claims side by side with other trade unionists, on the other that of claiming special status for themselves.

The impact of white-collar unions on the trade union movement as a whole is difficult to gauge. They contribute to numerous meetings and often propose motions (95). But this involvement limits itself to very precise issues: equal pay for women, pensions, raising the ceiling of eligibility for free medical care, taxes, and so on – in other words, issues which affect white-collar workers. Moreover, Congress willingly endorses such proposals. Their impact diminishes when it comes to questions of general policy, such as the decision whether or not to negotiate national wage agreements. Representatives of white-collar and professional unions recognise the weakness of their position and condemn the *de facto* obligation upon them to submit to policy laid down by the larger workers' unions; especially as white-collar unions do not agree among themselves on a common policy. The majority of them favour national agreements between employers and employees, and, conscious of their limited capacity for industrial action, prefer ordered negotiation to demonstrations of strength. Others, like the Civil Service Clerical Association, oppose such agreements, either because they deplore the reduction in relative salary differences between categories which these involve, or because they believe they can bargain better if they go it alone. Such disagreements illustrate once again the heterogeneity of the white-collar clerical sector and the difficulties they face in agreeing on common programmes of action.

Finally some groups within this category are capable of extremely organised action while keeping their distance from the trade union movement. Bank officials, represented by the Irish Bank Officials' Association, have on occasions gone on strike for long periods, and shown a determination and endurance that surprised many. They insist on the special nature of their profession, the quality of the service they offer and the skills and responsibility it demands; all of which, to their mind, justifies substantial material advantages. Their claims are limited to material demands, and they act alone. The few motions put to the vote at the general conference of their association concern only very definite claims, relating to length of holidays, banking hours, salaries, promotion prospects for women employees, pensions, overtime, and so on. The policy of the association finds expression in presidential addresses as well as in the editorial column of the *Irish Banking Magazine* (*94*). The latter is remarkable for the extreme banality of its contents, made up of marriage announcements, retirements, and articles on leisure-time activities. More serious matters are broached in the editorials, which often express the hostility of bank officials to national wage agreements, as well as their antagonism towards all forms of State intervention in banking affairs. They prefer, in other words, to go it alone and limit their horizons to banking affairs, arguing that their relatively high salaries are tied up with the prosperity of the banks. They wish to resolve their differences without outside help and resist all efforts to involve them in general policies which do not directly affect banking activities. This attitude, as well as proclaiming a superior status for banking officials, also suggests a defensiveness and an anxiety to protect the material advantages which result from it.

Clerical workers thus have developed several forms of collective action, but do not present themselves as a cohesive group, as a social force active in the building of Irish society. They prefer to fight their battles in a localised fashion, to entrench themselves in threatened positions for fear of losing their identity and being overwhelmed by the trade union movement. As a pressure group they are scattered, and oscillate between a desire to become involved in the larger trade union movement and thus fully assume their identity as wage-earners, and a need to reaffirm their traditional superiority over the workers. Caught between the two, clerical workers tend either to be absorbed by the trade union movement or to fall back on dubious and arrogant sectional demands. This hesitation reflects, moreover, the internal division within this category, whose lower levels are hardly distinguishable from the working class and whose upper levels overlap with junior administrative ranks.

The Petite Bourgeoisie

The category of petite bourgeoisie has already been referred to and described: small shopkeepers and businessmen, bringing together a great diversity of associations, each one defending the interests of a particular trade or business. The Federation of Trade Associations attempted to organise these associations and to co-ordinate their policies, but failed, since some of the most significant associations refused to be affiliated, or having agreed, subsequently left. Thus it can be said that the petite bourgeoisie have so far not harmonised their activities, and do not act as a group. One might stop there, on a purely negative note but it would be untrue to say that no traders' association has defined its programme of interests or defended it by resort to collective action.

The Retail Grocery, Dairy and Allied Trade Association (RGDATA) is the voice principally of the grocers and has been extremely influential in the domain of the small shopkeeper. The major preoccupation of retailers – survival in the face of numerous threats – has found an echo in all the pronouncements of RGDATA (*190*). Small retailers feel that they render an important service to the community, and that their hard work, as well as the responsibility and risks associated with it, ought to be duly rewarded by equitable profits. The interests defined and defended by the association do not evoke society at large, or embody a vision of a society that they might like to bring into existence. On the contrary, the claims of grocers are very much involved with the survival of small traders, the continuation of their services, and of course the income which accrues from these. The theme of survival reflects the anxiety of many small shopkeepers, permanently on the brink of bankruptcy. At the same time the demand for support for marginal and uneconomic trading enterprises allows the better-off shopkeepers to increase their profits. Once more concern for the survival of economically unviable enterprises turns out to be the defence of high profits.

RGDATA has from time to time reacted forcefully against certain governmental decisions. It resisted the introduction of value-added tax, later demanding a reduction of VAT on foodstuffs and finally backed the proposals of a number of politicians to abolish it altogether in this sector. It invoked as a pretext for this the cost in overtime and paper work and the responsibility for the administration of the tax, all of which would be shouldered by retailers, but was also afraid of increased State control over retailers' accounts. For similar reasons the RGDATA opposed the Retail Price Display Order forcing shopkeepers to display the prices of their goods. Vigorous denunciations of State intervention echo another favourite theme of the small shopkeepers: that of an inefficient, incompetent bureaucracy, of civil servants deciding and imposing regulations in ignorance of their possible results – the same State bureaucracy which continues to charge excessive prices for inadequate electricity and telephone services.

RGDATA fulminations against State interference are at variance with its policy of doing its utmost to enlist State protection in its own favour. Anxious to ensure fair competition among retailers, it supports the recommendations of the Fair Trade Commission to bring about a return to normal conditions of competition. But at the same time it declares its hostility to the price war, which, it claims, leads to monopolies. In this respect it criticises the lack of energy displayed by the State and demands more vigour in the application of Commission recommendations. It also demands of the State that it crack down on cross-border smuggling, that it curb co-operative trading outlets, that it enforce its own laws, that it put a stop to roadside trading, and that town planning should be such as to produce favourable trading conditions for shopkeepers. Thus, the attitudes of retailers towards the State reveal a remarkable ambiguity, in that they veer between open hostility towards the 'bureaucratic straitjacket' on the one hand, and various manoeuvres in favour of greater State intervention on the other. This contradiction parallels another: confidence in competition as the only regulating mechanism in the world of commerce and a hostility towards various kinds of competition.

Relations between the petite bourgeoisie and the bourgeoisie can be strained. On the one hand, small businessmen proclaim allegiance to the idea of free enterprise as the sole foundation of a healthy economy, and to this extent they participate in the project of the bourgeoisie. But this does not prevent them from fiercely opposing capitalist interests. Grocers accuse industrialists of favouring the supermarkets by discriminating in their favour. Further, capital, which finances the supermarkets, threatens the survival of many small shopkeepers. Supermarket chains dominate and manipulate the market, both in the wholesale and the retail sector. RGDATA constantly demands laws against concentration of retailing outlets by mergers and takeovers, insofar as these lead to a monopoly situation in which the small shopkeepers find themselves powerless. Moreover, this hostility often finds expression in denunciations of foreign infiltration and foreign speculative investment. The Irish petite bourgeoisie are as ready as any to play the patriotic card, especially given its nostalgia for the good old days of customs barriers, behind which, for a time, they prospered.

The petite bourgeoisie have no vision of a new social order, nor do they envisage audacious reforms. The management of a small business needs stability, and the status quo well accommodates the project of this category. Their prosperity depends on stable, ordered economic development, whereas inflation destroys stability and leads to social unrest. An over-vigorous campaign to slow down inflation, however, undermines purchasing power. To guarantee the profitability of capital investment while at the same time protecting the purchasing power of wage-earners: such is the dilemma facing the RGDATA. It reacts by favouring salary agreements negotiated at the national level, appropriate tax concessions, appeals for increased productivity, Buy Irish campaigns — measures which, while keeping everybody happy, would also hopefully protect the precarious balance necessary for successful trading. The petite bourgeoisie, in other words, are torn between capital in which, after all, they participate, and labour, whose purchasing power determines their prosperity, and in striking a balance between the two they hope to perpetuate the status quo. The latter symbolises, for the petite bourgeoisie, social order and the absence of conflict and disruption, and they are vocal exponents of law and order, denouncing strikes as destructive and praising the police as guardians of private property.

The analysis of the collective action of small retailers, taken as an example of the petite bourgeoisie as a whole, is instructive in formulating some general conclusions. The grocers, it is true, articulate certain interests, but they do not see them from the global viewpoint of society, nor have they any vision of a future. Their desire is to perpetuate the status quo, protect a stable social order, and guarantee competition among small shop-keepers for the indefinite future: a utopian aspiration, since it seeks to perpetuate a state of affairs which is irrevocably doomed. The fact that they ignore the future means in effect that the petite bourgeoisie have no project and that they are content to live in a present over which they have little or no control. Their interests do not take into account society as a whole and as such have only a limited relevance to society. This failure to link up with the larger social context is reflected in their interests. They always appear negative and in opposition to all measures envisaged by the State, which alone are capable of mobilising them. They express what this social category does not want, never what it wants. Their reaction to threats tends to be blind rather than reasoned or worked out in advance. They tend to see things in the short term only, and limited in their enter-prise, fluctuate with the tide. Finally, their programme is riddled with ambiguities and actual contradictions.

What we are analysing is not so much an absence of interests, but a failure to establish mediating channels between needs and interests. The needs of this social category – to survive in profitable trading – are immediately translated into interests, whose direction they determine, so that interests come more and more to depend on a constantly changing situation, and thus fluctuate with it. One might advance the thesis that the gap between needs and interests, as well as the complexity of channels of mediation, increases in accordance with the degree of involve-ment of society as a whole in the formulation of interests, and to the degree that the defence of these interests ties in with the defence of a particular type of society. Moreover, a social category does not become a significant social force unless it takes into account the social totality. It might even be said of Irish shopkeepers, as of the petite bourgeoisie as a whole, that they have no interests to be defended, only needs to be satisfied, and that they do so in an *ad hoc*, that is to say, inconstant manner.

The Liberal Professions

The liberal professions, influential, prestigious and relatively well off materially, occupy a place apart in Irish society. Nevertheless, they cannot be said to constitute a social force since their collective actions do not present a united front. Two examples, that of doctors and secondary school teachers, will help to throw light on the social orientations of this category.

Doctors represent a traditional elite in Ireland and have long con-sidered themselves as guardians not only of the physical but also of the moral health of Irish society. Their altruistic paternalism however is marked by a strong conservatism and at the outset they reacted in the moralising mode to the rapid changes being undergone by Irish society. In the face of mounting juvenile delinquency and drug-taking they reasserted the values of parental example. Confronted by the phenomenon of what they called selfish materialism they praised charitable activities in the community and disinterested personal commitment to the building of 'a society based on education, knowledge, wisdom and humanity'. In the face of technological change and State interventions in their professional activities, their inclination was to fall back on the theme of the family doctor. The tone and the traditional flavour of their pronouncements gave them a decidedly marginal relevance. However, these traditionalist stances did not prevent them from adapting to the new conditions of medical practice. The Irish Medical Association (IMA), the governing body of the profession, has endorsed the efforts of the State to rationalise hospitals and has even praised the introduction of a system of remuneration according to the number of visits by medical card holders. The IMA co-operated closely with the Department of Health and accepted increasing involvement by the State in the administration of health services. Claims by doctors did not trouble this harmonious relationship or at least did not lead to militancy on their part. The years 1972–3 represent the watershed in relations between the medical profession and the State (*104*).

On one point however, the IMA has always stood firm. It has persistently and fiercely defended the professional independence of doctors, demanding for example that family doctors have a direct say in the administration of health services in every county, and that they play a part in the management of hospitals. In short, that not only the practice but the administration of medicine should remain firmly in the control of doctors, as the sole guarantors of top quality medical care. This jealous defence of the independence which doctors have for long enjoyed, their right to set up the criteria by which they be judged, to control entrance to and education for the profession, and lay down an ethical code to govern their dealings with their patients never led to controversy. The situation, however, changed dramatically in 1974 when doctors rebelled against what they regarded as an intrusion by the State in their professional activities and denounced the danger of State domination of medicine.

In 1972 the local dispensary system was replaced by another, more flexible medical service. A balance was arrived at between the protection of private practice and involvement of the State: the payment by the State for medical services rendered to holders of medical cards was approved by the doctors. This system fulfilled two essential requirements of the doctors: the freedom of the patient to choose his or her own doctor and an appropriate fee for services rendered. Thus the doctors did not become salaried workers for the State and continued the fee-paying system, symbol of their autonomy as well as of their status. However, the medical profession became alarmed when it was proposed to extend the medical card system to the whole population, and when official rates of remuneration for their services failed to keep pace with galloping inflation. Doctors were shocked and angered when the Department of Health denounced abuses of the system and proclaimed its intention to penalise doctors who received too many visits, and even to refuse to register more patients with doctors who exceeded a certain level of visits. All this fed the resentment of the doctors but the storm broke elsewhere.

It was in the hospitals that relations between doctors and the Department were most difficult. The position of hospital consultants had always been a bone of contention. The IMA strongly disapproved of the idea of salaried consultants and proposed an extension to the hospitals of the system of remuneration already in operation in general practice. The association also successfully blocked the attempt to extend free hospitalisation to everybody, on the pretext that such a move would bring even more patients into already overcrowded hospitals and would lead to a deterioration in medical care. They doubtless also feared that the State would spread its control to the whole of medical practice, downgrade private practice to a marginal status, and dictate its own criteria of how the profession should be organised. In addition the material situation of the consultants – low wages, long working hours, poor facilities, which always figured on the agenda for discussions, again became an issue, with the professionals' new militant mood.

The collective action of doctors takes two forms. The IMA interests itself mainly in the professional aspects of medical practice. Since 1962 the Medical Union has been negotiating with the State for increased rates for the treatment of public patients and for improvements in working conditions for hospital consultants. It has often fought hard, and accentuated its character as a trade union by becoming affiliated with the ICTU. Relations between the two organisations have always been strained and so far efforts to merge them have failed. The medical profession displays two divergent tendencies. For a long time it remained content to run its own affairs, independently, since the question of pecuniary reward did not arise in private practice. But when the State intervention reached a certain level the question of remuneration became a priority. The profession then went on the offensive, organising itself and bringing pressure to bear on the State. The liberal vision of doctors offering their services to a passive and unorganised clientele no longer holds, since behind the patients lies the State, which, in the last analysis, must foot the bill.

The militancy of secondary school teachers, from the start, had a much more trade unionist character to it. As salaried employees, for the most part of religious orders, their professional experience is radically different from that of doctors. The State and the Church dominate the educational system and continue to control the recruitment of teachers and the content of their professional activity, at the same time denying them their professional autonomy. Teachers exhibit almost all the characteristics of the liberal professions: teaching demands a university degree, and consists of personalised services. Moreover, the whole ideological atmosphere of Ireland propagates a view of education as a preparation for life rather than the simple acquisition of skills. This preparation for life is regarded as including personal development, and confers upon the educator a highly responsible role which he can only fulfil satisfactorily on the basis of a privileged relationship between him and his pupils. Such a relationship demands not only acceptable working conditions and the recognition of a certain social status but also that pedagogical criteria be given priority in the school. This is borne out by the claims of the teachers' union, the Association of Secondary Teachers of Ireland (ASTI), which fights simultaneously on two fronts. The first concerns their position as wage-earners which, moreover, undermines their claim for professional status. Their salaries, they say, ought to reflect their status, reward their long years of study, recognise the special qualities demanded of the teacher and attract people of quality to the profession. Inadequate working conditions do not favour the necessarily personalised relationship between teacher and pupil. The ASTI also protests regularly against job insecurity, which often reduces the teacher's role to that of a mere dispenser of skills, with no say in the way in which he carries out his responsibilities. These several factors deny the teacher's autonomy, as well as the priority which ought to be given to the teacher-pupil relationship.

These claims automatically raise the question of the control of professional standards, the second front on which teachers engage in collective action: entrance to the profession, continuous education, the independence or at least the preponderant influence of teachers in everything that concerns schooling. For this reason they demand access to positions of responsibility as well as significant representation on boards of management. They favour the setting up of an Educational Council which would keep a register, monitor school programmes, lay down regulations for the profession, and thus eventually become an autonomous self-regulatory body for teachers. However, this autonomy, which is the fundamental characteristic of the liberal professions, continues to be denied them.

The liberal professions represent one pole of social differentiation in Irish society, but, unlike, say, the working class they exhibit an incapacity to involve themselves in coherent collective action. On the contrary, each profession worries about its identity and its autonomy, and seeks to control entry to it and to regulate its internal operations. The liberal professions as a whole could not be said to embody a single social group, since whenever they undertake group action they invariably end up by accentuating their particularism and their lack of cohesion as a group. Each profession acts collectively, but in its own interests, and while both the teaching and the medical profession belong to the Irish Congress of Trade Unions, neither sees itself as wage-earners in the way other trade unionists do, and their collective actions serve only to isolate them from the rest of society. Teachers resort to industrial action to affirm their status as a liberal profession, while it was only the more insistent presence of the State in the administration of medicine that drove doctors to such action. The obsession with professional independence does not necessarily reflect a corporatist conception of the social order: on the contrary, it could equally be regarded as a form of liberalism whereby each social category regulates its own activities and derives maximum economic benefit for services rendered. Doubtless, the liberal professions do manage to preserve their autonomy, their ability to govern themselves and to maintain their bargaining power in a situation dominated by the State. The existence of State control necessitates the exercise of special pressures and efficacious collective action. The doctors are learning this lesson by hard experience as are secondary school teachers, in even more bitter circumstances.

The constant attempts of the liberal professions to isolate themselves, to retire behind their codes of professional ethics, betrays their lack of a social project and their deliberate refusal to participate in the building of the social order. Their collective actions never challenge the status quo, and are usually in reaction to what are perceived as outside threats. Their interests are defined in purely defensive terms, and remain unmediated by the presence of a social project, since they do not directly involve society as a whole and have no influence on its development. The ASTI has been criticised for its tendency to react to situations created by others rather than taking the initiative itself. The Irish Medical Association languished in self-satisfaction until the early seventies, when, suddenly feeling threatened by ministerial interventions, it became militant.

Medicine and teaching are not, however, neutral forces in society. An educational system, for example, reflects a society and contributes directly to its development; but the implications of this rarely receive expression in the definition of their interests by teachers. The liberal professions thus preoccupy themselves almost exclusively with the carrying out of their professional tasks and with ensuring adequate revenue for doing so. In other words, their needs concern the control of their activities and a favourable bargaining position for the sale of their services. And these needs can only be satisfied by the professions in isolation from each other and from society. But because they suppress all mediations between needs and interests, in ignoring larger social considerations, the liberal professions have failed to become a coherent social force.

Conclusion

This chapter ends on a negative note since it points to the lack of a collective project among the categories considered above. Its conclusions, nevertheless, possess a wider theoretical significance since they put to the test and modify the notion that collective interests cannot exist in the absence of a common project; the notion that in affirming its interests a social group projects a vision of itself and society as a whole, and of a future to which it wishes to contribute. Clerical workers, petite bourgeoisie, and liberal professions certainly engage in (admittedly dispersed) forms of collective action and, without advancing a social project, defend their interests. Clerical workers remain extremely fragmented as a social group. The petite bourgeoisie cling to a precarious status quo, caught between conflicting social forces, and, since their interest lies in social order, they are continually adapting to shifting circumstances. Their interests only envisage the short term and lack a vision that would confer firmness and stability upon them. The liberal professions react in isolation to whatever threatens their desire for autonomy and their bargaining power. Their interests are thus characterised by this purely defensive aspect as well as by great instability. In short, these two social categories seek to satisfy their needs without reference to society, without involving themselves in the construction of social reality. By suppressing all mediations between needs and interests they in fact limit their horizons, denying themselves a 'sense of direction', and closing off a field of possibilities in which they might rationalise and stabilise their interests. Instead of which, their interests fluctuate indefinitely with the social situation itself, which in turn directly determines their activities and orientation. They have not succeeded in finding a point of anchorage, and drift with the four winds.

10

The Catholic Church in Irish Society

The exercise of power presupposes both a will to gain power and the capacity to wield it. Most studies of the power of the Catholic Church in Ireland have concentrated on the extent of the influence of the hierarchy and the clergy, but the concern of this chapter is more down to earth as well as more fundamental: it seeks to establish whether it might be said that the Church embodies a coherent social project or advances a particular social philosophy. Recognisably a moral force, may it be said that the Church is also a social force? Does it uphold the notion of a particular type of society; does it consistently agitate towards a definable end? To seek an answer to such questions demands that we study the way in which the Church has participated in the fashioning of Irish society over the years.

In the course of its history, and right up to the present day, the Church has displayed great flexibility and political realism, so much so that one observer had been led, not without a touch of irony, to comment on 'the remarkable feat of nineteenth-century Maynooth, simultaneously orthodox enough for Rome, loyal enough for the British Government and national enough for the Irish people' (quoted in *195*). Thus, the Church was able to come to unenthusiastic terms with the British government; it opposed the rise of Sinn Fein within the nationalist movement, but subsequently accepted the *fait accompli* (*151*); it condemned the hardline republicans whose rejection of the 1922 Treaty led to civil war and excommunicated some of their leaders, only to become reconciled to them when they acceded to power as Fianna Fail in 1932 (*124*); it orchestrated a bitter campaign against the Labour movement at its beginnings but later relaxed its attitude so that dialogue at least, if not agreement, was possible (*152*). This agility in coming to terms with those who hold the reins of power attests the political realism of the Church, but at the same time betrays its conservatism, since it is seen as always trailing behind events, acting as a barrier to any social changes that might upset the status quo. The ability of the Church to accommodate itself to the dominant political entity does not necessarily indicate opportunism, and may prove no more than a flexibility of approach to the solution of problems as they arise: in other words, that while remaining pliant in matters of strategy the Church never loses sight of its ultimate essential goals – its own survival and expansion. The faithful must remain faithful, continue to follow the religious and moral norms laid down by their Church. The continued survival of the

Church cannot be taken for granted, and the Church as an institution must consciously and persistently reaffirm itself through time. The process by which the Church guarantees its survival and development involves a certain mode of participation in society as well as preferences and compatibility with certain types of society as opposed to others. It is obviously to be expected that the Church will always be favourable to the type of society which facilitates its own survival.

The Continuing Presence of the Catholic Church in Ireland

The flexibility of the Church's organisational structure has enabled it to weather changes which might have been expected to threaten and undermine such a conservative institution. This flexibility derives from the dual nature of its organisation: on the one hand a diocesan clergy which caters for the daily needs of the flock, and on the other a variety of regular religious orders whose functions are more specialised. These orders, to a great extent autonomous, compete among one another for recruits. They prosper as long as they are seen to accomplish tasks felt as essential to the community, but decline as soon as their functions are perceived as inessential. The autonomy, the freedom of initiative and even the competition between the religious orders assures the near omnipresence of the Church in Irish society, as well as channelling energies and vocations in directions where they can be put to most use (such as teaching, nursing, charitable works, etc.).

The flexibility also shows itself in the plurality of languages in which the Church manages to express itself at any given time. The language spoken by the bishops is not necessarily that of the local clergy or of the heads of religious orders. Without actually generating contradictions — though occasionally giving rise to tensions — these languages differ in their emphases as well as in their priorities. Further plurality manifests itself in the extreme diversity of opinion to be found within the ranks of the clergy themselves. During the Church's campaign against the nascent labour movement several pro-socialist voices were to be heard from among the clergy, which in the event kept open channels of communication between workers and the Church. This surprising ability of the Church to contain tensions which might threaten disintegration helps to preserve contact even with enemies of the moment. The compartmentalisation of relations between Church and people in Ireland is yet another illustration of the same plurality within unity. It has often been remarked that the Irish tend to be selective when it comes to interpreting Church teaching. They tend on the whole to follow clerical direction but on occasions they are apt to ignore episcopal declarations, especially those touching the national question and the question of political violence: 'When the Church denounces patriotic violence the Church becomes inaudible without losing its authority in other fields such as sex' (*163*, 283). The Irish, it would

90

appear, heed the voice of the Church when it suits them, and lend a deaf ear when it does not. They will even on occasion express anti-clerical sentiments when they feel, inevitably, that the clergy do not live up to those Christian values which they profess. Paradoxically, anti-clerical sentiment serves as a support mechanism for religious institutions, since it activates the religious values which serve as criteria for the criticism of clerical shortcomings. This plurality of voices within the Church contributes yet further to guaranteeing the continued presence of the Church in Irish society.

The survival and expansion of the Church depend upon maintaining an adequate level of clerical recruitment. Priestly vocations in Ireland came until recently mainly from the countryside, thus reinforcing the affinity between the Church and the rural community (211). This affinity finds expression in an idealisation of farm life, which is seen as embodying the Christian notions of family autonomy, neighbourliness, community and personalised social relations. Rural recruitment of clergy also reflects the Church's suspicion of over-rapid industrialisation, especially since in the urban environment the authority of the Church tends to be a lot less strong than in the rural environment. The Church's preference for rural life as opposed to the city life may also be gauged by the degree of clerical involvement in various projects for rural development, by its advocacy of the installation of small factory units in the countryside, by its support for the co-operative movement, and even for the setting up of large single industrial enterprises in the vicinity of country towns. Today, the predominance of clerical recruits from rural backgrounds is on the wane, due in some measure to the decline of the farming community. Ireland has always sent missionaries abroad and these undoubtedly constitute a possible reservoir for the future, but the falling off in vocations cannot be redressed by recalling Irish missionaries without weakening the global position of the Catholic Church. In the event, the Church in Ireland has no need to resort to such extreme measures since the decline in religious vocations has bottomed out. The present rate of recruitment is being maintained, possibly by lowering intellectual and other standards of entry to seminaries, though this policy might well jeopardise the stature of the Church in Irish society in the future. Another possibility for the Church would be to appoint lay members to positions up to now reserved to clerics, such as happened in secondary schools where religious have gradually abandoned their teaching in favour of a purely administrative role. In summary, the question of clerical vocations is forcing the Church into some delicate decision-making.

Flexible organisation, a contained pluralism, a renewed clergy – all these are essential for the maintenance of the Church's position in Irish society. But the development of the Church depends, in the last analysis, on the support which it can command, and on the continued commitment of a large segment of the population to the faith which it proposes and to the moral tenets which it propagates. This commitment can obviously wax and wane, but it needs to be activated at times. The Irish Catholic Church has always affirmed its preference for denominational education, and has never wavered in this affirmation (1). It sees education as, among other things, the single most important institutional means of reinforcing Catholic precepts, and fears that the Church would lose its authority as soon as it lost control over the schools. Priests, especially in the smaller towns, tend to exercise their authority in a petty fashion and keep a tight control over religious and moral practices. But this authoritarian exercise of power is becoming less and less popular, even in the country; nevertheless it is a constant reminder of group norms, and thus tends to strengthen communal religious feelings. Nowadays, a more considered acceptance of religious doctrine is taking the place of traditional, unthinking conformity. But the Church has to fight for this acceptance, and to convince the faithful of its reasonableness, a task in which it does not always succeed, so that often its teaching is in conflict with prevalent values. One might mention contraception here, condemned by the Church but practised by many Irish Catholics, especially the young. Such conflicts lead to scepticism and undermine the Church's credibility in other areas, as well as losing it support. In any event the Church finds itself caught by the need to preserve its traditions while retaining its relevance. Theology faces this task by consistently reaffirming the continuity of the Church in times of social, cultural and moral change, while at the same time cautiously adapting itself, by redefining its values, reinterpreting its dogmas, and sanctioning new departures. This is not to say that the Church bows to every wind, but that it sees the necessity of adjusting its teachings to the realities of a world in which it wishes to flourish.

Finally the Irish Catholic Church fiercely resists any threats to erode its base. It has in the past objected to the adoption of children of Catholic parents by Protestants through Protestant adoption societies. Also, the Catholic Church in Ireland continues to extract of the Catholic partner in a mixed marriage a promise to bring up the children in the Catholic faith, or at least to pass on his/her religion to them, a practice which is deeply resented by other denominations.

A religious institution like the Irish Catholic Church cannot take its survival for granted but must recreate and reproduce itself at every moment of its existence. Different mechanisms (organisational flexibility, the plurality of its languages, methods of clerical recruitment, control of schools, strategies for maintaining support, measures to protect itself against numerical erosion) all contribute to this end. But within this process of continuity and change, preferences and affinities for certain types of society appear. We have already commented upon the Church's affinity for rural life and its distrust of life in the city. The social control often exercised by the clergy is in the authoritarian mould often associated with traditional society, and the puritan moral hegemony of the Catholic Church extends to society as a whole. This authoritarianism may be interpreted as a choice of type of society since it sets itself up against social permissiveness. By demanding that Catholic doctrine be reflected in the law and by tightening its control over the schools the Church rejects the pluralist society which might be able to unite and reconcile in their diversity the different religious currents in Irish society. In such ways the strategies by which the Catholic Church seeks to reproduce itself reveal certain affinities between it and certain types of society, but not to such a degree as would allow us to pinpoint the type of society which the Church would favour.

The Social Doctrine of the Irish Catholic Church

Social questions are not a matter of indifference for the Church. A number of papal encyclicals have offered answers to social problems, but always in general terms, by enunciating basic principles. We shall now take a look at the way in which the Church in Ireland has interpreted and applied these principles in the Irish context, as well as at the different emphases to be discerned in its social doctrine. The latter has been enunciated, communicated, and popularised in the review *Christus Rex*, and a rapid analysis of the contents of this review gives some indication of its major outlines (*22*). The results are given in Table 3.

Numerous articles concentrate on rural Ireland. Emigration attracted a great deal of attention in the early fifties, when excessive emigration was draining the countryside and drawing Catholics to urban centres in England, beyond the reach of clerical authority and thus exposed to the risk of losing their faith. The interest in rural Ireland intensified when the debate centred on industrialisation and the modernisation of Irish society. Here the Church proposed to halt the decline in population along the western seaboard by setting up industries in small towns. Papal encyclicals have invariably expressed the particular affinity of the Church for small farmer communities, which embody essential Catholic values: family-based production, the virtues of communities formed by smallholding farmers, individual autonomy. But nevertheless the extreme preoccupation of the Church in Ireland with the rural scene has something obsessive about it.

Very mixed feelings towards industrialisation and rapid modernisation emerged from the pages of *Christus Rex*. Urbanisation, it was claimed, encourages a materialistic outlook, sows the seeds of secularisation and nourishes atheistic humanism. As for industrialisation, it exacerbates class struggle and undermines individual and family autonomy. During the sixties, which were racked by bitter industrial confrontation, *Christus Rex* opened its pages to employers and trade unionists, in the hope that involving the protagonists in dialogue would help in the formulation and clarification of their respective positions, and promote reciprocal understanding. This policy reflected the position of the Church, its horror of

	1947 1948	1949 1950	1951 1952	1953 1954	1955 1956	1957 1958	1959 1960	1961 1962	1963 1964	1965 1966	1967 1968	1969 1970	1971	Total	%
Rural Ireland	16 (2)	22 (2)	109 (9)		277 (26)	170 (15)	31 (3)	54 (9)	82 (8)	18 (2)	132 (12)	55 (6)		966 (95)	15.50 (15.63)
Industrialisation	8 (1)	56 (5)	20 (2)	10 (1)		51 (5)		40 (4)	24 (2)	24 (3)	18 (1)	82 (8)	7 (1)	340 (33)	5.45 (5.43)
Industrial relations	5 (1)	173 (12)	34 (4)	31 (3)	81 (5)	109 (8)	28 (4)	21 (2)	83 (10)	43 (4)	60 (7)	27 (2)		695 (62)	11.15 (10.20)
Capitalism, Socialism	69 (8)	21 (3)	139 (13)	181 (17)	17 (1)	14 (1)	16 (3)	10 (1)	37 (4)	16 (1)	55 (6)		71 (5)	646 (63)	10.37 (10.36)
Poverty, inequality	20 (2)	10 (1)								7 (1)		27 (2)		64 (6)	1.02 (0.99)
Education		26 (1)	41 (4)	68 (5)		4 (1)	15 (4)		70 (7)	23 (2)	137 (12)	29 (3)		413 (39)	6.63 (6.41)
Youth	18 (2)	7 (1)					66 (8)		16 (1)		7 (1)		52 (5)	166 (18)	2.66 (2.96)
Community, Local Gov.	12 (1)	17 (2)	12 (1)	11 (1)			58 (6)	17 (2)				27 (3)		154 (16)	2.47 (2.63)
Media				93 (6)	45 (6)	33 (2)		34 (3)		61 (6)				266 (23)	4.27 (3.78)
Family			142 (9)		24 (2)		65 (6)	12 (1)				25 (3)		268 (21)	4.30 (3.45)
Social welfare	35 (2)	29 (1)	10 (2)	24 (2)	21 (2)			7 (1)			80 (7)			206 (17)	3.30 (2.80)
Civil rights		10 (1)		36 (2)		43 (3)				10 (2)	17 (2)	75 (9)		191 (19)	3.06 (3.13)
Church affairs	78 (8)		7 (1)	29 (4)	8 (1)	46 (4)	36 (2)	124 (20)	84 (7)	177 (17)	146 (15)	105 (9)	18 (2)	858 (90)	13.77 (14.80)
International issues	88 (11)	104 (11)	19 (2)	6 (1)	73 (7)	59 (8)	100 (8)	109 (11)	48 (5)					606 (64)	9.72 (10.53)
Diverse	26 (2)	28 (3)	34 (3)	48 (5)	11 (1)	17 (2)	50 (6)	15 (2)	21 (2)	71 (7)		69 (9)		390 (42)	6.26 (6.90)
TOTAL														6229 (608)	100% (100%)

Table 3. Distribution of articles in *Christus Rex* by general themes. (The first line indicates the number of pages; the second, in parentheses, indicates the number of articles.)

94

social antagonisms and its appeal for solidarity among the classes.

The Catholic Church has always spoken out very strongly against any socialist tendencies in Irish society, favouring a society based on small-scale capitalism, family property, small businesses and farms. The insistence on the right to private property injected a particular virulence to denunciations of communism – a somewhat blanket term applied to all forms of State intervention. The role of the State, an obsessive theme throughout the period, was the keynote of the debate, and a 'corporatist' solution to the problems of industrial society was constantly advanced: a society in which socio-professional groups would organise themselves into corporations and collaborate in decision-making, and in which the independence of the family and of voluntary organisations from the State would be guaranteed. This corporatist organisation would ensure that all voices would be heard and that institutionalised dialogue would lead to class harmony. The corporatist or 'vocational' vision early on found expression to some degree in the composition of the Irish Senate but has left little trace on Irish society as a whole. However, the question of the limits of State intervention has been at the root of some of the most violent clashes between Church and State. The Irish Church recognised that a certain amount of State intervention was necessary for the smooth running of society, but not to the extent of either encroaching on other institutions, such as voluntary organisations, or threatening to weaken the authority and freedom of choice of parents. Which is not to say that the Church espoused the liberal cause, in defence of individual initiative against encroaching bureaucracy. The hierarchical organisation of the Church, the absence of the laity from positions of power within it, the tight control exercised by the clergy over the schools are hardly characteristics of a liberal or democratic institution. On the contrary, in defending the family unit and the independence of voluntary organisations, the Church was seeking to consolidate its own authority and influence. By means of voluntary associations the Church can dominate such spheres of activity as health and social services. Further, it is in a position to exercise greater influence on a family which has not been integrated into a State-controlled, welfare framework, and is therefore dependent on the State. Thus, the bitter opposition between Church and State can be seen as the clash of rival notions of the place of the family in society, and an expression of the Church's determination, by keeping the State at bay, to hold its ground in those areas where it has always maintained a preponderant influence.

Questions of corporatism, of illegitimate State intervention, of the autonomy of voluntary organisations arise time and time again in the pages of *Christus Rex* and are the dominant themes of Catholic social doctrine of the time. In fact, these fixations lasted up to the mid fifties and subsequently declined in frequency and intensity. From then on discussion focused on the need for social planning and the building of closely-knit communities. The Church had sought to exclude the State from the social and health services; now it placed ultimate responsibility for such matters squarely on the shoulders of the State – in recognition no doubt of the fact that no voluntary agency was in a financial position to shoulder such a burden.

A significant number of articles in the review are devoted to the study of countries other than Ireland. They tend to begin by illustrating applications of Catholic social doctrine, then furnish information about mission work and finally, in a change of tone, appeal for international solidarity (between rich and poor, etc.). This type of article became rarer at the beginning of the sixties, and subsequently the theme was completely dropped. Curiously the number of articles devoted to Church affairs increased considerably over the same period. The Church was beginning to have doubts about itself, to look to its future, to consider anxiously those necessary but fearful changes that lay in store. It was as if the Church had lost its certainties and, temporarily, its self-confidence: it no longer dared to pass judgment on what was happening elsewhere and turned its gaze upon itself.

Many other themes were debated in the review but an analysis of the contents of *Christus Rex* reveal that none were given the same scrupulous and persistent attention as those of Catholic social doctrine, which are the subject of the vast majority of articles: the necessity to retain the rural character of Ireland, the dangers of industrialisation, the idealisation of a society of small business men, the denunciation of State intervention and, for a while, the advocacy of a corporatist organisation of Irish society. *Christus Rex* clearly expressed the social project which the Church advanced for Ireland up until the middle fifties, but also records its abandonment. The Church has ceased to plead in favour of 'a Catholic programme for the reconstruction of society'. The question remains whether the Church continues to profess social concern.

The Present Orientation of the Church in Ireland

The public declarations of the Catholic bishops published in the *Irish Times* during 1976 systematically addressed themselves to general themes. Difficulties arise here since the editor of the *Irish Times* was in a position to decide whether a particular declaration was worth printing and to emphasise those declarations most likely to arouse controversy. Nevertheless, all statements by the bishops receive wide coverage and the hundred or so published in the *Irish Times* during the year bear this out. Moreover, the authority of the bishops enables them to make their voices heard and to rectify any distortions which they consider the media might project. So much so that we may assume the range of themes of their public declarations approximates closely to the message which they actually wished to communicate, as well as to the problems which they wished to examine and the anxieties they wished to express in 1976.

Peace	33
Personal morality (especially sexual)	28
Social questions	21
Internal Affairs of the Church	15
Education	6
Industrialisation	6
Nationalism	4
Media	3
Relations between the Church and Voluntary organisations	2
Others	13
Total	131

Table 4. The Frequency of Themes Occurring in Declarations of the Bishops (published in the *Irish Times* during 1976).

The figures indicate the frequency of respective themes (and certain declarations contain several themes). The violence in Northern Ireland is naturally a source of anxiety to the hierarchy who, in 1976, made numerous appeals for peace. Certain of these declarations couple an appeal for peace with an appeal for greater justice, and for an end to discrimination towards the Catholic minority in Northern Ireland. Others, very different in tone, simply evoke the Christian virtues of patience and forgiveness. The second theme, in order of importance, reaffirms the norms of personal morality and concentrates principally on contraception, abortion, and divorce. Unambiguous attention is focused on sexual and family morality, and on the dangers of over-permissiveness. The persistent preoccupation of Irish bishops with sexual morality is in keeping with a long tradition of sexual puritanism. Contemporary efforts of the Church to influence legislative decisions all concern this area of behaviour. The bishops had in the past campaigned against the proliferation of dance halls in the country as being 'occasions of sin' and of encouraging promiscuity, and had succeeded in curbing their number.

They disapproved of all moves to legalise contraception, which they saw as encouraging sexual licence. In the same way they oppose legislation on divorce. Although this does not necessarily imply a commitment to a certain type of society, the Church's opposition to the 'permissive' society does nevertheless express its determination to impose upon the State the responsibility to legislate for society according to Catholic moral principles, thus barring the road to pluralism. Legislation on contraception was delayed and diluted by the open hostility of the Church, a hostility which eventually expressed itself in sullen disapproval of the *fait accompli*. Divorce continues to elicit vehement denunciations. The laws of the country, goes the argument, must necessarily reflect the fact that the vast majority of the Irish population is Catholic. According to Bishop Newman of Limerick 'the Catholic people of our country have a political right to such indirect support from the State for their interest and institutions...' (*Irish Times*, 12 November 1976). The Catholic hierarchy proclaims aloud that the Catholicity of the Irish nation ought to be protected by the State and that non-Catholics can be accommodated only to the degree that Catholic morality is not threatened.

Social questions come third on the list and here the contents of the bishops' declarations differ considerably from the social doctrines of *Christus Rex*. Some bishops lament the extreme social inequalities which exist in Irish society, where the affluence of some contrasts so sharply with the poverty of many others. They express the wish that poverty be abolished and demand that the most vulnerable sectors of society, such as children, widows, the unemployed, and the retired, be protected. They thus concentrate their attention on marginal groups, and demand that society act collectively in their favour – through charitable organisations and improved social welfare services. The wheel has turned, and now the Church presses the State to make greater provision for the weak and the needy: to intervene more, that it care for necessitous children, that it build more houses and open the gates of the schools to all. Old quarrels have been forgotten and the hierarchy envisages the solutions to social inequities as dependent upon concerted action on the part of the State, as well as upon less selfish attitudes among organised social groups.

The theme of education comes low on the list of episcopal declarations. Declarations on the educational theme tend to be limited to praises of the denominational organisation of Irish schools. 'Short of banning religion completely there is no greater injury that could be done to Catholicism than by interference with the character and identity of our schools . . . we know of no way in which we can ensure the integrity of our religion – including matters of doctrine and morality about which we stand alone – except through our Catholic schools' (Bishop Philbin, *Irish Times*, 7 February 1975). The high level of religiousness in Ireland is thus attributed to the existence of Catholic schools, while it is supposed that lay schools would be productive of secularisation of thought, and atheism. It is questionable, however, whether the desire to furnish Catholic children with a Catholic education justifies confessional – and indeed clerical – control of the entire educational system. Pluralism does not mean segregation into groups, but respects the diversity of different groups within the same unified framework.

The theme of industrialisation frequently appears, expressing sentiments of worry and distrust of industrial and urban development. The bishops still favour co-operatives and small businesses as means of overcoming underdevelopment in the countryside. They denounce incessantly the materialism which results from modernisation. The national question is also evoked from time to time, generally expressing itself in sympathy for the nationalist cause; a special link between Catholicism and the Irish nation is claimed, along with the implicit or explicit identification of the Irish nation as a Catholic one.

Conclusion

Although the Church has a clear preference for certain forms of social organisation, it does not see its continual survival and development as dependent upon the existence of any single type of society. Nevertheless, the Church has in the past forcefully proclaimed a vision of society; it believed that the corporatist principle offered a third way between capitalism and communism, a principle which quickly became a catch-cry denouncing all State intervention. Irish capitalism in the past, comprising small businesses, never attracted the wrath of the bishops but today the Church regards with concern the increasing domination of society by large national and multinational enterprises. The Church has abandoned its corporatist positions but no coherent project for society has replaced them. The Church expresses its concern for the most vulnerable groups in society but relies on social assistance to achieve that end. Such problems are solved only within the context of the status quo or, more exactly, independently of it: it is enough that society should wish it and leave behind its selfishness. The puritan tendencies of the Church and its efforts to maintain control of the schools do have social implications — more for what they reject than for what they favour. The conservatism which underlies these positions testifies not to an enthusiasm for the status quo but to a reluctance to call in question a sort of accommodation to the established social and political order which in turn looks after the essential needs of the Church. Social changes will not come from the Church, but when they come anyway the Church will not hesitate to adapt to them. It will adapt to the society which is today in the making, but it will make no creative contribution to its elaboration. In the past it looked with aversion on the advance of urbanisation and industrialisation in Ireland and found itself incapable of holding it back. Today it no longer proclaims commitment to a particular type of society and to this degree it has ceased to be a social force. The Irish Catholic Church professes a social doctrine but no longer entertains a coherent social project.

11
The Paradox of Irish Revival

While there is no doubt that the Irish language possesses qualities particular to itself, the call for its restoration as the national language of Ireland is invariably couched in nationalist terms. The intimate link between the promotion of the language and the assertion of national identity is rooted in the alleged affinity between the two (*18, 168, 245*). Gaelic culture, it is claimed, embodies the true national consciousness, conferring a national identity on the Irish people, and the language through which this culture expressed itself provides a link with the sources of traditional wisdom and civilisation, the repository of authentic Irishness. The language, so the theory goes, is steeped in a particular mode of thought, in a philosophy of life and a type of humour, all forged in the distant past and whose echo comes down to us through the songs and epics of classical Irish literature. The enthusiasts of the Irish revival are not slow to wave the language as a flag in the nationalist cause, or to assert that Ireland will never achieve true national independence without the inspiration of the lost gaelic past.

It is doubtful, however, whether any nation can lay claim to possessing a national 'soul', a collective consciousness which records and interprets the shared experience of its people, and its history as a nation; particularly when, as in Ireland, the delicate task for revivalists was to pick up the broken threads of history by linking the present with a 'soul' which had long since become separated from the body politic. A strange national culture indeed which the vast majority of citizens neither participate in nor contribute to! And surely there is something paradoxical about a national language spoken only by a tiny minority. The present lack of communion between the Irish people and gaelic culture has even prompted certain nationalists to deny the existence of an authentic modern Irish nation. Which explains why the cause of this culture often goes hand in hand with claims for political and economic independence – the three, apparently, being essential elements of Irish nationhood.

The insistence upon Irish as an essential element of nationhood appeared late, however, in the struggle for national independence. It was the latter, in point of fact, which originally focused attention on the language, insisting on the importance of working towards standardisation and the creation of a single national dialect. In this sense it is inaccurate to assert that Irish reflects the national consciousness, since the language itself was taken up by the national cause for its own ends. Further, the alleged affinity between Irish and nationalism implies that English, originally imposed on the vast majority of the population, is not capable of expressing authentic Irishness. The predominance of English facilitates the flow of outside ideas and influences, and brings the Irish into contact with English mass culture. The assimilation of Ireland to the Anglo-Saxon universe goes deep. Apart from Irish political institutions, imitated almost detail for detail from England or, up to recently, the alignment of Irish currency with Sterling, everything encourages ever closer relations between the two countries: books published in Britain attract a wide readership in the Republic and the circulation of British daily newspapers in Dublin is high, while piped television brings viewers within reach of three to four different British channels. Emigration and travel, inevitable given the proximity of the two countries, encourage contact, so that many Irish people claim to feel equally at home in Ireland and England. London fashions never take long to reach Dublin, and English pop stars and football teams attract a large following in Ireland. This widespread assimilation of English culture, especially among the younger generation, made possible by the predominance of the English language, has attained the dimension of almost total anglicisation. In this situation, the Irish language has come to symbolise resistance to the levelling influence of English mass culture. The project for setting up a second television channel in Ireland crystallised opinions for a while around the question of the survival of the national culture. A proposal to simply retransmit BBC programmes in Ireland was bitterly denounced by Irish language groups as the first act in the anglicisation — the cultural conquest — of Ireland.

But in fact many people deny that a privileged relationship exists between the Irish language and national identity. The term culture designates the way in which people live, the ideas they believe in and the language in which they communicate. Only a small minority of Irish people speak the Irish language — those who live in the remote Gaeltacht districts and a scattering of enthusiasts around the country. The modern Irish communicate with each other in English and, ironically, the nationalist cause itself was propagated through the medium of English. Certain leaders in the national struggle made no attempt to hide their hostility to the language, while others remained at best indifferent. It could not be claimed that Irish identity was in any way diminished by the predominance of English, and the history of the struggle against Great Britain has sometimes ignored gaelic culture. The assertion of Irish national identity did not need to wait for the gaelic revival to come along. On the contrary, the nationalist movement was quick to perceive the usefulness of this culture in crystallising nationalist sentiments and in mobilising sympathy for their cause.

Paradoxically, the Anglo-Irish literary movement, originating as it did in an ascendancy class which had ruled Ireland for several centuries, contributed to the gaelic revival by its romantic conception of an Irish past, by its popularisation of traditional Irish epics and by drawing for inspiration on mythical sources in the distant past. A further paradox is contained in the notion of ancient Celtic society as an embryo of the modern Irish nation. Celtic society before the Norman conquest was riddled with clan rivalries, and held together by a hierarchy of inter-dependencies always threatened with disintegration: it bore no resemblance whatever to a nation as we know it. Moreover, the concept of nationhood is a recent one, which first made its appearance in Ireland under the influence of British political thought. The aristocratic past of gaelic society is used as an ideological prop to a nationalist cause — nationalism being a modern phenomenon — and, ironically, as a weapon of popular republicanism in the nineteenth century in the struggle to unseat another, later, aristocracy.

The urge to assert a specific Irish identity is not necessarily inconsistent with a desire to participate in the culture of the English-speaking world. The desire for cultural identity is never more strongly felt than in a society which finds itself part of a larger culture, especially one with claims to universality. English might be denounced as a levelling influence but it is also valued for the direct links which it provides with world culture. This dualism goes some way towards explaining the support for a bilingual solution in Ireland. It is thought that bilingualism could both protect Irish identity and at the same time allow participation in a larger cultural universe. On the other hand, an over-emphasis on gaelic culture runs the risk of provincialism, ethnocentricity, and isolation from outside influences. The Irish language movement tends to look too much to the past, to over-indulge in nostalgia and to be more preoccupied with symbols and rituals than with what people believe, live, and feel. The attempt to resist the levelling influences of mass culture is accompanied, however, by a national desire to participate in a less restricted universe. This could be said to explain in part the apparent contradiction, revealed by numerous surveys, between the widespread support for the Irish language and the unwillingness to translate this support into deeds; the contrast between the public lip-service regularly paid to the language and private indifference (*210, 252*). The symbolic use of the language on official and State occasions is considered to be a sufficient expression of national identity. The rift between appearance and reality, between wishful thinking and meaningful action, between thought and deed, has been noted by numerous commentators, who interpret the phenomenon in terms of a national schizophrenia attributable to the trauma of colonialism. Others simply attribute it to the poor teaching of Irish in the schools and a consequent inability to speak it (*252*). But both interpretations miss the essential point: the apparent contradiction between the almost general acceptance of gaelic culture as a symbol of nationhood and the inability or refusal to speak the language in everyday life constitutes a strategy in a sort of dialectical balancing act in which the particular (Irish culture) and the universal (Anglo-Saxon culture) are set off against each other and the claims of both partially satisfied.

Attitudes towards the Irish language differ considerably from one social category to another and the key to these differences might be found in the above mentioned dialectic. The people most determined to revive and speak the language belong to two social groups: those who live in the Gaeltacht, where Irish is the vernacular, and the educated professional middle classes. In other words, the peasants and the literati, the former group being cut off from English culture, the latter on familiar terms with it. All other social groups remain either indifferent or hostile to the language. Hostility can be discerned among the managerial class, indifference among the working class, who continue to pay lip-service to the language while not speaking it. A positive attitude towards Irish is to be found only among the urban middle and upper classes (252). Might it be suggested that the people in this social group who value the Irish language do so precisely because of their familiarity with and command of Anglo-Saxon culture? The desire of this particular group to affirm an Irish identity does not express itself in hostility towards their English neighbours and it would be interesting to investigate whether their attitudes towards the language enable them to distance themselves from other middle-class groups (administrative and office workers) who are untroubled by their participation in Anglo-Saxon culture and who possibly communicate in Irish with much less assurance. It would indeed be interesting to investigate the reasons why an upper middle class came to espouse the cause of a language traditionally associated with a society of peasants and small farmers.

Numerous organisations over the years took upon themselves the task of promoting the gaelic cause, but none more so than the Gaelic League, which still plays a central role in the revival movement (217). The Gaelic League insists upon Irish as an essential element in national identity. From its foundation, many nationalist leaders were recruited from the ranks of the League and close links were forged between it and Sinn Fein. Douglas Hyde, a central figure in the League, resigned his presidency in protest against the identification pure and simple of the League and advanced nationalist policies. The issue of direct political involvement, of a subordination of the movement to nationalist politics, again raised its head in the seventies and continues to be a source of serious dissension in the ranks of the Gaelic League. Certain members have been recently trying, without success, to prise the revival movement away from overt political positions, to tone down the militant nationalist image, in an effort to appeal to a wider public. In any event, overtly or otherwise, the sympathies of the revival movement are unambiguously nationalist and, as we have seen, mere political independence without an authentic Irish culture was never regarded by it as the realisation of true nationhood.

In its efforts to promote the speaking of Irish, the Gaelic League from its beginnings sought to popularise traditional gaelic culture. It organised language classes throughout the country, encouraged traditional music and dance, and launched various festivals. It thus offered leisure-time activities while at the same time managing to set in motion a national adult education movement. Even today organisations like Gael Linn publish, underwrite films and carry out research in modern language teaching methodology. But the emergence of a politically independent Southern Ireland, committed to a gaelic renaissance, radically changed the context in which the Gaelic League operated, as well as its activities. From being a promoter of gaelic culture it became a pressure group, determined to keep the politicians to their promises. The movement ceased to contemplate the restoration of the language without the support of the State and its constant backing. The thinking was that the language would recover its former prominence if Irish became obligatory in schools, if knowledge of Irish became a requirement for entry to the civil service and if a significant number of programmes in Irish were broadcast on radio and television. The institutionalisation of the language certainly bore fruit and its position improved considerably: today all Irish people possess at least the rudiments of the language. But many criticise the strategy of entrusting to the State the task of revival, or at least of depending on it to too great a degree (*215*). The decline in the strictly cultural activities of the movement, its withdrawal from direct participation in the promotion and expansion of gaelic culture, the obsession with historical legitimacy, the gradual slowing down of the creative pulse in literature in the Irish language, all testify to the profound changes in the very nature of the gaelic movement since the achievement of independence in Southern Ireland. Others doubt whether compulsory Irish, by itself, could ever transform English speakers into fluent Irish speakers (*17, 18*). A language is most strongly influenced by its immediate environment – by the home, the place where one lives. In this sense the schools are fighting a losing battle. Furthermore, the Irish language will survive only if people come to appreciate it – and not simply as a result of it being imposed on them. There is surely something curious about a cultural movement which, instead of seeking to attract people to it by developing its creative spirit, by expressing what people live and feel, allows itself to become hidebound by officialdom. The taking up of the cause of revival by the State and its consequent institutionalisation might turn out to be the kiss of death to the rich reservoir of the gaelic heritage.

These various considerations ought to help us in answering the real questions raised by this chapter: to what extent is the restoration of a gaelic language and culture tied up with the creation or the re-creation of a particular type of society, and what are the real relationships between the Irish language and Irish society? The paradoxes outlined above ought in some degree to cast light upon the nature of the involvement of the revival movement in Irish society. In a sense, by allowing itself to become submerged in the nationalist struggle the revival movement became associated in the Irish mind with a vision of a rural society of independent small farmers. Even today it is battling for the survival of the Gaeltacht, those remote idealised pockets of Gaelic culture still 'unsullied by the inroads of modern civilisation'. It is by no means difficult to understand why the defence of Gaeltacht areas, those last bastions of *fíor gaelige,* should be dear to the hearts of revival enthusiasts. Nevertheless a too close identity between the Gaeltacht and the revival movement tends to identify the language in the public mind with a backward and doomed peasant society. The Gaelic League has in fact realised that its task is to promote the language in the towns and cities and that the survival of the language itself depends on its success in doing so. In spite of everything many continue to question the relevance of gaelic culture to modern urban culture, or whether Irish can serve as an adequate medium of communication in a modern industrial society. But the rural affinities of the language cannot be said to constitute a commitment to a particular type of society. Rooted as it is in a rural past, the language movement is today trying to extricate itself from its past and project a new image. Will it succeed? If not, this will be because it is identified too closely with a particular type of traditional society and will inevitably perish with it. If it succeeds this will be proof of its capacity to adapt to different types of society, proof that it no longer embodies a social force contributing to the building of a new society. Here we have the ultimate paradox of the revival movement: it will fail in its aims to the degree to which it continues to identify with traditional rural values which are on the wane in Irish society. It will succeed to the degree to which it embodies no significant social force and becomes indifferent to the type of society in which it finds itself.

PART THREE

THE STATE AND IRISH SOCIETY

12
Political Parties and Social Forces

The preceding chapters have sought to identify the social forces at work in Ireland and to define the orientation that their actions take. These social forces act at every level of society, but particularly in the political arena, where relations of power are welded and where social action seeks political legitimation. Political life, at least where parliamentary systems are concerned, revolves around political parties, the privileged agents of political practice. Our task now is to study the parties which confront each other on the political stage and to seek and define how they relate to the social forces. This chapter thus focuses on the nature of these relationships in the Republic of Ireland. It does not, nor could it, regard one as simply mirroring the other, as if social forces simply disguised themselves as political parties before entering the arena, or as if they merely created organisations and subsequently manipulated them at will. But nevertheless political parties do not ignore those social forces on which they depend and even go out of their way to establish special links with some of them. It is obvious that political parties are engaged in political action and that to this degree they commit themselves in certain definite directions. This implies that social classes and political parties are involved in a complex interplay. Social classes strive to realise their social projects and lend their support to one or other party accordingly. Political parties decide upon programmes of action which they think will bring them political power, having worked out which sources of support will best enhance their electoral chances without binding them too closely to any one social category. We shall now attempt to trace the complex dialectic which pertains in Ireland between social classes and political parties.

Fianna Fail

Fianna Fail enjoys an extremely varied support in Ireland and draws its support from all categories of Irish society. So many opinion polls over the years have come up with this conclusion that it has become an unquestioned commonplace (*148*). But such a state of affairs raises fundamental questions. How can a political party attract the support of social classes which are often engaged in open conflict among themselves? How can it succeed in bringing together such contrasting social forces? What are these policies which, it would appear, keep everybody happy?

For this astonishing balancing act is precisely what Fianna Fail has succeeded in maintaining since the 1930s. That a party should solicit the support of a particular social class, by taking into account certain of its interests, is fair enough. But this does not imply that the political party become a plaything in the hands of this social class or even that the latter respond to the advances made to it. Nevertheless, all social classes in Ireland are receptive to the advances of Fianna Fail, and one is inclined to wonder whether some of them are simply being duped. It is necessary to understand how Fianna Fail can rely on the support both of the bourgeoisie and the working class, how it retains its popularity among small farmers, even though it accepts the agricultural policy of the European Community whose principal aim is to eliminate small farms, which it considers marginal and uneconomical. It remains to us to trace, with whatever precision possible, the links which Fianna Fail entertains with the social framework in which it operates.

It enjoys the confidence of a large section of farmers and is especially popular among small farmers. One recalls that out of the farming class in Ireland as a whole two contradictory visions of the future have emerged over the years. On the one hand it envisages the modernisation of Irish agriculture, necessitating land reform, and evolution in the direction of farms sufficiently large to sustain a standard of living comparable to that of the towns. This vision, of course, includes the elimination of small farms. Another project, entertained by a sizeable but shrinking minority of farmers, is dedicated to the regeneration of rural life through the intensification of agriculture in those small farms in danger of extinction. In short, it is difficult to imagine two more contradictory aspirations for the future of Irish agriculture. Fianna Fail accepts the agricultural policy of the Common Market in its broad outlines and is not opposed to the modernisation and commercialisation of agriculture based on land reform and on the creation of a smaller group of efficient farmers. But at the same time it speaks out in defence of small farmers, who are an important symbol of Irish nationalism. The party takes great care not to come down too categorically on one side or the other, thus giving itself a certain leeway in its agricultural policy. Its pronouncements on the subject of agriculture have a calculated vagueness which barely cloaks the ambiguity of its position. It is indeed a paradoxical situation where a political party continues to enjoy the support of a social category while doing nothing to defend its interests. Is it possible that small farmers do not care about policies that affect them directly in their lives? The public image which the party so carefully nourishes, associated in the public mind with national unity and the defence of gaelic culture (the halo of 'republican party', in the special sense that it has acquired in Ireland), would appear to be enough to retain the allegiance of the small farmers. This public image preserves a certain affinity with rural Irish ideology which, though in decline, has not lost its evocative power. It is noteworthy also that the same farmers, more than any other social group, have given their support to those marginal parties which from time to time appear on the Irish political scene and attempt to reactivate the 'republican tradition'. This would appear to demonstrate that small farmers are not altogether happy with Fianna Fail as an expression of their aspirations, and that they desert them whenever an alternative presents itself. Small farmers, who are to be found in the ranks of none of the other political parties, support Fianna Fail whose policies reflect their interests in only approximate and ambiguous terms, for want of a decent alternative. After all Fianna Fail does express from time to time its interest in the defence of the small farmer, regularly calls for an end to land speculation and for a more equitable distribution of the land.

Fianna Fail does not unduly concern itself with the almost automatic support of this group which in any event is shrinking in numbers and in electoral importance every year. But it cannot count upon similarly automatic support among the other farmers, divided in their allegiance between Fianna Fail and Fine Gael and who have tended in fact up to now to favour Fine Gael (*148*). Fianna Fail has striven hard to expand its electorate among this category; for example, it refuses to commit itself on the question of income tax for farmers, a proposal which, not unnaturally, was received with little enthusiasm in rural Ireland. Not wishing to alienate voters it was in the process of wooing, it affirmed its support in principle for taxation of those farmers who could afford it — to refuse to endorse at least the principle would have alienated voters in the towns. But at the same time it deplored the manner in which the tax was introduced by the Coalition government, and questioned whether it was opportune at a time when farmers, under pressure to invest and to modernise, were in need of all the financial means at their disposal. But the party avoids placing too much emphasis on those overheated topics and seeks a large base of agricultural support. It has found a rallying point for farmers in high agricultural prices. It also lends its support and favour to the co-operative movement, which embraces the two rival conceptions of the future of agriculture in Ireland. It would appear that Fianna Fail has momentarily succeeded in its wooing of the farmers, since its remarkable success in the general election of 1977 was partly attributed to the fact that the wealthiest farmers abandoned their traditional allegiance for the first time (*183*).

Fianna Fail, assuming in its entirety the project of the bourgeoisie, proclaims itself as the party of free enterprise and does not hesitate to preach the philosophy of capitalism. Free enterprise and the profit motive are considered the answer to the challenge of economic development and industrialisation confronting Ireland. The commitment in principle to the defence of private property, defined as a fundamental right, is not contradicted by the existence of a large public sector. Direct economic intervention by the State, although relatively extensive, is no more than a deliberate effort on the part of the State to create and improve those conditions which are necessary for the capitalist development of the Irish economy. Only the extreme hesitation of private enterprise to involve itself actively in the drive for economic growth rendered State intervention necessary. But priority is invariably accorded to private initiative and the extension of the public sector is condemned by the party whenever it appears as a threat to private enterprise. The whole economic policy of Fianna Fail may be summed up as a systematic effort to stimulate capitalist development in Ireland. It is from this perspective that one must interpret its vigorous opposition to the introduction of wealth and capital gains taxes proposed by the Coalition government in 1974. Despite their somewhat modest ambitions these new taxes symbolised for Fianna Fail a move to control capital, and a threat to drive it out of the country. Fianna Fail actually considered the abolition of this threat as an essential step towards a solution of the economic crisis of the mid-seventies.

Curiously, Fianna Fail policies, which conform in broad outline to the project of the bourgeoisie and proclaim it loud and clear, are not particularly framed with the latter's voters in mind. Electorally, the bourgeoisie constitutes a numerically feeble group. But the ideological defence of private enterprise and profit brings numerous indirect advantages. It is favourably received by the petite bourgeoisie, always receptive to ideological expressions of support for private property and profit. The emphasis placed on economic development attracts even the working class since national economic growth makes possible the essential task of job creation. At the same time Fianna Fail appears as a modernising force and a source of innovation.

The social policies of the party, somewhat vague and limited, would not by themselves attract working-class votes. Reduction in direct taxation, greater equality of educational opportunity, a limited measure of worker participation on boards of management, improvements in housing and health services — such are the main themes of Fianna Fail policy. Reduction of unemployment, proclaimed as a priority of Fianna Fail social policy, is directly linked to the capacity of the bourgeoisie to promote economic development and, paradoxically, serves as a fundamental argument in the justification of capitalist economics.

Social classes apart, Fianna Fail has been closely associated with all the principal social movements in Ireland. It was born from the ashes of the nationalist struggle and has carefully nourished this nationalist image. The national question has never entirely disappeared from the Irish political scene and the perpetuation of the border between the Republic and Northern Ireland has assured its persistence. Moreover, the troubles since 1969 have revived the national question, as well as old passions. In spite of this the Fianna Fail leadership has advanced no special policy on the unification of Ireland and the issue has rarely held a central place in its preoccupations. In fact, the main parties have retained a bipartisan line and subscribe to the notion of unification by peaceful means and with the consent of the Protestant population of the North. In this domain Fianna Fail and Fine Gael policy coincide, though the nationalist 'images' of both parties are quite different. Nationalist professions of faith therefore perform purely ideological and propagandist functions, but have little relevance to practical politics in the Republic. Fianna Fail regularly recalls its nationalist past and takes advantage of brief spells in opposition to reactivate this facet of its identity. Similar conclusions could be drawn concerning relations between Fianna Fail and the gaelic movement. Committed to the restoration of Irish as the national language of Ireland, Fianna Fail has never taken any particular initiative to achieve this aim. The nationalist and the gaelic movements, which overlap to some extent, add to the diversity of Fianna Fail's electoral support, since these movements to some extent cross social lines.

Finally, the Catholic Church has unambiguously declared its interest in certain sectors such as education and social policy and Fianna Fail has not opposed the Church's efforts to exercise influence in these areas. It is content to leave the control of almost all primary and secondary schools in the hands of the clergy, although ready to entertain serious requests for non-denominational schools. It also allows the Church to wield a certain influence in the social services, by leaning its social policies on charitable organisations often inspired and dominated by the Church; it encourages decentralisation of the social services and a return to the local community which makes possible the participation of a greater number of voluntary associations. The indecision of Fianna Fail in the matter of contraception – more and more accepted by the population at large but fiercely opposed by the Church – and the search for a compromise suggest also the influence of the Church in the formation of Fianna Fail policy, as well as the desire of the party to avoid clashing with the ideological bloc from which it derives, in part, its legitimacy.

There is nothing mysterious about the relations between the Fianna Fail party and the diverse social forces at work in Ireland. But it remains nevertheless to explain the astonishing capacity of Fianna Fail to hold on to such a wide range of support. The problem is not so much to discover which particular social classes determine Fianna Fail policies, since such an approach assumes that political parties simply mirror the interests of one class or coalition of classes. Parties actively mobilise their social support and are by no means passive instruments. They create a particular support by deciding on certain policies, and they manipulate it for their own benefit. This capacity of political parties to form and manipulate their supporters, instead of merely reflecting their wishes, is illustrated by the dramatic about-turn in Fianna Fail policy on the retirement of Eamon de Valera and the succession of Sean Lemass. The real question to be asked may be put as follows: given Fianna Fail policy, how has Fianna Fail managed to monopolise such a large and diverse following? The mystery deepens when one realises that Fianna Fail policies correspond to the project of the bourgeoisie and, in the final analysis, do not differ fundamentally from

113

those of Fine Gael, who can command nothing like the same support?

Different mechanisms serve to unify this social diversity politically. The personalised type of leadership favoured by Fianna Fail aims at creating a feeling of solidarity around a powerful, charismatic figure. It gives the group a greater sense of belonging and pushes conflicting interests into the background. Fianna Fail recognised early on the importance of personalised leadership. After de Valera, a nationalist hero, it consciously and systematically set about creating the personal appeal of Sean Lemass and later of Jack Lynch. Fine Gael and the Labour Party have never had recourse to such a strategy, since their socially more homogenous support does not oblige them to play the charismatic card.

Fianna Fail derives in some measure from a broad unified national movement and thus transcends all particular interests. It proclaims itself on the political stage not as a partisan force, but as the expression of a national ambition. The struggle for national unity in the past conferred some credibility upon this claim, and today the urge for modernisation has replaced if not eliminated the old aspirations. Fianna Fail can shamelessly play the republican card, whose appeal is not limited to one class. This involves a harping on the past which in time becomes an essential form of legitimacy by reaffirming a tradition in which Fianna Fail played a worthy role. Finally, a certain ambiguity enables Fianna Fail to gloss over conflicts of interests between the different social classes which support the party. We have already remarked upon agricultural policy, where Fianna Fail has been somewhat ambiguous as to its intentions, in case too much light would undermine its support.

Yet these various mechanisms do not always work and tensions appear from time to time. Certain members complain at party conferences about the evolution of the party; from being a popular party, supported by small farmers, shopkeepers and even workers to being the party of privilege closely linked to the business world. The party has become the defender of capital and speculators, exclaims a delegate. Doubtless it has, though this only half explains the relations existing between Fianna Fail and society at large. Neither can it explain the ability of Fianna Fail to hold on to its wide and diversified support. How is it that the past still weighs so heavily on the contemporary Irish political scene? Why are certain social forces so blind that they give their support to a political party that does so little to defend their interests and their projects? How is it that ideology plays such a large part in Irish politics, while apparently remaining totally divorced from social determinants? But these questions await a study of the Irish political system as a whole in its relations to the structure of Irish society. Chapter 13 undertakes just this task.

Fine Gael

The relations between Fine Gael and the social framework contain little mystery and are indeed much less complicated than is the case with Fianna Fail. The Fine Gael party traditionally draws support from the relatively well-off farmers, and seeks to promote agricultural modernisation, thereby increasing agricultural production and raising the standard of living among farmers. For this reason Fine Gael accepts the necessity for land reform and an increase in the size of farms. Its policy is in line with that of the EEC, which advocates the elimination of small farms and advances various projects to facilitate early retirement for elderly farmers or farmers incapable of attaining the threshold of economic viability. But Fine Gael also favours a policy of high agricultural prices, and encourages the co-operative movement. In fact, like Fianna Fail, Fine Gael shies away from controversial issues and is often ambiguous in its commitments, seeking to find common ground between those conflicting projects which to some extent overlap.

Fine Gael is also committed to industrialisation by encouraging private enterprise. However, its support of the project of the bourgeoisie is less triumphalist in tone than that of Fianna Fail, and its capitalist philosophy is more muted. Although it clearly proclaims its economic policies, it does so in a straightforward, sober fashion (60). The hesitation to formulate the philosophy behind its policies or the tendency to focus on short-term targets cannot be explained away as simple lack of imagination or inspiration, or even by an urge towards pragmatism – even though this impression might often have been conveyed under the leadership of Liam Cosgrave. These characteristics of Fine Gael must be interpreted in the light of another Fine Gael trait: its tendency towards authoritarianism. This is not to say that Fine Gael represents a threat to individual liberties, but its authoritarianism represents an affirmation of the power of the State, a determination that it perform its governing role, that it control and regulate the forces at work in society. Fine Gael witholds its wholehearted support for spontaneous private initiative, and refuses to let go of the reins in the race for profit. To this degree, it lacks confidence in liberal capitalism, and seeks to control it through the intermediacy of the State. It seeks to spur the economy and promotes a corporatist view of Irish capitalism in which the institutional framework would control the principal socio-economic forces for the attainment of common purposes; a capitalism based on negotiation in which the State plays an important part. Fine Gael policy insists upon full consultation between all social forces in Ireland. It seeks to integrate these forces into an institutional framework and is committed to a mixed economy in which a private sector and a large public sector co-exists under the watchful eye of the State, whose role is both a promotional and regulatory one.

Fine Gael and Fianna Fail both undertake to realise the project of the bourgeoisie, and both see the future with the same eye; both are committed to industrialisation through private enterprise and profit. But their respective political styles, as well as their ideological emphases, differ considerably, even though their economic policies are scarcely distinguishable. It might be said, however, that the two parties represent rival tendencies within the same project. Fianna Fail illustrates the reforming and swashbuckling zeal of a bourgeoisie impatient of obstacles and State control. Fine Gael, on the other hand, fearful of the social upheaval involved in wholesale modernisation, insists on the necessity of a stable social order upheld by a strong and efficient State. Both parties reflect perhaps the contradictions of the Irish bourgeoisie, simultaneously reformist and conservative. It is possible that the reformist orientation reflects the industrial bourgeoisie, whereas the commercial bourgeoisie might be said to favour a more ordered capitalist development. Both explanations are plausible, though further analysis would be required before either were substantiated.

Finally, Fine Gael does not question the predominance of the Church in certain domains. It endorses the denominational school system, while insisting on the right of the State to supervise academic standards. It also calls, though somewhat vaguely, for greater participation on the part of parents and would like to see lay teachers become school principals in greater numbers. But far from wishing to curb the authority of the Church, its policy of 'leaving teaching to the teachers' suggests the contrary. In Ireland the Church maintains tight control over all aspects of education, not only in the great majority of primary and secondary schools, but also in the training colleges, where it is in a position to inculcate its educational philosophy on generation after generation of primary teachers. As far as the social services are concerned, Fine Gael does not object to large-scale participation by voluntary organisations, so long as State pre-eminence is maintained, believing that final responsibility for the solution of many social problems lies with the State.

The Labour Party

Though difficult to establish, the basis of Labour support in Ireland is the working class. This fact is reflected in numerous opinion polls, and it is not difficult to see that Labour's greatest support comes from the industrial constituencies. Rural Ireland has little sympathy for Labour ideals and Labour fails even to attract the support of small farmers in remote western areas. It does, however, attract some votes in the rural constituencies of the South and East, which contain significant numbers of agricultural labourers (21). The Labour Party also finds supporters among office workers, small shopkeepers, the middle classes, and even among the liberal professions. Moreover, these social categories figure prominently in the party leadership as well as among local or national elected party representatives (24, 148).

But the electoral support of Labour throws little light on the relations between the party and the social forces in Ireland. Far from it! The Labour Party is the political expression of the working class, in that it organises and articulates its project. But to say this is to raise certain questions: after

116

all, the majority of workers vote for Fianna Fail. However, this electoral support represents but a small fraction of Fianna Fail voters, and although most workers do not vote for the Labour Party, the party remains the principal political expression of the working class. Several reasons account for this. Firstly, the party issued from the trade union movement, as its political wing, and the trade union movement organises the vast majority of workers. The modern Labour Party has gained its independence from the unions, but special links remain between the two. Certain unions are affiliated to the party and contribute funds during election campaigns. Finally, only the working class vote in numbers for Labour.

The Labour Party forms only a section of the Irish left – the most moderate section at that – and to complete the picture it is necessary to refer to what is usually called the extreme left. This political tendency has appeared in various guises in Irish history – whether as Saor Eire, Sinn Fein, Clann na Poblachta, and today includes a multiplicity of splinter groups. But political radicalism in Ireland is often born more from the national question that from social issues. More importantly, working-class support for the extreme left is difficult to gauge; the extreme left, in any case, exists on the far margin of the working class.

The Labour Party has largely embraced the dominant project of the working class as we have already defined it. However, unlike the trade unions who focus their attention on immediate working-class demands, the Labour Party advances a programme which claims to offer solutions to the principal problems facing modern Ireland – a political programme in the real sense of the word. Industrial development is given priority, as the only means of creating full employment and increasing the national wealth, in order to gain decent living standards for all and to suppress the widespread poverty still existing in Ireland. The optimum development of the economy demands planning, within which private enterprise and profit will play the role of ensuring economic growth. This tolerance of private enterprise, however, has its limits; the Labour Party campaigns for the extension of the public sector when private enterprise fails to achieve economic dynamism or when an industrial sector acquires strategic importance for national development. It seeks more to control the capitalist economy than to replace it. For this reason one can understand demands for direct State aid for ailing firms (for example, by protecting them from imports) and why Labour does not shy away from encouraging foreign capital to invest in Ireland, on condition that it is tightly controlled. In other words, the party calls for more intensive industrial development, directed by Irish capital but also planned and responsive to the needs of the Irish people. State intervention, extended by a programme of limited nationalisation, should aim to stimulate economic growth.

The Labour Party favours a moderate form of workers' control and greater employee participation in the management of industry. Participation may come about in several ways: by greater circulation of information

117

concerning the company and the decisions of management; by involvement of union or elected representatives on boards of management; by
allowing the workers to hold shares in the business. Occasionally it calls
for complete control of the firm by the workers. The demand for worker
participation in management oscillates between two poles: taken seriously
it means control of an enterprise by workers or their representatives, and
this claim belongs to the socialist project. In its more moderate form, it
easily accommodates itself to capitalism and presents no threat to it. The
Labour Party leans towards this latter interpretation, and softens it even
more by excluding the petite bourgeoisie from its plans. Worker-control
does not affect small firms, even though they form the largest sector of
Irish capitalism.

Economic growth facilitates the redistribution of wealth by progressive
taxes and by social services, without lowering the standard of living in the
wealthier classes. In other words, industrial development must be tied in
with the effort to support the underprivileged, poverty must be eliminated,
and the most vulnerable sectors protected. The Labour Party declares its
commitment to improving the lot of the least well-off sections of Irish
society, and this is the basic theme of the party's programme. It demands
that the working class receive a more equitable share of the wealth produced. This demand for equality is accompanied by a demand for State
interventions as the only guarantee that greater equality will be achieved.

But the Labour Party, while recognising its special link with the working
class, does not limit its sphere of influence to it. It also tries to attract
categories other than wage-earners. It is careful not to frighten off the
middle classes, and woos the small farmers assiduously, though with little
success. Labour recognises land reform as essential to efficiency in agriculture, and favours co-operative organisations, as well as greater mechanisation. It does not envisage, however, such changes taking place against the
will of the small farmers who, even when living at subsistence level, are
reluctant to abandon their farms. However, such labour policies have so far
done little to attract votes among the entrenched small farmers of Ireland.
In brief, Labour addresses itself to all social categories and advances its
resolutions to all the country's major problems. But the fact remains that
real commitment is lacking, in that Labour policies are rarely discernible in
party practice.

The Labour Party programme reveals certain fundamental ambiguities
which leave it open to different interpretations. Its realisation would lead
to a reorganisation of Irish society but not beyond the moderate reformism advocated by the parliamentary Labour Party and its leaders. In the
event, the participation of the party in the National Coalition government of 1973—7 revealed that the real commitment of the party lags far
behind even the most moderate interpretation of its programme. However
if stated party policies were followed through seriously, they would open
the doors to a socialist future in Ireland. This socialist urge for a time

found expression in the impatient reformism of the Liaison Committee of the Left. One of the relative strengths of the Labour Party resided in its ability to balance the two projects associated with the working class: the project of reforming the capitalist system through more and more State control, and the project of a socialist Ireland. Each project represents merely a different interpretation of the same political programme, and both interpretations occasionally find themselves in stormy confrontation. Both focus on the themes of greater equality, economic planning and State intervention, but they nevertheless lead in different directions. But indefinite peaceful coexistence proved impossible in the long run, due to a lack of flexibility in the Labour Party. In 1977 certain left-wing members of the party were expelled, and subsequently formed the Socialist Labour Party.

Conclusion

In spite of what is often said concerning the absence of a social base for political life in Ireland (*231*), relations between the different political parties and the social framework are not difficult to establish. Figure 1 traces the scheme of these relations. It must be pointed out that it focuses its attention on social classes, on social categories which engage in collective action to express a collective will and defend a specific social project. We know that a single social category may contain conflicting tendencies, and the figure takes this fact into consideration. But the social categories which express no collective will and defend no project do not figure here. This is not to say that they have no importance for Irish political life, but the manner of their intervention is beyond the scope of the present chapter and will be considered in the next.

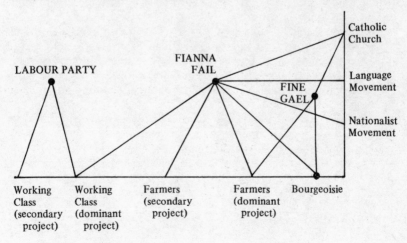

Figure 1: Political Parties and the Social Framework

119

Figure 1 reveals some interesting characteristics, such as the fact that Fianna Fail appears to receive support from almost all social forces in Ireland. We have attempted to explain this phenomenon but our explanations raise other fundamental questions. They send us back to an analysis of the political system as a whole and of its relations with other dimensions of Irish society (for example, the apparent dominance of ideologies from the past in debates upon social questions of the present). In the course of our analysis, it has however become clear that relations between social classes and political parties are not just a matter of one mirroring the other. Political agents can never be considered as mere appendices, as representing social forces in another guise. The two types of agents confront as well as complement each other, manipulate as well as co-operate with each other. Within this dialectic we are obliged to grant that political parties have both an identity and their own presence and this dialectic simultaneously complicates and illuminates their interrelations.

13

Political Activity

The preceding chapter drew attention to the apparent lack of correspondence, in the Republic of Ireland, between the social structure and political life. In other words, the political parties, around whom the political system is organised, maintain a somewhat loose relationship with the social forces. This does not signify that subtle correspondences do not exist between politics and the social life of the country and our task so far has been to trace the interrelationships of the two. This relative autonomy highlights the ideological nature of political life in Ireland, or at least, which is not quite the same thing, the apparent importance of ideology, in that the lack of a direct relationship between political activity and the social structure might result from the domination of politics by ideology. As we have seen, national issues are more important than social issues. The past still dominates the present and the most important difference between the two major parties remains rooted in the Civil War. Many doubt, and with good reason, whether treaty politics play a significant role in everyday political practice, where government decisions tend to be dictated by short-term pragmatic considerations. In other words, politics in Ireland blends cautious realism and nationalist rhetoric, from which blend it might even be said to derive its stability. But this rhetoric cannot be ignored as irrelevant, since it is integral to the image of the two major parties. We have already seen that certain social categories are liable to support a political party whose image is no longer in focus with its actual political stance. Small farmers, as well as the working class, provide a clear illustration of this in their continued support for Fianna Fail. The problem is not one of recognising that nationalist shibboleths pay electoral dividends, but of understanding why they continue to do so despite the records of the parties concerned.

Explanations for the persistent effectiveness of those ideologies (24) usually refer to the present nature of Irish culture, with its slow rhythm of life and its long collective memory. The nationalist question has also been given a new lease of life by the 'troubles', which have been raging since 1969. Another factor is the tendency to vote along family lines, thus automatically perpetuating partisan affiliations and ignoring the political content of party programmes. This is accompanied by the anti-intellectualism which has often been said to underlie Irish political life, and which is purported to explain why political divisions revolve around personal loyalty

121

rather than principles and policies. It is indeed both paradoxical and ironical that anti-intellectualism should produce a situation where politics are dominated by ideology. All this is probably true, but the reasons for the domination of the past must be sought not in the past but in the present: it must be assumed that the persistence of appearances whose sole function is to hide reality serves some present purpose. Appearances are never other than a particular form of the real, and there is no difficulty in pouring new contents into old forms. Fianna Fail offers a good illustration of this: a nationalist party *par excellence,* the standard bearer of tradition, it has become the party of modernisation and national development. This fusion of the myth with the reality principle explains the strength of Fianna Fail. While all the other parties promise modernisation and economic growth, none of them can draw upon the myth and the credit of the past. The reality principle, in Ireland, imposes itself by means of the myth.

Great attention has been paid to *political culture* in an attempt to cast light on the apparent lack of correspondence between the social and political systems, and on the apparently disproportionate role played by ideology. Observers of political life in Ireland go even further in granting causal efficacity to this political culture, which is often seen as a collection of national stereotypes. But such a view ignores that fact that 'political culture', far from being the point of departure or a determining force in politics, constitutes rather the end product of political activity, and changes when the latter shifts focus. Attitudes are forged in political activity and political beliefs fluctuate all the time. Even granting the relevance of such factors as attitudes, knowledge, political judgments, one would have to be naive indeed to believe that the illusions people cherish concerning their political system also fully determine its functioning. In short, even though ideology oozes from the pores of political activity, the latter always preserves a relative autonomy.

It is necessary, therefore, to take a closer look at the notion of political culture, since it contains different and even contradictory aspects. Two of these are immediately discernible: basic attitudes on the one hand, and knowledge, beliefs, opinions on the other. Is it possible that these two aspects go against each other? The authoritarian strain in Irish institutions has often been remarked upon. Surveys have also revealed certain attitudes which it is difficult to reconcile with the liberal democratic spirit: 50 per cent of the Irish people demand tougher and more violent measures against criminals, 75 per cent accept corporal punishment in schools, demand strong government, have no objection to curtailment of freedom of the press 'when necessary' and consider it natural that one imposes one's beliefs on other people (*187*). But how does one reconcile these authoritarian (in the sense of non-democratic) tendencies with the unquestionable belief in representative institutions? For, and we shall deal with the matter later, the legitimacy of parliamentary institutions in Ireland has never been in doubt.

122

Irish political culture, then, far from being coherent, constitutes a balancing act of opposites, apparently contradictory but in fact manifesting themselves on different dimensions – in any event an internal source of tension. The task is to discover how these two tendencies interact one upon the other and how they manage to coexist. But at this point another, more central and more fundamental question arises: that of the contribution of political culture as a whole to the continuity of the political system, and to the stability of parliamentary institutions in Ireland.

Political Culture and Parliamentary Stability

The predominance given to Irish political culture in explaining political phenomena may be attributed to the need to account for the political stability that has so far characterised political life in the Republic. How, in the light of the divisions we have noted, can this political life assure its stability? The question has often been asked, and different answers have been forthcoming. Certain analysts, such as Brian Farrell, explain it in terms of historic continuity, which was not interrupted by the establishment of an Irish Free State in 1922 (49). In the first place, the Free State modelled itself on the principle of parliamentary democracy, and conducted itself according to well-established electoral practices and representative procedures. Here we shall merely suggest as a source of continuity the administrative and policy legacy of the new State, which enabled it to weather its stormy beginnings – armed struggle with Britain, followed by bloody civil war. Moreover, the modernisation of Ireland before independence played an important role. Land reform, almost completed before 1922, had defused a rebellious peasantry; widespread literacy; a communications system for linking regions and towns; an efficient administrative machine; all have contributed to a relatively smooth transition from colony to an unified Free State. In spite of a short civil war the system quickly established itself on an already modernised social infrastructure. Finally, the Catholic Church itself, usually regarded as a conservative force, is here presented as an agent for modernisation, putting all its weight behind the effort to create a unified and stable nation. There is no doubt that political life in the Republic has profound roots in the colonial past, that this facilitated the transition to independence and accounts for the numerous resemblances to the British political system. But inertia cannot explain the continued stability of the system over a period of fifty years. Contemporary reasons must be advanced to explain contemporary stability, even when recognising the important role played by tradition.

Other analysts, such as D. E. Schmitt, turn their attention to nationalist feelings to explain the phenomenon. He suggests that these feelings, forged in the course of a long and turbulent history, constitute an important reservoir of support in a self-governing Ireland. But this argument can be easily refuted, since nationalist feelings, in their extreme form, regularly pose a

123

threat to the continuity of political institutions. More original is his suggestion that certain authoritarian tendencies, to be discerned in numerous aspects of Irish social life, have contributed to popular support for parliamentary institutions. This indeed is the basic irony of Irish democracy, that it owes its stability to an authoritarian tradition, which representative institutions were quick to take advantage of it, thus ensuring almost automatic support for their own authority (*199*). It would be a mistake to exaggerate the authoritarian strain in Irish society, which, though real, is confined to particular spheres such as education, family life, and personal morality. One may only guess as to its actual effect on political life. The argument rests on the notion that automatic deference towards persons in positions of authority naturally transfers itself to the State, the ultimate form of social authority. But here again, certain considerations limit the validity of this argument. In the first place the authoritarian strain is linked to the past of Irish society, and more particularly to traditional rural society (which dominated the country as a whole up to the mid-fifties). Nowadays the Irish family, even in rural areas, is not as authoritarian an institution as it used to be (*84*). The atmosphere in the schools is changing rapidly and the influence of the clergy is much less decisive, even in matters of personal morality. History shows that certain groups have never hesitated to defy religious authority, even at the risk of excommunication; the advice of the Church in political matters is not always followed, especially where the national question is concerned. Moreover, the assertion of an Irish authoritarianism has a contradictory side to it: the superficial deference towards the British authorities or towards the landed gentry during the colonial period by no means signalled acceptance of or obedience to them. Such ambivalences are to be found among groups who have experienced domination by external forces, and by peoples who have been colonised. But the important point to be made here is that ambivalence towards authority ought to qualify over-hasty generalisations about this facet of Irish political culture.

D. E. Schmitt also somewhat tentatively advances another theory that carries more weight. He suggests that the demands made to the political system are of the gradual and moderate type — nothing, in any case, which would threaten to disrupt the normal functioning of the political life. This argument suggests that Irish political institutions are accepted by the major social forces in Ireland, and that they do not seek to overthrow them or even to transform them in any fundamental way. We shall have cause to return to this point later.

All these explanations of political stability in Ireland revolve, in one way or another, around the question of the legitimacy of Irish political institutions. Where does authority in Ireland have its source? By authority is meant legitimate political power. Obviously, authority in Ireland is vested in representative institutions, in parliamentary democracy. This simply signifies that only those representatives elected to parliament have a right to take decisions for the whole of society, that the government is chosen by the parliamentary majority and that a bureaucratic administration executes its decisions as efficiently as possible. The representative tradition goes far back into Irish history, and the inclusion of Ireland in the British parliamentary system for over a century considerably facilitated the acceptance of democratic habits and of the procedures of political representation (52). In fact the British parliamentary system was simply adapted to the Irish situation with very slight modifications in 1922 (one such modification was the use of the proportional representation system in Ireland as opposed to the majority ballot system used in Britain). The legitimacy of the struggle against the British presence derived entirely from the first Dáil elected in 1919, and during the Civil War both camps justified their actions by invoking it. The Republicans, however, who violently rejected the Free State authorities, as well as any compromise on the issue of national independence, never succeeded in posing a serious threat to the elected government. It should be remarked that despite a long history of violent struggle, the army in Ireland has always been subordinate to the government and has never played an autonomous role in political life. Even the romanticism associated with physical force has never prevented the various paramilitary factions from being confined to the margins of political life. Also, no party defeated in a general election has ever rejected the verdict of the polls. However, 'legal-rational' legitimacy acquires certain subtleties in the Irish context. By itself participation in a parliamentary system does not confer legitimacy and for many years Ireland sent representatives to Westminster while denying the right of the London government to rule Ireland. Furthermore, the role of the majority becomes illegitimate if, as in Northern Ireland where an electoral framework was created to assure power for a well-defined political majority, this majority wields its power against the minority. Parliamentary representation needs to be based on a sense of nationality.

We have already referred to the persistence of the authoritarian strain in Ireland, which strain could be said to belong typically to the 'traditional society'. Deference, respect, and obedience are 'naturally' accorded to individuals in precisely defined positions: the head of the family, the elders of the community, the priest. Traditional societies are of diverse kinds but the authoritarian tendencies discerned above are said to belong to the 'peasant society' model, the type of society characteristic of Ireland's recent past and still persisting to some degree. Traditional legitimacy, instead of being opposed to the legal-rational authorities or in competition with them, supports and completes them. The Catholic Church has thrown all its weight behind parliamentary institutions, attempting to combine a commitment to liberal and democratic institutions with a corporatist philosophy. Education, conceived at the outset in the traditional mode, contributes to the moulding of youth in support of parliamentary institutions. A paradoxical state of affairs exists, then, where a legal authority leans heavily for support on traditional forms of authority.

Charismatic authority hardly appears in Ireland. Allegiance owed to the bearers of authority based on exceptional personal qualities is only, if ever, to be found in the case of the bishops. But we know that even the authority of the bishops is a blend of tradition and legality (the latter in the sense that their authority derives from the fact that they represent an organised and even bureaucratic Church). This is not to deny that certain political leaders individually command enthusiastic and even unconditional support. Eamon de Valera perhaps furnishes an example of a charismatic leader. But in spite of the personal qualities often attributed to him he only succeeded in incarnating Irish destiny when he abandoned armed struggle or — more significantly — political opposition outside the parliamentary framework. The charismatic leadership of de Valera always gave way to legal authority; it only affirmed itself within the parliamentary system. Further, this charismatic leadership of de Valera actually reinforced parliamentary institutions.

To come back to our problem: how to explain the apparent lack of correspondence between social structure and political activity. Explanations in terms of 'political culture' do not bring us very far. We shall now consider another aspect of the Irish political system: the different levels of political activity and the often problematical modes of interaction between them. This analysis hopes to provide a key to the understanding of political life in Ireland and of the role of politics in social organisation.

Levels of Political Activity

Observers give great importance to the peasant model, which is supposed to shed light on the essential characteristics of political activity in Ireland. The village mentality, the priority given to personal relations, a distrust of politicians, and a very ambiguous attitude towards all forms of authority — these, briefly, are the principal traits of this particular model. The village mentality dictates that political relations crystallise within the framework of the locality and the immediate environment. The majority of actors on the political stage, including patriots and nationalists, pay little attention to the national dimension. Great national debates and the activities of the central government do not affect them directly. The priority given to personal relationships in such a society accentuates the personal loyalties which flow from family and friendship ties. This also means that the personality of individuals becomes more important than their ideologies or their political programmes. This fact explains in part the phenomenon of political families, where the widow or son of a deceased politician can almost automatically count on the support built up by the husband or father. It also determines those partisan affiliations which, in certain families, persist from one generation to the next. 'The peasants' suspect civil servants of defending their own interests and have a low opinion of the honesty and uprightness of politicians. Their cynicism, or at least their scepticism, goes with an ambivalence towards all forms of authority, an ambivalence which manifests itself as a tension between an occasionally almost obsequious acquiescence and a sullen hostility towards those in whom authority is vested.

Two pieces of field-work, carried out towards the end of the sixties, have described and analysed political activity in Ireland at constituency level. They focus their attention on 'political machines', those groups which gather around a local leader, and which act as middlemen between the local population and the central government and civil service. Paul Sacks has studied political life in Co. Donegal, where the figure of Neil Blaney dominates (*197*). He describes the Blaney 'machine', whose task it is to organise the distribution of favours to voters. The electoral success of the leader, as well as that of the machine behind him, depends in effect on his capacity to render personal favours and to satisfy the private interests of the voters. The political machine serves as an intermediary between individuals and bureaucratic agencies, which most people prefer to approach through a person of influence. In fact according to Sacks the patronage involved is mostly purely imaginary since public agencies carry out their functions according to fairly well-defined procedures which leave little room for favouritism. But no matter, deputies and local leaders intercede in favour of their constituents to the civil service for pensions, social welfare benefits or planning permission which would in all probability be granted to them anyway. Which is not to say that the local leaders wield no influence; they decide municipal appointments on the local level, as well as building contracts and other matters. The machine, centred on the leader, is also composed of intermediaries who channel requests which can be dealt with on a local level, falling back on the leader when difficult manoeuvering is required for a particular request. Paul Sacks discerns rather intense competition between different deputies and local representatives within one party, in the same electoral area. This competition represents a permanent threat to the cohesion of every party, but the latter deflect the threat by dividing constituencies into reserved sectors, veritable electoral fiefs within which candidates canvas votes, arranging for second-preference transfer votes to be redistributed among one another.

A second field-study, carried out at about the same period in a southern county, gives a somewhat similar picture of political activity in the constituencies (*8*). Voters consider their political leaders as intermediaries, whose principal function is to render personal or collective favours in their locality. The politicians enter wholeheartedly into a game, and exploit it for their own political ends. The success of every deputy depends on his aptitude for 'pulling strings'. The study also reveals sharp competition between members of the same party.

The two studies, however, differ in important respects. In the first place, Mart Bax, author of the second study, refuses to describe politicians as 'patrons', distributing favours and privileges. He prefers to speak of 'courtiers' who cannot grant favours in their own right but who enjoy privileged access to other well-placed individuals, both in the administration and in the local business community (to whom they are linked by a similar network of reciprocal favours). Politicians put these and others in their debt through favours granted, so that when the time comes they may benefit where necessary from the good will they have built up in these quarters, 'pulling strings' and publicly displaying their powers of influence. Having become 'courtiers' the politicians now play the role of intermediaries between those seeking favours and those in a position to grant them. The study also shows that local politicians tend to belong to social categories which play a central role in rural social life — such as shopkeepers and far-mers. Another difference between the two studies relates to the nature of the favours distributed. Paul Sacks talks of imaginary patronage, which suggests that the politicians have practically nothing to give, that the majority of requests made on behalf of constituents would be automatically granted anyway. Marx Bax, on the other hand, insists that the favours granted through the agency of politicians are real enough, and that practi-cally the whole community is caught up in a dense network of transactions. But whatever the truth be, political activity at the local level rests on a belief in the politicians' capacity to deliver the goods, a belief carefully nurtured by the politicians themselves.

Also, although both studies concur in the observation of political in-stability within each party, they diverge in their interpretations of this in-stability, and of the contradictions which undermine the political machines. In the one case the instability derives from the difficulty in regulating electoral competition, and limiting the activity of politicians in their re-spective fiefs when, naturally enough, each seeks to enlarge his number of first-preference votes, even at the expense of candidates from his own party. In the other case, it is claimed that the instability results from com-petition between the politician and his aides. The latter, indispensable middle-men between politicians and constituents, develop and consolidate power bases of their own, so that the day comes when they are in a posi-tion to challenge the 'boss' in local elections. The bosses are forced to re-sort to all sorts of devices to contain these threats to their power, and not always with success.

There can be no doubt that practices described above are an integral part of the Irish political scene. Two independent studies both arrived at the same results, though the emphases in the two books are not the same, and both focus upon and systematise observations already made on several occasions before (23). Nevertheless the problem concerns not so much the reality or otherwise of these activities but their significance in Irish politi-cal life. Paul Sacks takes care to place this system of transactions in a larger perspective and shows that the links binding patron and clients have their origins elsewhere. In this context he cites extended family ties, ideological teachings, partisan loyalties, and so on. Here we encounter a serious diffi-culty, insofar as both studies give the impression that the whole of Irish political life revolves around competition within parties, rather than between parties. The distribution of votes between parties is not fixed once and for all; one might well ask whether a large share of local politics is not concerned with trying to shift allegiances from one party to another. One might also ask whether these practices limit themselves to remote outlying areas. Political transactions of this sort are practically a general phenomenon in rural Ireland, and are even to be found in Dublin (67), but their importance varies considerably from region to region. The political machine prospers in the most remote areas since it performs the conservative function of mediating between district and central authority. It thus perpetuates and exploits the isolation of the region by sheltering it from too much contact with the centre. More important still, how do these practices fit in with other forms of political activity? Paul Sacks points to a further conservative characteristic of the political machines. He observes, for example, the hostility of Neil Blaney towards the Irish Farmers Association, which seeks to organise farmers and encourages them to defend their own interests, without resorting to intermediaries.

It is not sufficient to describe in isolation a particular dimension of political activity, and assume its simple coexistence with others. It is necessary to discover how the different dimensions are co-ordinated as well as their reciprocal interactions and to place them in their global, national context in relation to the social forces. The above considerations cast light on one particular aspect of political life in Ireland. But they fail to explain how politicians and deputies obtain their electoral support. They explain the mechanisms whereby, within each party, certain individuals are nominated as candidates and are elected to the Dáil. However, insisting on intra-party rivalries, they pay scant attention to voting patterns, and exaggerate their stability. What then is the basis of party support? In this context local transactions lose their significance and we are once again obliged to pay attention to the political images and partisan activities already referred to in the previous chapter. The abyss dividing party image from party politics is reflected in the gap between local politics (centred on competition *within* parties) and national politics (organised around competiton *between* parties). Thus deputies are elected for reasons which have little to do with the policies which they seek to implement or with the decisions they will come to concerning society as a whole. This statement, however, must be qualified, since instead of talking in terms of a lack of relationship between the two dimensions it would be more appropriate to speak of mutual tolerance. The elections of 1973 and 1977 amply proved that party allegiances are far from fixed, and that they are subject to the vagaries of the political breeze. The measures proposed by a political party do influence the way people will vote, although a considerable degree of elasticity exists between electoral support and the concrete policy orientations of a party. The example of Fianna Fail has already been given; Fianna Fail enjoys a social support (small farmers, for example) and an ideological support (the nationalist, Irish language supporters' vote), which seems to contradict the declared political aims of the party: the modernisation of Irish society, the building of an industrial capitalist economy, and so on.

The political orientations of active party members have been analysed in a Dublin constituency (68). The results of the analysis would suggest that activists within Fianna Fail are more nationalist than those in Fine Gael or Labour, and on economic issues tend to be closer to Labour than to Fine Gael. When it comes to religion Fianna Fail and Fine Gael agree in most issues and disagree with Labour. The author, Tom Garvin, sees the network of affinities and oppositions between parties as a source of political flexibility, which finds expression in governmental alliances and coalitions. But, to come back to our point, parties differ principally on the ideological level and a study of party activists emphasises this. Economic and social policies appear less important to party workers than, say, the issue of secularisation, the national question, and cultural identity.

The fact is, however, that the working out of policies is reserved to the small inner circle of each party — to what is in effect a minority within the parliamentary party. The various local branches have little say in policy debates, and even less in policy decisions. They only come to life at election time, when they wield great influence in the nomination of candidates and play a preponderant part in campaign organisation. They also send delegates to the party ard fheis every year. The ard fheis is officially the supreme decision-making forum of the party, where votes are cast by delegates on a series of motions put to them by the platform. But in fact they have become little more than well-orchestrated rituals, efficiently organised and manipulated from the top, an occasion to unite around the leader and reaffirm the spirit of the party. As soon as the party wins power, pragmatism takes the place of rhetoric, the government takes into consideration the interests of organised groups, involves certain representative individuals in the decision-making apparatus. Partisan differences disappear and the only things that distinguish one party from another are certain differences as to political tactics. All this contains implications which are of vital importance in a consideration of the nature of democracy in Ireland.

Unity in Contradiction

The relative independence of the various levels of political activity in Ireland does not signify a lack of integration in the total political structure, any more than it signifies fragmentation or contradiction. It might even be said that this autonomy renders the working of the system smooth and more efficient. It suggests that each level has little interference in the affairs of the others. The politician looks after his interests in his constituency and seeks to reinforce his position through an exchange network of reciprocal favours; 'transactional' politics are what characterise the constituency. On the other hand, government policies are shaped within a restricted group which integrates in a more or less regular fashion on the representatives of forces in a position to bring pressure to bear. Such autonomy isolates governmental activity from the debilitating influence of over-rigid principles and restrictive ideologies. The ideological debate is preoccupied with nationalism and the Irish language, while political decisions concern the day-to-day development of the economy and social problems. The ideological debate concerns itself however, with certain realities and more and more tends to reflect changing circumstances, so that the distance between nationalist rhetoric and day-to-day pragmatism which has for so long characterised Irish political life is diminishing.

The relative autonomy of each level of activity means that government activity is to some extent freed from electoral control, insofar as voters cast their vote locally according to the logic of patron-client relationship, and pay little attention to the policies advanced by the different parties. However, elections fulfil an essential function in Irish political life, not as a mechanism for exerting control over deputies and government, but as a renewal of the legitimacy of political activity. Democracy, in the form of parliamentary representation, acquires a ritual dimension and becomes a sort of integrative ceremony. Elections, parliamentary representation, and inter-party competition are no longer at the strategic centre of the political system, since the real centre of power is located where decisions are arrived at and put to execution. There are several reasons which justify our referring to the ritual character of parliamentary representation. In the first place, the two main parties contending for votes pursue, despite their different political styles, almost identical policies. This has already been remarked upon in the preceding chapter. When voters choose between Fianna Fail and Fine Gael, how much real political choice is involved? The similarity of the two parties results from the fact that whatever differences exist between them have their roots in the distant past: born of the Civil War, with different views on the national question they have both taken up pragmatic stances on all other issues. Moreover, in Ireland, as elsewhere, elections are to a large extent decided by the floating vote. Political parties know that electoral success depends on the fluctuations of unstable voters, noncommitted and moderate by definition, and they adjust their programmes accordingly. Secondly, and even more importantly, the process of governmental decision-making involves the direct participation of several interest groups. Each ministerial Department keeps in contact with the various consultative committees of the interests concerned, and, both formally and informally, senior civil servants and ministers are known to communicate with organised interest groups on a regular basis (*122*). This network of consultation and negotiation tends to exclude deputies from the decision-making process, and contains the range of possible decisions within narrow limits.

The fact that parliamentary activity no longer finds itself at the strategic centre of the political system does not necessarily mean that it has become irrelevant to Irish political life. After all it is the mechanism by which political personnel are chosen, even at the highest level. Put somewhat more cynically, it constitutes an incomparable form of collective entertainment, and electoral vicissitudes are discussed at the counter of every bar in the country. It might also be mentioned here that television coverage of the elections is said to have played its part in personalising election issues around party leaders. In other words, general elections, even if they only produce the illusion of participating in political life, nevertheless give a certain outlet to the electorate and strengthen the legitimacy of the parliamentary system — which legitimacy constitutes a significant factor in the political stability of the Irish Republic. As well as conferring legitimacy on the Dail, the electors make a further contribution: that of furnishing the State and the government with a valid base, and giving it a certain authority in its dealing with the social partners; so that the government acquires a definite identity, becomes a social force in its own right, and promotes particular programmes which it seeks to impose on the other social forces by means of consultation, negotiation and even confrontation. The dynamic role which the State is able to assume is possible precisely because, being founded on the system of parliamentary representation, it enjoys a degree of relative independence and a power base which diminishes its dependence on the social forces, and allows it to work its own policies.

Universal suffrage contributes directly to political stability by integrating into the system those groups without any real or conscious collective project, groups which, incapable of transforming themselves into social forces, would otherwise remain outside the political process. It mobilises the passive participation of those social categories which have already been identified: petite bourgeoisie, office workers, and the liberal professions. With no vision of the future these groups more than any others tend to vote according to the mood of the moment and to drift according to the flow of events. More subject to ideological manipulation than the more powerful social forces, they are also more inclined to be moderate in their political views. The petite bourgeoisie tend to idealise the status quo and seek to reconcile social antagonisms. Clerical workers derive their sense of collective identity only from proclaiming their superiority to the working class — a superiority which they feel to be under constant threat and which must be protected. The liberal professions enjoy their privileged status while failing to act as a group. In short, none of these groups participate directly in political life, but they constitute a passive support for the political system, voting for proposals they consider reasonable and which are unlikely to upset the established social framework. Their status as voters gives these groups a political reality, saving them from what would otherwise be political impotence, as well as assuring the continuity of parliamentary institutions. Finally, these categories, by creating buffer zones, considerably diminish the likelihood of direct confrontation between those social forces which count. They function, if not as mediators, then at best as moderators.

The analysis of the political culture, then, which confers legitimacy on parliamentary institutions to some degree dispels the mystery surrounding the operation of the social order in Ireland: the stability of Irish political life, the uninterrupted continuity of political institutions, and the regular functioning of the State. Political culture – a very large label – embraces contradictory phenomena but underlines the significant fact that the Irish parliamentary system enjoys an almost unquestioned legitimacy. We have sought to establish the existence of different levels of political activity and have seen that the relative autonomy of each level, far from producing conflict, contributes to this stability by binding a network of highly personalised political relations to highly centralised and bureaucratic State institutions. We have also suggested that parliamentary representation and the activities that go with it no longer occupy the centre of the decision making stage but function more as a ritual of political and social integration. Finally, it was suggested that universal suffrage introduces into political life categories whose politics tend to be moderate, who have no desire to upset the status quo – who serve as buffers between rival social forces. We have already analysed the different social forces on the political stage, and their respective projects, as well as relations between these projects, and the interests that derive from them. The farmers, for the most part, look to modernisation of agricultural techniques and land reform. The working class is committed to industrial development, which it sees as the only way of satisfying the needs of workers. The bourgeoisie is also committed to industrial growth, but within the private enterprise system and inspired by the profit motive. These projects diverge considerably and envisage the future in very different terms. Nevertheless they are all thrusting in the same direction, and all reiterate the theme of development. They overlap to some degree, and have a great deal in common. In a sense the different social forces speak the same language, and despite their often contradictory aspirations they manage to agree, if not on entente, at least on the necessity for peaceful coexistence. They do not invariably seek confrontation, but where possible adapt to one another. The zone of State activity corresponds to the intersection of these projects. The stability of Ireland's political institutions derives from the peculiar way in which the differing social projects overlap and interrelate. None of the social forces question the legitimacy of State institutions, or wish to rock the ship of State, upon whose fate they all equally depend.

14
Ideology in the Republic of Ireland

Every group of individuals or every society produces ideas, beliefs and values which enable it to judge and situate itself in relation to other groups or societies. These preferences and beliefs are often deeply embedded in people's consciousness, and represent what the members of the group consider to be self-evident; what they accept without too much thought; as well as what they are prepared to fight for when threatened. We are thus dealing with a type of knowledge which is not necessarily aware of itself as such, and which cannot easily be questioned. But these ideas and judgments also manifest themselves as the privileged themes of public debate, the subjects of endless discussion, since, in the final analysis, they alone count. This system of ideas, beliefs, and preferences defines the atmosphere and cultural climate of a society. It is this climate that we are attempting to describe in the present chapter. One might refer to it as culture, were this term not used in anthropological works to refer not only to the beliefs but also to the behaviour of groups or societies. For this reason I have chosen to use the term 'ideology' to designate such beliefs and dominant themes.

Each individual participates in the ideological phenomenon, and in fact lives and embodies it in spite of himself. But one cannot expect to define the ideology of a given group by focusing on individual expressions of it, since it is to be found in the individual in an extremely partial and personalised form. Public opinion constitutes another expression of a society's ideology, so do the diverse political discourses, such as literature, and the more systematic and generally more complex contributions of the intellectuals. Of the various forms of ideological expression, which could be said to be the most complete, the most revealing? We have chosen to study the letters to the editor published daily in the *Irish Times,* in the belief that here is a unique field of ideological expression in Ireland. The ideological universe which we have chosen covers a wide field, and is especially appropriate in that here we observe ideology in its raw state: the give and take of ideological debate, and the crystallisation of spontaneously expressed beliefs and judgments. In other words, these letters, where the writer is unhampered by strategic considerations, express ideology in a more spontaneous form, since it is not transformed by being censored or polished for political or polemical ends. Which is not to say that the letters to the editor of the *Irish Times* never contain bias or distortion.

In the first place, to compose a letter to publicise one's opinions presupposes a certain confidence and competence, which are usually the result of a good education. Let us remember also that readers of the *Irish Times* come from the middle and upper-middle classes, and from the most educated sectors of society. Further, it can be seen that certain enthusiasts write frequently and are doubtless satisfying an urge for ideological expression. It is also obvious that editorial control intervenes and choices are made to publish some letters rather than others. One must suppose, however, that editorial intervention does not distort in any important way the ideological picture represented by the page.

The themes touched upon in letters, which cover several different periods, may without any great difficulty be divided into fourteen categories (see Table 5). The stability of our classification has considerable importance: it reveals that the questions raised and the opinions expressed in the letters are activated by a myriad of day-to-day events, but that, in spite of this, they revolve about the same themes, which come up again and again. Nevertheless, this reduction of the Irish ideological field (reduction in the sense that it focuses on fourteen principal categories only) does not result in any greater coherence. One might have thought that certain themes would dominate the others; one might have hoped to discern a hierarchy of importance among the different categories. This, however, did not happen, and from week to week the relative importance of each category fluctuates. Certain topics monopolise the attention for a time and then disappear almost completely, or at least fade into the background.

The tables measuring the relative importance of each category of ideological expression reveal no regularity. But the letters themselves are marked by considerable repetition in respect of the principles which they invoke. Whatever the events which provoke readers to write, the same themes occur over and over. But, on the other hand, the same events produce contradictory reactions and judgments, as well as, occasionally, endless debates. However, the same divergent judgments appeal to the same sets of principles, and in this sense reveal a certain regularity. In any event, it is necessary to pay special attention to the themes and principles which underlie each category of ideological expression.

The Principal Ideological Themes and Their Underlying Dichotomies

Letters grouped under the heading environment, or *ecology*, concern the protection of nature against pollution, the preservation of animal and mineral resources, the generation of energy, the preservation of tourist sites and of archaeological treasures threatened by urban and industrial development. (The numerous letters concerning Wood Quay have been classified under the heading environment although, because they concern the national heritage, they could equally validly be classified under 'nationalism'. Such difficulties of classification occur from time to time when there is an overlap between two categories. In such cases the solution must sometimes be arbitrary.) The destruction of a long established traditional order of things, the threat to balance between man and nature, strikes a profound chord. It stimulates a resistance which has its origins in the attachment to a rural past. Large-scale, unplanned industrialisation and an increasingly avaricious materialism alienate many who oppose the modernisation-at-all-costs attitude to Ireland without, for all that, wishing to cling to the past (spiritual—material opposition). This conflict invokes an opposition between adaptation (whether traditional or modern) to nature and the domination of nature which is almost invariably involved in economic and social modernisation. But it also invokes another principle, since the critique of industrialisation relates to the preservation and affirmation of national identity. Modernisation undermines the relevance of that fund of experience which has made of Ireland a nation, since it destroys the past upon which nationalist sentiment in Ireland draws almost exclusively for nourishment. In another, more concrete way, economic development, which relies to such a great extent on foreign investment, is seen as a threat to the control by the Irish people of their own destinies.

Questions of *morality* (especially as they relate to contraception, abortion, the right to divorce, mixed marriages, censorship, etc.) invoke directly the religious-profane dichotomy. The discussion almost invariably revolves around attempts by the Catholic Church to impose, by means of the State, its moral code on the whole of the country's population. The religious-profane opposition is immediately duplicated in the spiritual (idealist)-materialist dichotomy, the latter being identified with an excessive preoccupation with material comfort. Naturally enough in this context, religious is linked with spiritual and the profane with hedonism. But other principles begin to appear in the background when, for example, divorce, contraception, abortion, and pornography are perceived as foreign imports, alien and a threat to Irish culture and morality. In contrast contraception and divorce are sometimes defended as individual civil rights, being withheld by the combined forces of Church and State (an example of the opposition State—individual). A further opposition appears in the family planning debate: conformity to nature—interference with nature. Certain forms of contraception are classed by the Church as artificial, and therefore condemned, while others are classed as 'natural', and therefore morally acceptable.

The third category, *religious affairs,* covers a wide range of issues: purely internal matters such as changes in the liturgy, others such as the ordination of women, which overlaps with the question of sexual equality. It also includes such issues as the increasing gap between rich and poor in developing Ireland. Numerous letters express anxiety at the rapid rate of change in Irish society and at the moral void that has ensued, arguing that only Christian values can transform society into a caring and generous community, attentive to the needs of all. Over and beyond the religious-profane,

136

spiritual-material dichotomies appears a more general and fundamental opposition between *community* (altruistic and harmonious) and *society* (selfish and discordant). Finally, the individual–State opposition finds expression in the humanitarian concern with the erosion of civil and family rights, particularly in relation to prison conditions in Northern Ireland.

Naturally enough, sharp attention is focused on the *Northern Ireland conflict.* Here two themes prevail, each one activating different principles. In the first place the nationalist position denounces the British presence in Ireland and demands unification of the country. The other is also concerned with the division of Ireland into two entities, but concentrates instead on the theme of *rapprochement* between the two, on co-operation, on working towards a federal solution, and so on. The presence of the British army and the continuing armed struggle lead to repressive legislation (even in the Republic), which presents a constant threat to individual rights (individual–State). The religious dimension to the Irish conflict is often denied, though some claim that the only solution to the Northern conflict lies in the secularisation of Irish society.

The defence of fundamental *civil rights* is involved in varying contexts. The introduction of safety belts in cars, and even the introduction of an angling licence were vehemently denounced as curtailments of personal freedom, and recall the issue of the limits of legitimate State intervention. At the same time many letters complain of a lack of serious commitment by the State to law and order and ask the State to exercise its role as defender of its citizens more efficiently. A further question that often arises is the unequal access by citizens to legal redress. Invariably, the theme of conflict between individual and State plays a central role in this category.

The *affirmation of national identity* occupies a large place in the universe of ideological debate and appears in various guises. It most often finds expression in denunciations of British influence as well as of all forms of economic and cultural dependence. It appears whenever national sovereignty seems threatened – in particular in the context of the Common Market. The national–cosmopolitan opposition underlies most discussions in this category since its concern is to define what it is that makes for collective identity. The Irish language receives a lot of attention in this context, being held to embody traditions and a history without which modernity would seem to be meaningless. Finally, and somewhat on the margin, relations between socialism and nationalism raise the often ignored questions as to the nature of a truly national society of the future – a moral question since it consists in judging a type of society according to whether it is equitable or not.

The *feminist movement* also figures regularly in these letters: the right of married women to work; equal pay; the place of women in Irish society; and so on. Two oppositions appear in this context. One, the general opposition between tradition and modernity is at the heart of the debate and concerns the traditional role of women. The maintenance of the traditional status of women is justified (and after all, ideology is about justification) by recourse to Catholic doctrine which insists on the spiritual and affective role of women and which places women at the centre of family morality. Those who criticise this definition of women's role do so by invoking the notion of equity.

Letters dealing with international affairs do not concern us directly, since they are not normally governed by the principles which structure the Irish ideological universe. However, some letters are not devoid of ideological content: for example, appeals for closer ties with the third world are often couched in religious terms. The relative importance of this category, which gauges the degree of attention given to the outside world, varies from week to week, but on whole the category is of secondary importance.

The many letters which focus on *education* concentrate on two aspects of the theme: the aims of education, and entrance to university. The former concerns the aptitude of the school system to create rounded personalities, the over-competitive nature of school life, the obsession with examinations, the lack of education in art, and so on. The spiritual–material opposition again appears in connection with the choice between types of education: whether schools should concentrate on trying to develop to the full the personalities of their charges, or whether they should be preparing them for a competitive world where qualifications are all. Should education be training young people to make a positive contribution to the community, or should it be arming them for the future in a world where only the fittest survive. University education involves different controversies: the difficulties of university entrance, the problems as well as the privileged nature of student life. The call for equality of opportunity for young people who aspire to university education directly invokes the equity – inequity opposition.

Urban problems, generally limited to Dublin, also receive attention: the decay and the filth of Dublin's inner city, vandalism, impossible traffic conditions, the loneliness and impersonality of city life. Significantly, letters rarely mention rural problems, which is perhaps a reflection of the attachment to rural life, and a perception of the urban environment as being unnatural and therefore problematic (natural–artificial opposition). Moreover, the concentration of poverty in the cities and its greater visibility automatically gives rise to concern and indignation (equity–inequity).

Letters reiterate a long list of *social problems* (the elderly, the young, delinquency, alcoholism, unemployment, poverty . . .), and in view of such concern one might expect discussions of social policy to predominate in ideological expression. But this is not so. Social policies are unequivocally discussed in terms of helping the disadvantaged (equity–inequity), and of encouraging altruism and fellow-feeling. Again the spiritual–materialist and religious-profane oppositions appear, and here it must be recalled that social policy in Ireland mainly finds expression in charitable organisations,

138

	equity — inequity	individual — State	national — cosmopolitan	conformity to nature — interference with nature	religious — profane	spiritual — material
Ecology			X	X		X
Morality		X		X		X
Religion		X			X	X
Northern Ireland		X			X	
Civil Rights	X	X				
Nationalism	X		X			
Feminist movement	X			X		
International Affairs						X
Education	X					
Urban problems	X			X		
Social problems	X					X
Economic policy	X					
Industrial Relations	X				X	X

Table 5: Dichotomies underlying the major themes of the letters to the editor.

in which the Church exercises great influence. But the three dichotomies referred to together polarise the ideology of social problems around the community (altruism)—society (selfishness and normlessness) opposition.

Letters concerning *economics* tend to concern themselves with taxation and unemployment, questions involving equity and the just distribution of the national tax burden — a moral consideration in fact (equity—inequity). The same principles prevail in the category *industrial relations,* these always discussed in terms of an equal share for everyone in the national wealth. But this theme overlaps with another — that of the choice open to the Irish people: of a society exclusively preoccupied by material well-being in which different groups struggle to achieve maximum advantage for themselves, or of a society in which individuals and groups assume collective responsibility and look to the results of their actions.

Finally, the category *diverse* includes all themes which are difficult to classify, questions which are neutral or on the margin of the ideological universe. Certain themes re-appear from time to time, such as coursing with live hares, which provokes widespread indignation on several grounds: cruelty to animals, the preservation of nature, and even on religious grounds, when the animals in question are defined as God's creatures. Occasionally letters resist all classification, when in denouncing materialist society or deploring the decay of community spirit, they go to the heart of the ideological debate.

Associations Between the Principles Underlying the Categories of Ideological Expression

Although it was not possible to discern a regular pattern (in the sense of one particular theme consistently acquiring more importance than others) in the above-sketched ideological universe, certain underlying dichotomies emerged. The field is organised around a limited number of these dichotomies, which are clearly discernible in that the ideological utterances themselves (the letters) do nothing but manifest them. Table 5 summarises the preceding account and shows, at a glace, the tendency of these associations to manifest themselves simultaneously.

- The equity—inequity opposition associates mainly with the idealism—materialism opposition, but less so with any of the others.

- The individual—State opposition appears in particular with the religious—profane opposition but hardly with the equity—inequity one.

- The national—cosmopolitan opposition and the conformity to nature—interference with nature opposition develop no privileged associations.

140

- The spiritual—material opposition most often associates with the religious—profane opposition, but also with nearly all other oppositions.

- The religious—profane opposition, even though it associates with all the others, reveals some affinity for the equity—inequity opposition, and also for that of individual—State.

We have suggested already the existence of a very general opposition dominating the field of ideological expression: that of community versus society. This opposition is not a pure one, insofar as it is the result of a fusion between basic dichotomies. Another general opposition (tradition—modernity), crystallises around affinities between four dimensions: national—cosmopolitan; adaptation to nature—interference with nature; religious—profane; idealism—materialism. One final remark on this point: the general community—society opposition exerts greater influence on ideological expression than the tradition—modernity opposition.

Combinations Between Dichotomies

The above oppositions form associations with one another but they also combine. Can it be assumed that a value which appears in one dimension (equity—inequity, for example) involves a particular value in another dimension (religious or profane, national or cosmopolitan, and so on)? We shall define positive and negative values that appear in each dimension in the following manner (for the moment the terms positive and negative carry a purely conventional meaning):

+	−
equity	inequity
individual	State
national	cosmopolitan
conformity to nature	interference with nature
religious	profane
spiritual	material

It must be stated that in five cases the oppositions do not combine at all. But if they do the most common case of combination consists in an attraction between negative poles, that is to say that a negative value in one dimension combines with a negative value in another, without, however, the positive values combining. Thus the value *cosmopolitan* combines with the value *interference with nature,* when denouncing the destruction of national resources by foreign industries or when condemning 'non-natural', imported methods of contraception while the value *national* would not appear in any way to relate to *harmony with nature. Cosmo-*

141

politan combines with *profane* when ideological discourse declares that ir-religiousness and atheistic humanism are alien to Irish culture. Or again, when industrialisation is condemned as leading to pollution, it invokes other negative values such as *materialism* and *interference with nature,* the former creating the latter. *Materialism*, the negative value *par excellence,* combines with the *profane,* another negative value, where secularisation of Irish society is seen to involve both moral decline and an unrestrained quest for material comfort. Social problems are usually regarded as products of an urban rather than a natural environment (while rural problems tend to be passed over in silence), thus combining *inequity* and *interference with nature.* Occasionally the combination is entirely congruent (positive value with positive, negative value with negative), and in such cases we have a harmony of values. The combinations *religious–profane, conformity to nature–interference with nature* illustrate such a harmony. *Religious–conformity to nature* coincide when ideology considers maternity as the natural vocation of women. On the other hand the *profane* coincides with *interference with nature* when it advocates 'non-natural' methods of con-traception. Another harmony brings together *spiritual–material* and *equity–inequity.* Appeals for social solidarity, for a more caring, respon-sible community, bring together *equity* and *spirituality.* On the other hand, selfish demands, taken as evidence of an ever-increasing materialism in Ireland, are regarded as expressing a lack of consideration towards the weakest, least privileged sections of the community, and an indifference in matters of social equity.

One encounters, however, more complex areas: in the first place, the negative value in the *individual–State* dimension invokes that of *national–cosmopolitan:* but it combines equally well with a negative value, *cos-mopolitan* (when the State is condemned as encouraging a foreign politi-cal, economic and cultural presence) as with the positive value, *national* (when the State is seen as the guardian of national identity). One thus ob-serves a neutrality, an absence of combination between the positive value *in-dividual* and the dimension *national–cosmopolitan* while the negative value *State* combines indifferently with the two values of this same dichotomy.

A more complex case again is that of combinations between the dicho-tomies *national–cosmopolitan,* and *equitable–inequitable.* The positive values combine when it is proclaimed that only a really national Irish society can be equitable. But one observes also certain *criss-crossing* com-binations (+ –) when it is sought to show that over-emphasis on national-ism often fails to take into account the inequities of the social system *(national–inequity)* or when it is pointed out that equity in Irish society is more important than nationalist claims *(equity, cosmopolitan).*

A similar network of combinations occurs between the *religious–secular* and *individual–state* oppositions:

- A positive combination *(individual–religious)* since religion ultimately

142

concerns itself with individuals and demands the exercise of individual responsibility.

- A criss-crossing combination *(individual—profane)* when the defence of what are often regarded as individual rights, such as contraception, divorce, etc. conflicts with the State, which tends, on these issues, to concur with Catholic dogma.

- Another criss-crossing combination *(religious—State)* occurs when the State is encouraged to enforce Catholic morality by legislative means.

What conclusions may be drawn from the foregoing? With the exception of a small number of crossed combinations (+ —), ideological discourse combines oppositions in a relatively determinate way: positive values tend to combine with positive, and, with much greater frequency and intensity, negative values with negative. Moreover, the words 'positive' and 'negative' ought by now to be understood in a much more literal fashion than at the outset, since the negative term or value of each opposition tends itself to be subject to negative judgments in Ireland. It can also be seen that the more stable associations *(tradition—modernity, community—society)* rest on harmonious combinations.

Tradition	*Modernity*	*Community*	*Society*
+	—	+	—
national	cosmopolitan	equity	inequity
comformity to nature	interference with nature	religious	profane
religious idealism	profane materialism	idealism	materialism

Further, without denying their own efficacy, these two general oppositions possess elements in common which, in the Irish ideological universe, tend to combine harmoniously, thus reinforcing each other.

+	—
tradition	modernity
community	society

Conclusion

Ideological debate in Ireland revolves around the oppositions that we have identified above, and ideology as such does not exist outside these confrontations, dissensions and contradictory points of view. It thus finds expression in diverse forms, and in none of these is it to be found in its entirety.

To state the case thus is to suggest that ideology is not a simple matter of ready-made, stereotyped ideas — though it is that also. It is not a system of ideas, choices or values. It does not suppose that everybody, or nearly everybody, shares the same views and agrees on all the basic issues. The letters to the editor of the *Irish Times* contain animated, even impassioned confrontations on numerous themes in which often conflicting conclusions are reached. Ideological unity, therefore, is to be found not in the various conflicting points of view, not even in the issues which give rise to debate, but in the principles that underlie and activate such debates. One cannot reduce ideology to a culture, to a collection of definite ideas, values, and beliefs, although it is true that in Ireland a number of those values which we have defined as positive do enjoy a privileged support: it is a framework within which to develop moral and intellectual orientations. However, it has to be said that true as this might be, the outlines of the Irish ideological universe should be sought in debates arising out of day-to-day events. Ideology cannot be perceived empirically, since it is an abstraction, a network of oppositions which manifest themselves under various forms, but subject to precise rules of association and combination.

The above considerations afford a glimpse of certain forces at work in shaping the ideological universe in Ireland. The *religous—profane* and *idealism—materialism* oppositions are to be found at the centre of two essential dichotomies already analysed (community—society, tradition—modernity) which would suggest the profound influence of the Churches (directly or through the medium of voluntary organisations) in the formation of the ideological climate. We have also observed the strategic place occupied by the *equity—inequity* opposition, most often invoked by such socio-economic forces as farmers, workers and entrepreneurs. The second general opposition, *tradition—modernity,* includes the *national—cosmopolitan* dichotomy which betrays the presence of effective organisations concerned with the promotion of a national identity in Ireland. But the analysis of forces which fashion ideology in Ireland requires an investigation of a different sort, in which it will be necessary to distinguish between those social forces which dominate the ideological field, and others which use ideology for their own ends without actually fashioning it.

15
The Shaping Forces behind Ideology

Newspapers in Ireland regularly carry reports of declarations not only by government ministers and politicians, but also by representatives of numerous interest groups and voluntary associations, of dignitaries and personalities of all kinds. These declarations express points of view, give rise to disagreements, and contribute to public debates. They mobilise public opinion for or against particular causes, and in doing so have recourse to principles that they simultaneously both activate and enunciate. Nevertheless, ideology is not everywhere present in these public statements nor is it to be found there in pure form. Partisan commentaries naturally contain partisan bias and may be ploys in a wider strategic confrontation where often ideology is no more than a cover. In other words, ideological expression is already mediated, and can no longer be regarded as an end in itself. However, it does allow us to observe those agents who have most recourse to ideology, as well as the themes which they most often draw upon. In the first place it will be noticed that the socio-economic forces do not participate in the wider ideological debate but confine themselves to those issues which affect them directly. They play on the underlying ideological structure by means of the mass media and in this fashion attempt to manipulate public opinion on issues as they emerge from day to day. The economic theme thus dominates this ideological field and, interestingly, is resorted to by the three principal social forces in Ireland. The unions, employers and farmer organisations tend, moreover, to restrict their interventions to this economic field, as well as, to a lesser extent, to social policy.

Both the government and politicians generally contribute to discussions concerning economic themes but their intervention does not stop there. The politicians make their presence felt in all public debates; but the question arises whether they are content to use ideology for their own purposes, or whether they contribute in a significant fashion towards its elaboration.

Voluntary organisations, as well as the liberal professions (academics, various experts), also play a significant ideological role. The intervention of these groups and individuals tends not to be of a specialist kind but principally in a less material, more intensely ideological area: morality, religion, civil rights, education, national unity — though also on social and economic issues. The relative pre-eminence of the liberal professions as a source of ideological expression well illustrates the prestige and privileged position which this social category enjoys in Ireland. Both the prestige and the intellectual character of their work mark them out for positions of moral leadership in society. The participation of various voluntary organisations in debates on moral and social issues adds to the influence of the Churches, with which they are often closely related. Moreover, the clergy also intervene directly in the ideological field, and are in themselves a significant source of ideological expression. Neither must it be forgotten that numerous academics and experts, although classified as belonging to the liberal professions, are in fact clerics. Through these three voices, the Churches exercise a significant ideological influence, even though in the universe which we are studying their influence is considerably less than that of the politicians and the socio-economic forces. A final remark on this point: with the exception of members of the liberal professions, individuals rarely contribute to public debates or initiate campaigns. They are condemned to live with ideology, while being excluded from participating in its elaboration.

The religious and social forces occupy a position of secondary importance here, whereas our study of the letters to the editor of the *Irish Times* would seem to suggest their preponderant influence. Might one advance the hypothesis that the clergy principally influence ideology at its roots, in a more determining fashion that is discernible in their day-to-day contributions to public debate? But where do we situate this more profound, perhaps more fundamental, level at which ideology is fashioned and elaborated — where basic attitudes and orientations are formed, ways of perceiving and judging are inculcated, where beliefs and a sense of what is important in life are instilled? Various institutions may be seen as being involved in this inculcatory process, but obviously education must be accorded the position of foremost importance. Thus, a study of the educational system in Ireland ought to allow us to perceive the impact of the social forces on this strategic focal point of ideological elaboration.

Education and the Forces Shaping It

Ideology simultaneously projects the obvious and the controversial, what everyone accepts and what the individual cherishes and will defend against all opposition. The efficiency of the school system in the ideological formation of its charges or in the creation of those ideas and stereotypes which are universally taken for granted, has by no means been proved. It is doubtful whether it can compete with or supplant the family in the socialising process, but its great importance cannot be questioned. The following pages will attempt to trace those forces which, by their effects on the educational system, play a major role in the creation of the ideological climate in Ireland.

By 1831 the British government had set up a network of schools throughout Ireland, directly controlled and answerable to the State. The contemporary Irish school still bears the marks of its origins, and is very

	Government	Politicians	Pressure groups*	Other pressure groups	Voluntary associations	Bishops	Professionals	Diverse authorities**	Local authorities	Individuals	TOTAL (%)
Political issues	2	4	3						1		10 (3.26)
Media	3	4			1			1			9 (2.93)
Diverse	4	1		8	3	1	2		1	1	21 (6.84)
Industrial relations		2	19	6			4	1			32 (10.42)
Economic policy	8	8	41	1			2	1		1	62 (20.20)
Social policy		5	2	1	10	5	4	3	2		32 (10.42)
Urban problems		2	2		3	1		3	12	4	27 (8.80)
Education	1	2		15	1	2	7	4			32 (10.42)
International affairs	2	4			2	1					9 (2.93)
Feminist issues		1		1						1	3 (0.98)
Nationalism	2	3		1	2	1	1	1	1		12 (3.91)
Civil rights		5			1				1		7 (2.28)
Northern Ireland	4	3			1	3					11 (3.58)
Religion					1	2	2				5 (1.63)
Morality		1		4	5	1					11 (3.58)
Ecology	5	5		1	3		7		1	2	24 (7.82)
TOTAL	31	50	67	38	33	17	29	14	19	9	307
%	10.09	16.29	21.82	12.38	10.75	5.54	9.45	4.56	6.19	2.93	(100)

Table 6. Ideological expression according to theme and source (as reported in the *Irish Times* for diverse periods: first week of February and August in 1976–9; 1 to 14 March 1979).

pressure groups: unions, employers' associations, farmers' associations.
**diverse authorities:* Garda, semi-state bodies.

147

much the child of the British system. Moreover, in Ireland the past is often more closely studied and analysed and thus better known than the present. Education is no exception to the general rule. The line-up of forces at work in education and the evolution of educational institutions during the last century are already well known (*1*).

The British colonial authorities thus decided to finance a national system of education, a network of primary schools, in Ireland. Surprise has often been expressed that the British should have chosen Ireland, the poorest and least industrially developed part of the United Kingdom, for such an experiment. Ireland possessed none of the characteristics which go with a high degree of literacy: it had undergone no industrial revolution or significant degree of urbanisation; nor had it broken with traditional agrarian social structures. But other factors compensated for the absence of normal conditions of school development. Ireland had already experienced State intervention in educational matters, since a network of State-financed schools had long existed in Ireland for the purpose of proselytising the population in the Anglican religion. Moreover, the Irish peasantry had demonstrated a remarkable determination to educate themselves, probably in reaction to numerous attempts to suppress Catholic Irish education. Peasants had persisted in sending their children to the semi-clandestine hedge-schools which survived all attempts at repression. Finally, the interested parties succeeded in arriving at a sort of compromise, and on an educational system acceptable to all. Thus in 1831 the authorities decided to offer substantial financial aid to those schools willing to accept State control. The management of schools was left in the hands of local managers, generally parish priests, but the Commission in charge of schools imposed a strict control on course content and timetabling. The curriculum, as well as carefully circumscribing the place of religious education in the schools, concentrated on developing skills in reading, writing and arithmetic. It carefully excluded all references to Ireland, to its history, geography, language or traditions. British determination to exclude from the schools anything that might stimulate nationalist sentiment led in time to much tension and resentment. As well as this direct control the State influenced Irish education indirectly due to the fact, for example, that the British Treasury, which controlled the purse-strings, further reduced the range of subjects available in these schools by discouraging the Commission from distributing allocations for extra subjects.

The Churches had a profound influence on the new system, in that they succeeded in transforming schools which might have been, if not lay, at least neutral in religious matters into institutions which were directly controlled by the clergy, divided along religious lines and more and more committed to catechising. The Catholic Church unhesitatingly agreed to accept the offer of financial aid. Financially incapable of keeping going an adequate number of schools for the education of Catholic children it deplored the large number of them attending Protestant schools, where they were at the time subject to intense proselytisation. The educational system set up in 1831 at least enabled the Church to remove Catholic children from Protestant influence, while in effect returning the management of schools to the local clergy. The Catholic Church, however, became progressively tougher in its demands, so that the schools gradually acquired a more and more confessional character. The control of education has always been and continues to be a fundamental principle of Catholic doctrine and this principle was in practice embodied in the educational system of nineteenth-century Ireland. The Church had succeeded in getting State support for a system of confessional primary schooling while continuing to directly finance its own secondary schools, and eventually succeeded in getting recognition for a Catholic university in Dublin. The Church of Ireland, having first refused to submit to State control and having disdained financial assistance, put the *de facto* seal on religious segregation in the schools, since only Catholic children attended the subsidised schools. But financial difficulties gradually drained Protestant resistance and before long the Church of Ireland agreed to join the State system and quickly adapted to it. In any event, in the course of the nineteenth century the Churches radically transformed education in Ireland, completely subverting the secular spirit of the initial proposals, and instituting a system of confessional education throughout the country.

The nationalist movement, powerful though it was towards the end of the nineteenth century, left little mark on Irish schools. Hostile towards an educational system which systematically ignored Irish reality, it contributed little to rectify the anomaly. Utilitarian considerations also entered the picture, and influenced in some degrees the evolution of secondary education. Almost all secondary schools were affiliated to the University of London, which set examinations and granted diploma certificates. In this the schools were doubtless ceding to pressure from parents, since chances of employment were higher for possessors of these diplomas from London. The result was that to a great degree the schools prepared their pupils for administrative and business careers, and this utilitarian emphasis in turn modified to a significant degree the importance of the other aims of education, insofar as school activities became more and more geared to success at examinations. This led to even greater rivalry between the schools, and could even be said to some extent to have deflected schools from their declared confessional purposes.

Such was the base on which the new Free State was to build its regenerated educational system. To date very few serious studies of the forces at work in Irish education has been carried out (2) so that the following is but the sketch for an analysis of developments since. Three significant changes in the history of educational institutions may be easily identified. The first concerns the taking over of the educational system by the Irish authorities in the early twenties. In fact, the new State changed very little, underwriting the *de facto* control by the clergy of primary and secondary

149

schools, and thus assuring continuity from the old regime to the new. But the loosening of the imperial grip led to significant transformations of the school curriculum: 'Irish reality' was introduced into primary schools for the first time and primary schools were actually charged with the responsibility of reviving the Irish language. Two phenomena summarise the changing philosophy of primary education at this time: the reaffirmation of clerical control and the undertaking by the schools to inculcate nationalist ideals in their pupils. The secondary schools were also affected by the new mood, and the humanities now took pride of place. A few years later the State intervened to take direct responsibility for technical education, and to train young people for those manual occupations which were disdained by the clergy. In 1930 the Vocational Act (followed in 1931 by the Apprenticeship Act) set up a system of technical or vocational schools, to be managed by local authorities but financed entirely by the State. Practical training meant in effect preparing boys for manual occupations, and introducing girls to the 'domestic sciences'. The technical schools enjoyed a doubtful status, cut off as they were from the secondary schools, which monopolised academic training as such. But, in spite of the few criticisms which were voiced, the setting up of the 'techs' stirred up little political or ideological debate. The educational system thus constituted was to function without change for almost forty years. Towards the middle of the sixties, however, education became a burning issue in Ireland, when the clamour for reform became so insistent that the State was finally forced to take the initiative. It is worth noting that the new found reforming zeal of the State was accompanied by a push towards industrial development, so that it is not difficult to conclude that the two were closely connected. In any event, the government opened up the door to secondary education, by abolishing school fees and providing transport facilities for children living at a distance from schools (*170*). Some years later the Department of Education launched a new concept in education, that of the community school, which would dismantle barriers between the secondary and vocational schools, offer a more balanced curriculum as well as rationalise existing resources. In the sixties, then, the old system was subject to a total rethink, and the dust from the debate has still not settled. Keeping in mind this brief survey, which only takes account of the most salient developments, what forces can now be discerned at work in the Irish educational scene?

There remains little ambiguity about the position held by the Catholic Church, still the most powerful single force in Irish education. The Catholic hierarchy continue to insist that religion should penetrate every aspect of education, and that education play an active role in combatting the materialism and secularising tendencies of modern society. The purpose of education is to develop knowledge, but it should also strive to instil wisdom, the moral sense and, according to the bishops, morality must be founded in religion. The Catholic bishops insist not only on Catholic schools but on

150

direct control of Catholic schools by the clergy. By contrast, Protestant schools encourage much greater participation by the laity. These schools, moreover, resent their minority position and the difficulties arising therefrom: the distances often separating them from their pupils, and lack of finance for the maintenance of their secondary schools. State aid is not sufficient and Protestant schools do not have religious institutions at their disposal which, like the Catholic religious orders, may supplement government grants. But these complaints do not alter the fact that the Church of Ireland continues to support the educational system in the Irish Republic. In any event they nowadays represent a marginal force in education, and cater for a much reduced Protestant community.

The Catholic Church effectively manages the great majority of primary and secondary schools, which they also own. It presides, directly or indirectly, over the training of teachers. To the school then, falls the task of producing, year after year, new Catholics. In this it is largely successful, since a large proportion of the population continues to define itself as Catholic and to conform to Catholic religious practices (*162*). The question is often asked whether the schools produce good Catholics or merely inculcate ritual observance rather than conviction. However, the Catholic Church seems happy with the products of the schools and accommodates itself to them with little difficulty.

The fact that the educational system remained stable for so long doubtless is testimony to the Church's success, and to the fact that no significant force has ever dared challenge its domination. Catholic educational ideologues make great play of the distinction between education and mere instruction. Of course education must prepare young people for the future, but it must focus on development of the personality, the stimulation of enthusiasm, and the encouragement of creative activity. They refuse to subordinate education to economic interests, to the so-called necessity to industrialise. After primary school level the Church favours the teaching of humanities, based on classical culture (and the use of Latin up to recently as the universal language of the Church no doubt created an affinity between Catholicism and classical culture). The Church's disdain for the vocational schools is partly explained by this philosophy. The Catholic Church had no interest in these schools and did not consider them as rivals to their own secondary system. It has occasionally criticised their secular character, and their lack of a spiritual dimension, but never with too much vigour. However, the exhortation to educate rather than instruct has not prevented the Church from running its own schools in an illiberal and often authoritarian fashion. Despite the resounding formulae, the Church in Ireland has not been noted for stimulating intellectual enquiry or the critical spirit. The following criticisms have often been levelled at secondary schools (*130,167*).

- The intellectual development of students gains from memory work, but an over-exclusive emphasis on memory does not encourage intelligent use of knowledge, maturity of personal judgment, understanding, or initiative.

- The importance of examinations in the educational system partly explains the emphasis on memory work, leading to the excessive competition so deplored by many. The race for diplomas reinforces the utilitarian bias of schools which, despite denials, have taken upon themselves the career ambitions of the parents.

- The overweighted school curriculum has also produced imbalance. Modern languages, as well as the more practical and scientific subjects, are neglected. Academic faculties are cultivated to the detriment of artistic talents, maturity of judgment and the emotional balance of the student.

The contradiction between ideology and practice is only apparent when the ecclesiastical authorities, while claiming that the aim of education is to form the whole personality, simultaneously exhort educators not to lose sight of the moral and spiritual dimension − which means in effect inculcating the Christian message. Teaching ceases to be a mere job and becomes a 'vocation'. The answers to moral and religious questioning are furnished by the doctrines of the Church; the intellectual and spiritual quest stops short since the answers are predetermined and provided in advance. Taking seriously their task of producing Catholics, Irish schools tend to become authoritarian in tone, and this in turn fits in with the dominant authoritarianism of Irish Catholicism which has long been characterised as excessively puritan, especially in the domain of sexuality, and extremely hierarchical in its relations between clergy and laity. Seen from this perspective, education has as its mission to develop the personality in a very precise direction, to control and channel thought, to encourage certain attitudes while repressing others.

The recent reorganisation of Irish education threatens the privileged position of the clergy in the schools. This is not to say that they are in danger of losing their hold over schools, but that they might be obliged to share it. Secondary school principals reject the notion that the traditional educational system over which they preside might have impeded the growth of the national economy. They oppose the programme for amalgamating schools, raising as it does delicate problems of ownership and control. The religious orders have no intention of letting go of their schools, or of sharing power, even among themselves. Neither do they accept the notion of a 'viable' school, emphasising the dangers of uniformity and impersonality inherent in overcrowding. Finally, they denounce the notion that educational policy should be dictated by the demands of the labour market.

The State plays a significant role in education and is in a position to intervene in a very direct way. It has nominal control over the national schools, which belong to the State, pays for maintenance of school buildings as well as teachers' salaries, and sets the curriculum. Secondary schools do not belong to the State, but the State contributes towards building and maintenance costs, pays teachers' salaries and exercises direct control over curricula through its inspectors and State examinations. Despite this omnipresence, the State has left it to others to decide on the content of education in the schools. It has reinforced Church dominance in education, and given an institutional framework for the propagation of nationalist principles. After a long absence, the reality of Irish history, traditions and culture has at last penetrated the schools, which were also given the task of reviving the Irish language. In all national schools, at least up to the fifties, junior classes were conducted in Irish. After that age, not only Irish but history and geography were taught through Irish. The promotion of Irish through the schools has not been an unqualified success. At the outset it was necessary to remedy the situation whereby the linguistic knowledge of the teachers themselves was lacking. More importantly, the language was rarely spoken outside of the school, so that learning Irish became a painful, artificial, purely academic exercise. Fifty years later practically all Irish citizens speak some Irish but they assign to it a purely ceremonial role and continue to speak English in everyday life. Despite this lack of success the revival project remains institutionalised in Irish schools, with the blessing of the State (*156*).

The State also exercises a direct influence on, and responsibility for, technical training and has undertaken a profound transformation of the technical education system. Fearing that the system was no longer adapted to the needs of rapid industrial development, which required a high level of general education, it has echoed widespread appeals for modernisation. The State admits that schools must furnish the service sector with well-educated personnel, and it was this that prompted the move towards free secondary education, the raising of the minimum school-leaving age and free travel to and from schools, all of which were intended to increase the number of students attending secondary schools. The schools ought also to be able to satisfy the technological needs of industrial society: the demand for skilled workers and technicians increases as the demands for unskilled labour is expected to diminish. The setting up of Regional Technical Colleges opened new perspectives in the once despised field of technical education, which often tended to end up in a cul-de-sac. Vocational schools may now prepare students for university entrance, which has contributed to raising their status. Finally the new community schools seek to narrow the gap between secondary and vocational schools, to provide programmes which balance academic, technical and artistic capacities. In short, the State is trying to erect a bridge between the schools and the economy. It has become the voice demanding a greater recognition of the use-value of education and of the need to adapt to the modern world. Greater attention is being paid to the teaching of modern languages and to scientific, technological and commercial studies. That the State has not been entirely successful in these efforts is proof that it is faced with significant opposition.

The State is supported in its efforts at modernisation by the business community, which insists that the schools provide training more relevant to the needs of industry and commerce and to the needs of the modern world. They look to the schools not to inculcate academic knowledge but to provide a flexible work force. The universities also lack 'relevance', in the opinion of the business community, which insists on the importance of realism, initiative and industrial progress. A university education might be proof of intellectual capacity, which is necessary for industry, but it does not promote leadership or initiative. Industrialists do not demand of schools and universities that they train the personnel they need: they assume this responsibility themselves. But they would like to find in their recruits a bit more realism and sense of practical possibilities, and attitudes towards work upon which they could graft their specialised needs. Parents also insist on the practical aspects of education. For parents an investment in education is an investment in their children's future in which thinking they are only being realistic, since even if education no longer guarantees a good job, salaries are in any event graded according to qualifications.

The teachers themselves have not made their presence felt strongly in the educational system. However, they occupy an extremely strategic role since all the fine resolutions would fall flat if it were not for the working contact between teachers and pupils. In a certain sense teachers represent the most typical product of the Irish school system. Their training, especially that of primary teachers, has been very closely supervised. For the most part they accept without question the division of the schools along religious lines and willingly teach religion. They have been profoundly influenced by nationalist ideas and among them are to be found the most enthusiastic defenders of the gaelic tradition. None of which has prevented teachers fighting for their own interests, such as the securing of employment, control over their professional activities and participation in school management. That they are a long way towards achieving these testifies to the weakness of their position. Teachers are also very aware of the role of education as a factor in individual development, and of the need to lead pupils towards self-expression and the formulation of personal judgments. Refusing the role of mere conduits of information, they see the school as a centre of liberal education, which makes them a force to be reckoned with in the educational field.

The universities, somewhat special educational institutions, exert strong influence on the system as a whole. In the first place, they assert their autonomy and are self-governing to a large degree. Secondly, entrance requirements to university dictate almost directly the secondary school curriculum, and in turn a school's reputation to a great extent depends upon the number of its pupils who go to third-level education. Moreover, the universities themselves train the teachers. However, the university is not immune from tensions, especially where its role and identity are concerned. Should the university aim to provide a liberal education, or should it train people for particular careers (such as lawyers, doctors, engineers and so on). This tension between usefulness and general culture even appears within departments preparing students for the liberal professions (*10*). But, in any event, is the university not destined always to drag its feet when faced with social change?

To conclude, and despite what everyone says, the encouragement of initiative and of creativity cannot be a priority in Irish schools. Too many forces are contending to influence them in one direction or another. The Church demands that the schools produce good Catholics. Nationalist forces demand that they produce good Irishmen, and that they reaffirm national identity through the Irish language. The State echoes the anxieties of industry and demands of the school that it adapt to the modern world and provide skilled workers for industry. More recently it has been suggested that the schools should undertake the task of working towards a more egalitarian social system, by those who forget that schools more often perpetuate the past than point to the future. Finally, the State puts forward proposals for rationalisation and amalgamation and would like the schools to be cheap. Perceived above all as a process of socialisation, in which attitudes and beliefs are imprinted upon still malleable personalities, the school channels, controls and directs the development of its pupils. As long as it is regarded as a means of moulding young people's minds in a preconceived framework, it seems likely that the Irish educational system will continue to perpetuate those authoritarian strains which have so long characterised it.

Conclusion

The socio-economic forces are a very important source of a great deal of ideological pronouncements in Irish newspapers. But they occur only in very particular contexts, such as economic questions or issues concerning industrial relations. The specialised nature of such pronouncements contrasts with the less frequent but more diffuse presence of the liberal professions, various voluntary organisations, of the clergy, and behind all three, the presence of the Catholic Church. The analysis of those forces shaping the school, one of the sources of ideology, reverses the situation. The clergy above all and the nationalist movement move into the foreground, while the State seeks to adapt the schools to the modern world. This inversion in the order of relative importance does not necessarily involve contradiction. The day-to-day activation of ideological debate remains on the surface, and the socio-economic forces use ideology for their own ends rather than creating it. In this context religion and nationalist forces have been institutionalised in the schools, which indicates the privileged role they play in ideological production.

16
Economic Activity

In the 1960s growth established itself as the dominant and uncontested project of economic activity in Ireland. That it should be a priority for all socio-economic forces appears to be taken as self-evident, as if the economy could have no other goals or ambitions. Yet full employment or a reduction in the working week are realistic options for which a given society could sacrifice indefinite material growth. In other words, the fact that Ireland is aiming unhesitatingly for optimum growth does not mean that she is merely recognising the necessities of life; she is making a definite choice.

The choice having been made, what means does Ireland choose to attain its goal? It is perhaps important here to recall the history of Ireland's colonisation by Britain and to point out the impact on Ireland of integration with Britain, how Ireland lost most of its newly acquired industrial wealth (through the combined effect of the free trade legislation passed in Westminster and the revolution in communications brought about by the railway) and was given the unenviable role of supplying industrial England with cheap agricultural produce. But can agriculture, which became the primary economic pursuit in Ireland, provide acceptable living conditions for all or create opportunities for development? The agricultural revolution was slow in coming: advances in productivity, the introduction of new techniques and even changes in attitude, have failed to bring about the kind of growth in agricultural production that would stimulate the general development of the economy. Today it is not that agriculture has no role to play in the economy, or that its contribution is not recognised or appreciated, but simply that its role is secondary, and that the experience of the last few decades suggests that only the industrial sector has the capacity to promote growth and to achieve it. While the relative contribution of the service sector has remained constant at about half of the gross domestic product, agriculture's contribution has declined (from 31.9 per cent in 1926 to 16.2 per cent in 1971) according as the relative importance of industry has grown (from 18.1 per cent to 35.6 per cent in the same period) (*116*, table 1.6). What is more, the higher growth rate of industry shows its greater dynamism. For example, the annual rate of growth of the Gross National Product (GNP) was 3.9 per cent for the period 1961–72, but it breaks down as follows (*116*, table 1.8):

agriculture	1.7%
industry	5.8%
services	3.5%

Hence the project of economic growth boils down to an industrial growth project, following, as something of a straggler, the economic model of all those countries that have successfully pursued sustained economic growth.

Ireland had no hesitation in placing industrial development in the hands of private enterprise, and in fact refused to envisage anything other than a capitalist economy based on individual profit. Can capitalism in Ireland fulfil these expectations? The old dream of self-sufficiency or even of economic protectionism has no longer any support. Economic growth, centred on industrial development by means of private enterprise within a context of international trade, is the dominant project in the Irish economy. We will now take a closer look at the economic mechanisms associated with this project, and try to judge their effects.

The Dominant Project – Aggressive Capitalism?

Regular industrial growth depends both on the general level of demand for manufactured products and on the capacity of industry to satisfy that demand (productive capacity, largely controlled by investment). Strong demand without development of productive capacity only leads to rapid inflation; productive investment without a corresponding demand leads to economic recession. This very simple economic model will be helpful in defining the precise nature of the dominant economic project in Ireland. As regards demand for industrial products, it is easy to discover its sources: private domestic consumption, State expenditure and, naturally, external markets. Ireland's economic growth, it is often said, depends on exports. The emphasis laid on exports takes on a quite definite ideological sense, and everything must fall in line with the constraints of international competition. Employees are exhorted to moderate their wage demands in order to safeguard a relative advantage; firms are urged to make substantial improvements in productivity. It does appear that there is a close relationship between the growth of industrial output and the growth of exports. The 1960s were characterised by increased industrial vitality and the proportion of exports in national industrial output grew considerably in that period: from 13.8 per cent (1961) to 30.2 per cent (1972) (*116*, table III.3). Hence the idea that exports caused the growth of the economy.

Without denying the importance of exports for industrial growth, some economists have recently re-emphasised the importance of domestic demand and have suggested that exports and economic growth are not as directly linked as had been thought. Firms concentrating on exports are not necessarily more advanced, or better able to improve the productivity

157

of their investments. In fact, the growth of exports is largely based on increased imports. Foreign firms established in Ireland and concentrating entirely on exports are often only the last link in a long international chain, and their contribution is very limited. It may well be that industrial growth and economic progress act as boosts to exports rather than the contrary. Indeed, the relative importance of exports and of the internal market varies from one period to another. K. Kennedy and R. Dowling state that it was the growth in internal demand that created economic growth up to the beginning of the sixties and that afterwards exports took over (*117*). In any event it is unwise to neglect the contribution that internal demand makes to economic development: it is sometimes vital, sometimes secondary but always important. Private domestic consumption does not increase as rapidly aş national income, since an increasing proportion of this goes into savings, but it nonetheless increases regularly. Finally, public expenditure, which sooner or later becomes domestic demand, increases regularly – the average yearly increase for the period 1961–72 was 13.8 per cent (*116*, table VII.1). The need to maintain the expansion of overall demand is widely accepted and the role of the State in this regard is uncontested.

However a regular increase in overall demand is not in itself sufficient to guarantee industrial development. We must also consider investment, which determines the productive capacity of the economy. Like demand, investment comes from different sources. Personal savings, taken overall, make a substantial contribution to investment – about 12.7 per cent of the GNP in the period 1949–61 and 17.8 per cent for the period 1961–68 (*117*, 166-7). Economic development requires a high level of savings, but at the same time it broadens the base of savings, since a developed economy creates conditions favourable to saving. The general increase in the standard of living, especially in the sixties, and, later, the increase in agricultural prices, gave a powerful stimulus to savings; in this context it is worth remembering the propensity of farmers to save a large proportion of their income. Self-financing by firms, by which I mean that portion of profit which is neither paid out in tax nor distributed in dividends but reinvested in the firm, is another source of investment. Self-financing accounts for 50–60 per cent of profits after tax on average but it varies considerably according to the economic climate (*117*, 166-7). The State also invests a great deal and here again the rate of growth of State investment is increasing every year (*116*, table VII.1). The State directly finances the national infrastructure, or encourages modernisation, expansion, job creation indirectly, through grants (*213*, 24). The State draws part of these monies from taxes but that source is insufficient and it then borrows, by issuing loan stock (the public debt). The State also borrows externally, from international financial institutions. Finally, much of industrial development in Ireland arises from the establishment of foreign firms. The Irish government has actively encouraged investment by foreign capital, a driving force in industrial expansion.

Investment has different destinations and effects. The systematic pursuit of industrialisation which began in the late fifties was founded on the distinction between productive investment which expands the productive capacity of the economy and social investment which only satisfies immediate needs without producing anything (*244, 281*). The validity and usefulness of this distinction has been questioned: a reduction of so-called non-productive investment contracts internal demand, one of the sources of expansion. In addition, social investment can directly stimulate industrial demand, such as the building of hospitals, schools or even private houses. It creates jobs without increasing the volume of imports or having an adverse effect on the balance of payments. On the other hand, so-called productive investment, which is supposed to expand the productive capacity of the economy and improve productivity, does not always promote industrial development: sometimes it leads to an increased level of imports, which detracts from the stimulus it gives the economy.

The dominant project of economic development, of which we have just seen the relation between its principal variables, places all its trust in the profit motive. But this insistence on private enterprise and the mechanisms of trade and competition does not eliminate the economic role of the State. Indeed the project would not succeed at all without the systematic support of the State and its direct and constant participation. It creates external demand by encouraging exports with a whole range of grants, tax exemptions and even sales promotion on foreign markets. It also affects the internal market through its economic policies. Itself a major consumer, its fiscal and budgetary policy determines the level of domestic consumption. The State is also very heavily involved as an investor. The public debt has become a very high proportion of GNP and absorbs a high proportion of personal savings (*116*, 100, 106). Finally, the State encourages the establishment of new firms by numerous grants. Yet the intervention of the State, while it is a determining factor in the economy, does not conflict with or intentionally compete with the capitalist project, since it is in fact essential for its success. But the paradox of a State devoted to private enterprise could easily become a source of bitterness when the situation arises where it is impossible to check the dynamic of State intervention, and when industrial development demands a continually increased commitment from the State.

This project can be realised by means of different economic policies, and, indeed, economic debate is largely concerned with particular government decisions in the context of this project. Rarely are questions raised about the major assumptions: the need for economic growth, the idea that industry can accomplish it, capitalist organisation and the integration of Ireland into the vast network of international trade. Discussion centres more on the often delicate balance that must be struck between economic variables, or the manipulation of domestic demand according to the requirements of the overall situation, sometimes stimulating it, sometimes restricting it, or the method of encouraging exports as well as the appropriate levels and geographic location of investment. All these decisions or choices are reflected in the fiscal and financial policies of the government, since through them it strives to manage a more or less coherent economic system, to lead it in a particular direction. But these fiscal and financial policies only compete within the same overall point of view.

Yet the social dimension also directly influences economic policy. For example, job creation is presented as one of the primary aims of industrial development, because unemployment is seen as a major social problem. Maximum job creation rarely corresponds to an optimum industrial development policy, which requires increase in the productivity of labour as much as expansion of the labour force — in this sense economic development creates as much unemployment as it solves. In fact, the aim of full employment is not taken very seriously in Ireland, but there is an unacceptable level of unemployment, a limit not to be exceeded — a social and political question — which has a fairly direct effect on economic activity. Another 'social' question that weighs heavily on economic policy is the distribution of material resources. This question affects wage demands and demands for greater profit; it sometimes expresses itself as a desire for a more equitable distribution of wealth, through redistribution or a narrowing of the scale of wages in favour of the less favoured categories. It introduces an unstable variable into the economy: the notion of equity and class conflict.

The dominant economic project raises problems that affect the fundamental principles. First, it proposes to insert the Irish economy into a network of international trade, exposing it to the four winds and subjecting it to the whims of the international market. Ireland thus loses control of the strategic factors that determine economic growth. The development of the Irish economy depends more and more on the very changeable capacity of world markets to absorb Irish manufactured products. Of the three principal variables that determine the success of exports (cost of production, rate of exchange, and overall economic situation outside) only one, the cost of production, can be determined on a national level. This cost depends on the cost of labour, or in other words the living standards of employees, and also on productivity and the cost of raw materials. Let us not forget that in Ireland manufactured goods for export rely upon a high level of imports (*128*: a comparison between Table 4.1 [p.28] and Table 5.4 [p.47] shows the relation of a high level of exports to a high level of imports, even though the tables only deal with new industry). The ever more insistent demand for increases in productivity and the obsession of industrialists and the State with wage restraint, show how limited is the power of the authorities to manipulate the levers of development, since so few of them are under domestic control.

160

Economic growth also requires additional investment. It is well known that the growth in industrial production in recent years has almost entirely been due to new industries brought to Ireland by the grants of the Industrial Development Authority (*128*), and largely composed of foreign firms attracted by financial incentives. The investment that powers economic growth comes from outside Ireland and public expenditure does little more than create favourable conditions for it. The demand and the investment that create economic growth come from outside the Irish economic system, and form an unstable base for industrial development, particularly since international capitalism in Ireland coexists with national capitalism without establishing a network of trade or interaction with the local economy, without becoming integrated in it or even stimulating it (*117*, 286–8). To this economic dualism is added another difficulty. Foreign industries established in Ireland specialise in final assembly, the last stage in the industrial process. Industrial development in this form will only create a kind of sub-proletariat since there is no need for research or heavy industry: it does not need skilled workers or technicians or researchers. Finally, the added value at this stage of industry may not be very great (*128*, 10–12). In spite of these reservations, can it be said that government grants are justified, or that foreign investment can ensure continuing industrial growth?

The capitalist flavour of the dominant economic project is not without its difficulties. Private enterprise, represented by the Irish bourgeoisie, does not fully play the role it has been allotted but leans heavily on the State, on development incentives and export incentives, investment in infrastructure and grants of all kinds. It has also left to foreign firms the development opportunities offered by the State. In short, the project based on private enterprise is possible only through permanent stimulation by the authorities, the establishment of a plethora of incentives, grants, exemptions, undertakings – and the greater and greater involvement of international capitalism. The project of economic development through private enterprise and the profit motive is supported at arm's length by the State. But this increasing State intervention in economic activity undermines the project itself and denies it in practice. This tension, inherent in the dominant project, could easily become exacerbated into a contradiction and lead to another project explicitly centred on the State and dispensing with the bourgeoisie. This internal contradiction adds to the uncertainty that arises from lack of control by the State over the major economic variables.

Economic Alternatives for the Future

Any economic activity crystallises around certain principles and fundamental choices. The dominant project in Ireland, far from the only possible one, is the result of a choice between different options. The future, even in economic terms, holds a number of choices, each with its constraints and its difficulties but also its advantages, between which a decision must be made.

The project of an economy based on private enterprise and developing behind protective barriers comes up against considerable obstacles in Ireland. Indeed it was tried and failed. The erection of customs barriers was intended to discourage imports and to permit substitute industries to come into being and to prosper in the national context, sheltered from competition which, for historical reasons, the industrial sector could not meet (*126*, 610, 144). In fact a group of national entrepreneurs came into prominence but, working in too small a market and without real competition, producing expensive products and little inclined to improve the productivity of their firms, they developed very slowly. Small-scale capitalism does not represent a realistic possibility for development. A restricted internal market will not support sustained growth. The lack of competition and stimulation to improve productivity, resulting from the small size of the domestic market, does not spur firms into making an effort, or to make growth a necessity. The policy of protection seems to have broken the will to develop and expand firms, which, in a capitalist economy, is the only stimulus to expand production. The relative isolation probably acted as a brake on the improvement of living standards among the population, because Irish manufactured products cost more than similar items on the international market. It is also said that this form of small-scale capitalism creates great inequalities because consumers pay a great deal for products, and the industrial firms compete very little among one another, often enjoying a quasi-monopoly and very high profits. It is true that such an approach to economic development keeps the centres of economic influence and decision-making in Ireland, but in that kind of situation the will to develop the economy, to make the effort to harness economic activity to the task of reducing unemployment or of eliminating the obvious social and regional inequities, requires a strong political commitment and large-scale intervention by the State.

This paradox keeps recurring: economic development through private enterprise and the profit motive requires increasing State intervention; in order to succeed the private enterprise project constantly pushes the State into the major role. Yet, for all that, the dominant project is not a 'socialist' one because it does not eliminate private enterprise, it simply entrusts the State with the task of orchestrating its activity. The State then acts on the strategic elements of growth, so as to increase the prosperity of the private sector. It compensates for the deficiencies of capitalism and keeps it in good working order.

On the other hand, in a project of development really centred on the State, the public and private sectors would have a quite different relationship. The State dominates the economy and takes full responsibility for this domination, taking control of the mechanisms of the market and deciding on the level and the forms of production, consumption, investment, etc. It gives itself the means to carry out its policies.

Up to the present the project of economic growth centred on the State has been simply described as the negation of capitalism. In fact there are various, widely different, forms that this negation can take. One possibility is to increase the number of nationalised firms to reinforce the public sector while continuing to apply to it the criterion of profitability. Another possibility is to integrate all the public sector into one overall plan and eliminate the autonomy of each firm. This scheme is that of authoritarian socialism, which could easily be transformed into State capitalism. The Irish economy would enter international competition and base its growth on exports. Competition and the pursuit of profit would then reappear on the level of the economy as a whole and would provide the basis for domestic planning. The inclusion of the Irish economy in a wide network of international trade reintroduces competition and profitability, not for firms but for the economy as a whole and at the same time the economy is subjected to all the vicissitudes of the international market.

The combination of effective protection and predominance of the State is a realistic alternative to the dominant capitalist project because the two elements would combine easily together and reinforce each other. The State would exercise tight control over a much smaller demand but on the other hand it would be up to the State to stimulate it. At best the fact of being restricted to a small market would only lead to a slow but regular growth in the economy. Once in a position to manipulate all the economic variables, would the State be able to overcome the many limitations of the protected economy? A very strong political commitment is required to compensate for the lack of competition, of internal pressure to expand production, and to get over the inability of the economy to absorb large quantities of products and hence to produce cheap products over a wide range. In a scheme such as this, the economy would no longer have to follow blindly on the workings of the market but would be more responsive (given a political commitment on the part of the State) to the need to solve the social problems created by the unequal distribution of wealth. But is this kind of socialism viable in a small country such as Ireland? Ireland could be able to control its destiny and cease to be the toy of forces beyond its control; is this worth the price of greater frugality and slower growth?

The socialist project may also mean participation and collective responsibility, organised co-operative effort. The co-operative movement has a long history in Ireland but has confined its activity to the agricultural sector, scarcely touching industrial activity. In fact, today the co-operative companies compete with one another and, even though they guarantee a stable outlet and a high price to farmers, have become businesses like any other. They obey the laws of supply and demand and fall short of realising the original aim of the co-operative movement — which was not

163

only to eliminate the exploitation of farmers by middlemen and to ensure stable and dependable outlets, but also to protect the more vulnerable groups from the effects of the open market, to negate the law of the marketplace by controlling it.

Economic activity fully centred on the State, workers' control — neither of these ideas is defended by any major social force, not even the working-class movement. Yet the dynamics of economic development in Ireland have brought the State into the centre of things, if only as an instrument, and given it the principal role in the economy.

17

Social Forces, Political Elites and the State

The distribution of power, the primordial question for political analysis, has a direct bearing on relations between the State and society. It is important to know if a particular group concentrates power in its hands, power being defined as control of decision-making or as having a determining influence on decisions. In other words, is there in Ireland what some call a political elite, a power elite, or a ruling class? First of all we must. define these terms, which are closely related. So far as we are concerned, for present purposes, a political elite means quite simply the group of people who occupy the uppermost positions in the political system, what we would term positions of authority. It includes the limited group of elected representatives who alone are entitled by law to make decisions in the name of the Republic of Ireland, decisions which bind the citizens as a whole. The members of the government, Dáil deputies and, less obviously, senators are all members of this political elite. A study of the political elite in Ireland published a few years ago proposes another categorisation of this elite: the ministers, the President and also the senior civil servants (28). The senior civil servants probably influence government decisions but they do not possess any authority. Their ability to influence decisions would place them in the power elite, not in the political elite. The study referred to also excludes the members of the Dáil from the political elite, since many of them do not attempt to influence decisions of national importance. Nonetheless in Ireland the Dáil is really the only institution that can make laws. It appears that the author of the study is defining not the political elite but the power elite, even though the group he studies belongs to neither one nor the other, but lies between both.

A group of individuals occupy positions of authority at the summit of the political system. But that in itself is not sufficient to designate that group as an elite. There must be something else, since the idea of an elite implies relative stability (the same individuals remaining in place), control of entry to the group, and above all a certain internal cohesion. The relative stability of the political elite in Ireland can be ascertained by studying its rhythm of change. Table 7 shows the turnover in political personnel since the foundation of the State. It shows the rate of renewal of parliamentary deputies and indicates, for example that 40 per cent of those elected deputies in 1927 were already deputies in 1923. The percentage of deputies elected in 1923 diminishes progressively, of course, over the years, through electoral defeats, retirements and deaths. A political generation disappears about every thirty years. The first generation, however, the majority of whom quickly dropped out of sight, was an exception, taking about forty years to disappear entirely. This exception can easily be explained by the fact that the generation of deputies that came out of the nationalist struggle was largely composed of young men who came early to political prominence. This situation did not recur. In fact the first decade of the Irish Free State saw a great turnover of deputies and of the political elite: of those who were deputies in 1933 only a quarter had been deputies in 1923 and less than half survived in 1923–7 and 1927–33. Such low figures were never to be repeated. In the following decade, which saw Fianna Fail come into power, there is evidence of the stability of the political elite. From this period on the proportion of survivors from one election to another, from one section of the table to another (representing a period of 4–5 years on average) is in the region of 60–70 per cent; in each generation approximately 25 per cent of the deputies were in the Dáil twenty years before. There are, however, two exceptions to this great political stability, two periods which saw a more significant renewal of personnel. The transitions from 1945 to 1951 and from 1965 to 1969 show a greater elimination of deputies, a greater renewal. This is clearest in Table 9 which shows the losses in each group from one period to another. There, we again come across these two periods 1945–51 and 1965–9, as well as a further period 1961–5, so that the 1960s as a whole saw a relatively high turnover of deputies. Once this change was made the early 1970s witnessed a great stability in the political elite, the greatest in the history of the Irish Republic.

In fact the figures in these tables underestimate the stability of the parliamentary elite, because another assembly, the Senate, opens its doors to certain deputies who have lost their seats temporarily, thus allowing them to remain in politics, still members of the political class, and wait for the next election. The senators are a secondary but not negligible element in the political elite. Movement between Senate and Dáil is not revealed in these tables and that leads to an underestimation of the stability of the political elite, since that movement takes place within the elite. Indeed the turnover among senators follows a different rhythm to that among deputies: renewal is much more rapid (a generation lasts little more than twenty years), the rate of survival is much lower from one election to another. It is only at the foundation of the State that senators were characterised by greater stability than the deputies. The Anglo-Irish nobility at first enjoyed high representation in the Senate, no doubt to alleviate the fears of the group ousted from power. But the arrival in power of Fianna Fail changed all that; from the 1930s on the Senate no longer had a political role. The stable group in the Senate today is prin-

Table 7. Renewal of personnel in the Dail.

	1927	1933	1937	1944	1951	1954	1957	1961	1965	1969	1973
1923	40%	25%	23%	13%	12%	10%	8%	6%	4%		
1927		45%	39%	28%	19%	16%	10%	10%	4%		
1933			66%	50%	33%	28%	22%	12%	7%	2%	
1937				68%	43%	33%	27%	16%	9%	4%	
1944					54%	46%	39%	27%	16%	11%	6%
1951						70%	56%	45%	32%	21%	15%
1954							67%	62%	44%	28%	21%
1957								70%	52%	31%	24%
1961									71%	46%	38%
1965										62%	55%
1969											79%

Table 8. Renewal of personnel in the Senate.

	1927	1933	1937	1944	1951	1954	1957	1961	1965	1969	1973
1923	80%	42%	12%	10%							
1927		63%	13%	6%	5%						
1933			18%	13%	5%						
1937				56%	28%	20%	17%	–			
1944					38%	28%	22%	–			
1951						48%	38%	–	12%	3%	
1954							43%	–	20%	2%	
1957								–	35%	8%	2%
1961									–	–	–
1965										40%	25%
1969											45%

These tables show the proportion of TDs (Table 7) and senators (Table 8) returned at a particular general election, who had already been returned at a previous given election. (For example, 8 per cent of deputies and senators returned in the 1957 election had been members of the Dáil or Senate in 1923.) These percentages do not represent a rate of survival (the proportion of parliamentarians who survived from one election to the next) but only the proportion of TDs or senators who were already in the Dáil (Table 7) or the Senate (Table 8) in a given previous year. Thus the figure takes account in the variations of the total number of TDs or senators, that is to say the increase or diminutions in personnel which make political survival easier or more difficult.

	1927	1933	1937	1944	1951	1954	1957	1961	1965	1969	1973
1923	40%	−15	−2	−10	−1	−2	−2	−2	−2		
1927		45%	−6	−9	−9	−3	−6	0	−6		
1933			66%	−16	−17	−5	−6	−10	−3	−5	
1937				68%	−25	−10	−6	−11	−7	−5	
1944					54%	−12	−7	−12	−11	−5	−5
1951						70%	−14	−11	−13	−11	−6
1954							67%	−5	−18	−16	−7
1957								70%	−18	−19	−7
1961									71%	−21	−8
1965										62%	−7
1969											79%

Table 9. The progressive diminution of political generations.

The table shows the percentage diminution of each generation of deputies. It allows us to identify the periods that witnessed a significant diminution in each generation, in other words a greater renewal in Dáil personnel.

cipally composed of people of high social standing, honoured by nomination to the Senate, or else of politicians who have failed to get elected to the Dáil and who wish to return there, or who are in danger of disappearing from the political scene.

The slow turnover of the political elite suggests a certain stability; the mode of replacement reinforces this suggestion of continuity. The existence of political families has often been noted in this context, underlining the inheritance of positions of authority: 28 per cent of the deputies elected in 1965 and 1969 had such family connections (50). Sons, nephews, or widows of deceased or retired TDs are favoured in electoral competition, and the phenomenon of political families is all the more marked when it comes to ministerial positions.

There is, therefore, empirical evidence to support the idea of the existence of a political elite. It is extremely difficult to establish its cohesion but the stability of the group in itself produces cohesion: the individuals meet frequently, get to know each other. The fact that most are recruited in a relatively narrow and homogeneous social group also suggests common experience, favouring internal cohesion in the political elite. Members of the Dáil are almost exclusively recruited from clearly defined social groups:

the professions, the petite bourgeoisie, and farmers, other social categories being practically excluded from positions of authority (*24*). One also suspects an ideological cohesion, shared values and choices: unquestioned assumptions, a common vision of social reality accepted without discussion. Certain questions never become political issues. Denominational education, parliamentary representation, the nationalist ethos, the relationship between the State and the moral principles of the Catholic Church — none of these questions have ever really entered the political arena, as if there were a convention requiring these questions to be left out of party politics. Finally, the cohesion of the group is founded in social life, on a network of informal contacts such as, for example, membership of the same social circles or of the same clubs. But there is no systematic information available on this point.

Stability over a period of time, recruitment from a restricted social group, ideological coherence despite all differences and oppositions, all of these characteristics render very plausible the notion of a great cohesion of the political elite, but fall short of proving it. It thus appears not entirely fanciful to speak of the existence in Ireland of a political elite, a relatively stable and quite cohesive group, which holds the positions of authority.

A Governing Class

Attention has often been drawn to the exceptionally important position which the professions occupy in the political elite. Why is it that this social category above all others should be so profoundly involved in political life and so able to reach the highest positions? It is, of course, often said that this category possesses essential qualities for success in political activity. First, a university education, a characteristic of the professions, gives both intellectual flexibility and the ability to appreciate the complexity of social, economic and political problems. It fosters fluency and public speaking is still the essential medium for creating a political image, communicating one's positions, proposing solutions and stimulating support. The political advantage generated by university education is not measured in diplomas but is nonetheless a definite product of that education. We must however make this reservation: the more intellectual professions contribute relatively fewer people to the political elite, leaving the field open to persons who have a less speculative and more practical training. But the presence of the professions is certainly linked to advantages such as the above in the process of political selection, even if it cannot be entirely explained by them.

Perhaps one should seek the explanation in other characteristics of this social category. In Ireland, more than anywhere else, the professions enjoy great prestige, which can readily be converted into a political resource. In addition the professions are seen as having a great deal of leisure, or at any rate a greater than average flexibility in the organisation of their activity,

169

and this leisure or flexibility fits in well with political activity. Professional activity is generally concerned with personal service, which greatly helps in the development of social *savoir faire*, and an easy manner in society. The network of personal contacts which the professions create is no hindrance to political ambitions. All of this can be capitalised on, if occasion requires, for political ends, either directly or indirectly. In the latter case the characteristics mentioned above are advantages, qualities sought after in officers of voluntary bodies. Positions of authority in such bodies quite readily serve as springboards for political ambitions, giving a quasi-political experience and a platform of interests to promote or defend on the basis of which a political career can begin and progress. Close links with certain organised interest groups are part of the strategy of any politician.

Thus, professional people possess qualities which are strategically important for electoral success. But they also have to be politically acceptable. They enjoy great job security, high social status and on the whole a high standard of living, all of which encourages an enlightened conservatism, a defence of the status quo or of moderate reform. This conservative and moderate trait helps them in their political activity but in itself would not make them into a political class, a fertile ground for the recruitment of the political elite. The fact that they have no interest and little desire to change society makes them worthy of confidence. On the other hand they are not attached to the perpetuation of society as it is at present in all its details. For we know already that the professions have not succeeded in producing a project, a collective plan of action. Thus they will not use their authority to advance their own interests, and lacking collective aims, they do not closely identify with any of the projects that compete in Irish society. In addition, they keep a relative distance from all of the projects and thus have a certain flexibility and the ability to raise themselves above immediate conflicts. Their conservatism is not inconsistent with a certain tendency to be reformist in certain matters. Such is the magic power of the professions, their place in Irish society, between the social forces; all of which singles them out as well suited to political life. This does not mean, however, that the professions belong to that much sought after social category, which is at the same time part of society and above it, beyond its intrigues, its special interests, and its conflicts. For the fact that they lack a project and their independence from particular projects does not mean that they are autonomous or without bias. It is simply that their social position encourages them to link essential projects, and to use their influence to establish points of contact and possibilities of compromise. Hence their political talents in the administration of society.

If it is true that the professions do not seek positions of authority in order to protect their collective interests, which they would be hard put to define, does their pre-eminence tell us something about the structure of power? It is often said that the professions belong to the middle classes, which dominate Irish society and that the large number of members of the professions in positions of authority expresses this domination in political activity. According to this theory these influential members of the middle class act with a systematic bias in a particular perspective, with a precise ideological orientation. If this is true one would expect to find a basic conservatism, a resistance to change, the trademark of dominant classes anxious to preserve the status quo from which they profit. The broad support for Fine Gael in the middle classes in part illustrates this conservative attitude. But this is only a mood and is indicative neither of the defence of common interests nor of a common ideological orientation. Indeed certain categories of the middle classes show no conservative tendencies and, as we saw in the case of industrial managers, often demand profound changes, so as to favour industrial activity. What is more, the professions in particular are characterised by a relative independence from competing projects, by a flexibility that enables them to contemplate social changes that are not always agreeable for other elements of the middle classes. Finally, the political parties that are working for a radical transformation of society are often led by individuals from the ranks of the professions (although there appears to be a predominance here of the lower ranks of the professions, especially teachers). In short, the attempt to link the predominance of the professions to the defence of a vague and politically diverse middle class does not hold water.

Can they be described as a governing class? What is meant here is not that the professions as a whole participate in the government of Ireland; that is much too literal a meaning of 'governing class'. It is clear at least that this social category is a privileged recruiting ground for the highest positions of authority. It does not govern for itself, or in order to promote its own interests above all (in this sense the governing class never becomes a ruling class or dominant class, even though it may take advantage of its position). Nor is it the much sought after category which is above all special interests and beyond their conflicts. The fact that it does not participate in any project does not give it access to a mythical 'common good', but that does not take away its capacity, which is essential for its political survival, to adapt to the balance of social forces. We are not concerned here with whether that balance of social forces is changeable or well structured and stable. One could even envisage a situation in which the governing class would carry out its function of governing in a situation completely dominated by one social class, which would impose its outlook, a framework within which the governing class would exercise its authority, keeping its autonomy but also respecting well-defined limits. Some commentators go so far as to define the governing class as the docile instrument of the ruling class. But what is this ruling class and by what means is it supposed to control the governing class?

The professions are not the only group from which the governing class is recruited. The petite bourgeoisie also contributes to it, although its role in the political elite is relatively secondary and decreases as one ascends the political ladder. The participation of the petite bourgeoisie in the governing class is of a very different nature. First of all, it brings to the political elite an element of local colour and local outlook, at the point where the cosmopolitanism of the professions is in danger of losing touch with certain realities of Irish life. The petite bourgeoisie, among whom many important local figures are recruited, acts as a link between the political elite and a whole network of local contacts (a network of contacts which makes an important contribution to the progress of the political careers of these shopkeepers and small industrialists). In addition, their 'social nature' makes them acceptable in positions of authority. Like the professions, the petite bourgeoisie is incapable of collective action, whose only project is support for the status quo. Caught between the rival projects of the bourgeoisie and the working class, the petite bourgeoisie insists on stability and social order, the need for compromise, and ordered competition ending in dialogue and negotiation. The petite bourgeoisie seeks to reach and to create a balance between the social forces, but a balance headed towards the defence of private enterprise, a conservative balance with itself in the centre. In striving to accomplish this task it can call on neither the same talents nor the same political flexibility, nor indeed the same imagination as the professions. Perhaps that is why the petite bourgeoisie has only a secondary role as a recruiting ground of the political elite, and that its role is that of moderator and speaker of home truths. In short, with the professions it forms a marriage of opposites.

The Senior Civil Servants

Fears have often been expressed that the growth of the State brings a growth in the power of the State bureaucracy, and of these civil servants who hold offices of responsibility in the various departments. According to this theory senior civil servants constitute an important group within the governing elite. In Ireland can the State bureaucracy exercise an independent influence, does it constitute a centre of power? Officially, of course, the bureaucracy is merely an instrument and does not make decisions about important political policy.

There is no doubt that senior civil servants can influence policies of the departments in which they are employed. That, in fact, is their function: advising ministers who take responsibility for decisions, outlining possible options and making clear the consequences of each (246). Their advice and recommendations carry a lot of weight because civil servants know their files thoroughly and are expert in the eyes of the minister. They represent bureaucratic continuity as opposed to the relative instability of ministers. In addition, the growth of the State and the extension of its sphere of influence has increased their power, forcing them to take decisions that ministers have neither the time nor the interest to consider. The considerable increase in matters that come up for ministerial consideration, the growing complexity of legislative activity, the development and planning activities in which ministerial departments are called upon to play a creative, stimulating role, all of these create new possibilities for the exercise of their influence. Finally, more power is delegated to civil servants today than in the past (47). Laws as well as ministerial policy must be put into practice; they require interpretation, a sense of judgment, and flexibility on the part of the civil service.

Certain administrative tasks are by statute made quite independent of the minister. Commissioners, civil servants independent of the minister, choose recruits to the civil service, or assess tax liabilities, etc. The delegation of tasks of semi-state bodies has become quite common in Ireland, relieving the minister of the burden of daily control of certain activities. But in spite of all this the ultimate responsibility rests on the minister, and the constitution does not make it easy to delegate power. In practice and of necessity ministers give their senior civil servants great latitude and place a heavy burden of personal responsibility on them. Senior officials meet delegations from interest- or pressure-groups and often negotiate with them; they are members of numerous committees; they also represent Ireland at international conferences. They are beginning to emerge from anonymity and sometimes defend publicly the policy of their departments. Civil servants are no longer presented as simple instruments and are now supposed to show creativity and initiative in the promotion of economic development, as well as in the social and cultural development of Ireland.

That does not mean that the various government departments are not subject to certain controls. The parliamentary assemblies keep a careful watch on their activity. Allocations in the budget effectively control the financial resources of the different departmental activities. Ministers are regularly called on to answer for the activities of their department before the Dáil — which could even require a senior civil servant to answer questions. The State bureaucracy is also subject to judicial control, in that citizens can go to court to defend themselves against the often arbitrary decisions of civil servants. But taking legal action can be long, intimidating and expensive. Administrative tribunals have been set up, composed of civil servants independent of the departments, to act as courts of appeal where decisions are contested.

In conclusion it is clear that civil servants influence ministerial decisions both on legislative proposals and in the application of government decisions. Indeed their function is defined as the exercise of influence and the assumption of such responsibility. But the independent activity of the bureaucracy is kept within rather narrow limits by governmental and parliamentary controls, and, to a lesser extent, by the right of citizens to go to court to overturn decisions of government departments.

It is hardly surprising that civil servants influence the exercise of power. But do they all push together in the same direction? If their power is arbitrary and dispersed, they lose all unity of action and cease to exist as a collective force: their inclusion in the governing elite would not then be justified. Thus, group cohesion is a condition of inclusion in the political elite. But little is known of the cohesion of the senior civil servant group and any conclusion in this regard can only be very tentative. It has been observed that the group has a great homogeneity in its origins, being recruited mainly in urban areas from the sons of office workers and middle executives. The greater majority of civil servants have also in common that they have been educated by the Christian Brothers and this secondary school education may show in their characters: a practical education little inclined to speculation, with a tendency to produce rather introverted and cautious personalities, encouraging political and cultural ethnocentricity (*179*). Their internal cohesion is also aided by their activity, and by the development of an *esprit de corps*. 'In practice (the civil service) cannot be neutral. It develops its own value systems, its traditions and precedents, its *esprit de corps*, its corporate image' (*206*). In this context it is interesting to note that senior civil servants are never recruited by open competition, but by internal promotion. A selection is carried out and the highest levels are reached only by those who, *inter alia*, have shown that they can be trusted. The continuing education and training that many of them engage in and their network of informal contacts also favour greater integration. Opinions on this point are divided: some commentators stress the lack of solidarity or personal contact among civil servants while others hold that there is such contact. The relative independence of senior civil servants *vis à vis* the political authorities encourages the creation of a group identity, reinforced by their expertise and protected by the secrecy that envelops their activity. Perhaps one could also speak of an ideological coherence, such as their reputed tendency to turn all political questions into administrative ones. Finally, one could attribute a systematic orientation to their influence, in defence of their group interests: obtaining favourable conditions for their careers; regular promotions by seniority (and not by merit or efficiency duly measured); the protection of their independence; and so on. All of these suggestions are quite plausible but the available data is not conclusive on this subject.

Civil servants are not regarded as exerting any great influence in Ireland, either by the public or by politicians (*186*). Observers of the political scene in Ireland are, on the contrary, surprised by the relatively modest and even subordinate role that bureaucrats have accepted for themselves. Since they embody no particular vision they only act as docile instruments of the political authorities, never putting up a serious challenge — although clearly the bureaucracy delays or activates certain policies according to its preferences. One hesitates therefore to include senior civil servants in the political elite, not because they do not influence government decisions but because that influence does not appear to spring from group cohesion.

174

Power elite or dominant class?

To affirm the existence of a 'political elite' does not greatly advance our analysis and leads in the end only to a somewhat neutral conclusion. It would be more informative to discover a small group that had no authority given to it but nonetheless exercised a determining influence on government decisions. But in that case who would be the members of this power elite? We have already commented on the rather special place of the professions, which however does not arise from group unity or from a specific collective orientation. The military institutions are extremely hierarchised and their senior officers are identifiable; but the army chiefs have always kept their distance from the political scene and do not intervene. The State bureaucracy, as we saw, is a rather doubtful case: senior civil servants influence government decisions but their influence does not run counter to the authority of parliament or of the government, both of which supervise and control their activity. The Church acts in a highly co-ordinated manner and, through its bishops, speaks with one voice. Occasionally it intervenes directly on the political scene and secures the defeat of certain proposals. Apart from this power of veto, limited in fact to specific issues, the Catholic Church exercises a diffuse political influence of low intensity. It is obvious that the Catholic Church, though without political authority, exercises a certain power: but does this make it an element of a power elite, a cohesive and conspiratorial group? One also thinks of the economic elite (meaning the leaders of the unions, of the employers' federation, the farmers' associations). Government policy is largely determined directly in relation to these socio-economic forces, through a network of consultations and negotiations. A special study would be required to establish the impact of these pressure groups on State activity, a study which would be very difficult to carry out. Nonetheless conflicts of interest occur between the State and these groups and that makes one doubt, not their great influence, but their participation in a hypothetical 'power elite'; the distance between these groups and the State shows that they have influence but are not in control.

The enumeration of influential groups is not sufficient to prove the existence of a power elite. One would also have to show that these elements combine, develop coherence and cohesion, act together. But this way of examining the distribution of power in Ireland is not fruitful. The idea of a small organised group, conspiring to pull all the strings, does not go far; at least it helps to remind us of the fact that power and authority do not coincide, that behind the political elite there are other forces. If there is no power elite, is there perhaps a social class influencing the political elite, controlling it maybe, a dominant class or even a ruling class in Ireland?

18
The Social Forces and the State Project

The existence of a political elite, a cohesive group of individuals in positions of authority, does not really help us to throw light on the relations between the State and society. The attempt to discover behind this political elite a power elite does not offer us a realistic or even a useful perspective. But can one say that there exists in Ireland a ruling or even a dominant class which can effectively influence the State? We must first clearly note the distinction, which is highly important if we wish to prove our statements, between a ruling class (a social class which controls government decisions either directly or indirectly) and a dominant class (which exerts a decisive influence). The mere possibility of a conflict of interest between the State and any social class eliminates the hypothesis of a ruling class: no force exercises a direct, effective and absolute control over the State. But the possibility of conflicts, of a lack of correspondence between interests, is not incompatible with the existence of a dominant class which can exercise a determining influence. Indeed, as the previous chapters have shown, the interests defended by a class are unstable and variable. In short the test of interests is not conclusive in relation to determining the existence of a dominant class.

One can also look at the particular affinities between the State and certain social classes, in that they either share a similar orientation or perceive social reality in the same way. It has even been said that the proof of the domination of the bourgeoisie lies in the fact that the State defends private property. But this is a generalisation which does not take account of certain different or even divergent orientations within the property-owning classes. The defence of private property is a trait not only of the bourgeoisie but also of farmers and the petite bourgeoisie.

The observation of a convergence in interests or even of ideological affinities is not a very convincing test or means of discovering the relationship between the State and the social forces. In the preceding chapters we have analysed the social forces active in Ireland, forces that can engage in collective action and define policies for the future. In the same way, the State, the collective action of society as a whole, bases its activity upon a project. The comparison between the State project and the various particular projects in Ireland is the most useful and the most conclusive test of the relations between the State and the social forces. It enables us to observe the similarities between projects and thus the possible domination of one social class over the State, to measure the extent of the relative autonomy (if any) of the State from the social forces and to investigate the source of this autonomy. The study of the different projects is a point at which the question of the relations between the State and society, that highly controversial topic, can find an empirical answer.

The dominant aspect of the State Project

The drive for economic growth is the principal preoccupation of the State. It defines its policy for the future, is the fundamental principle of its activity, the cohesive force behind its actions, and the explanation of its modernising zeal. This is clearly expressed, in the declarations of successive ministers and various official publications, as a determination to develop and increase material production. But the economic circumstances in which Ireland finds herself qualify and define that preoccupation. Industrial growth is based on too narrow a national market and must seek to conquer external markets, to export. The degree to which Irish manufactured products can sell abroad becomes, therefore, a strategic focus of the State project. The State envisages a capitalist development of the economy only, and private enterprise is the foundation stone on which it hopes to build the transformation of Irish society. But this orientation can only be considered an essential aspect of the State project if it is more than an ideological expression or a 'rationalisation' of its actual policy, if it underlies all its activity and is in fact the principle and the coherence behind that activity.

A great number of State actions can be fully understood only as attempts to advance the development of private enterprise. A whole range of incentives to promote industrial activity has been created, to modernise existing firms and attract new industries. The Industrial Development Authority was established to seek out new investors, to distribute often substantial grants, and to attract new industries by direct assistance. It also seeks to create a climate congenial to productive investment. Profits on exports are exempt from tax. The State contributes to the promotion of manufactured products abroad (Coras Trachtala). It finances research and advice services for industry, such as the Institute for Industrial Research and Standards, and the Irish Productivity Centre. It worries over the quality of management, which it sees as an important factor in industrial success and contributes to the funding of the Irish Management Institute, which carries out management research and training. At the same time as it strives to attract new industries, the State tries to reform the structure of existing industry so as to produce greater efficiency, more thoughtful management, greater attention to market outlets. Wishing to increase the productive capacity of Irish industry it not only stimulates private enterprise but gives it grants and makes up for its deficiencies by its own

177

commercial and industrial agencies. Ireland's desire to join the EEC is in part explained by its concern to find a framework within which Irish industry could prosper: Ireland would become an important location for industries wishing to gain access to the Common Market (287). The establishment of a broad market without restrictions would assist exports.

The economic management that is carried out principally by the annual budgets must be understood in the light of this project. Public expenditure, principally the programme of public investment, has greatly increased over the last decade. The State spends a large amount of its resources on industrial investment, whether by investment in the infrastructure necessary to industry or by direct stimulation of private enterprise. This public expenditure, in the form of credits or exemptions, direct grants or even purchases, is designed to lead to private investment. In the annual budget great care is taken not to hinder efforts to encourage industrial development. Controlling inflation, stimulating production, channelling supplementary resources to the State, encouraging demand or restricting it — all of these economic imperatives must be satisfied without threatening the spirit of State policy. The function of the budget is to adapt that policy to an ever-changing situation, to carry it through in spite of obstacles, difficulties, and restrictions placed in its way (247).

The mobilisation of public resources through taxes reflects this project in an exaggerated way. Direct taxes are almost entirely borne by employees, who pay their taxes every week or every month, when they are paid, in the PAYE system. The liberal professions have little difficulty in avoiding high taxation and do not pay their share of taxes. Farmers were practically exempt from income tax until 1974. Since then the most well-to-do farmers have been brought into the tax net, and the prosperity of agriculture following Ireland's accession to the EEC made it difficult to continue exemption from tax for the majority of farmers. It is true that farmers pay local taxes, calculated on a valuation of their property (indeed all property owners used to pay these taxes or 'rates' until 1977, when rates were abolished for private houses). But even with regard to rates substantial reliefs and exemptions reduce the burden of taxation for farmers (266). Finally, the State draws part of its revenue from taxes on industrial profits and business profits, taking an average of 40—50 per cent of profits (250, 251). But, concerned as it is not to hinder industrial development, it grants numerous exemptions to firms contributing to industrial expansion. Deduction for reconstruction, capital depreciation, exemptions for additional exports, various arrangements with investment institutions (building societies, insurance firms) soften the impact. All of these opportunities for decreasing the burden of taxation are fully exploited; in 1975 company taxation accounted for only 5 per cent of direct taxes, whereas in 1960 it accounted for 31 per cent (247).

Ireland is one of the few countries in Europe that has not established

178

taxes on capital and wealth; property is affected only by an inheritance tax which has numerous loopholes. In 1974 the government proposed to introduce taxation of capital gains and of wealth, as well as a new inheritance tax (249, 261). These measures became law in spite of fierce opposition but were later abandoned by the new government in 1977. Such taxes would conflict with the whole industrial strategy, which is to attract investment by creating a favourable economic climate. Thus the tax system in Ireland weighs heavily on employees, directly by taxing a high proportion of income and indirectly by taxes on commodities. The State is careful not to affect private enterprise, either capital gains or the enjoyment of property itself, a circumspection which it justifies as an anxiety not to frighten off investment. Indeed the State uses taxation as a very important instrument in the application of its economic policy, through the effective manipulation of the principal economic variables.

But it is not only in economic policy that the orientation we have described plays a dominant role; it also controls a large part of the work of the various ministerial departments. The Department of Industry and Commerce has a very important role in the carrying into effect of decisions for the encouragement of industrial development. It has, of course, broad general tasks, such as supervising the operation of competition in business and preventing the introduction of monopolistic practices. It keeps a watch on prices (for the most part following the recommendations of the National Prices Commission), keeps a register of companies and of patents, introduces regulations for industrial activity, and allocates licences for exploration and mining of natural resources. It follows closely the indicators of industrial development, the indices of growth of industrial production and even changes in industrial structure (242). In sum, it supervises industrial organisation as well as carrying out general tasks. (This section was written before the 1981 general election, which resulted in changes to the structures and nomenclature of certain departments. The functions of the Department of Industry and Commerce, for example, are now discharged in part by the new Department of Industry and Energy and in part by the Department of Trade, Commerce and Tourism. Since such changes do not affect the points raised in this section, however, the old nomenclature has been retained.)

The Department of Industry and Commerce is also concerned with scientific research and technological progress. Economic growth, we are assured, requires that constant attention be given to technological development and the State must encourage its application. A National Science Council advises the minister in this field and administers certain grants. The Council has recommended certain tax exemptions, granting of allowances and amendments to the anti-monopoly legislation, and suggested that greater importance be placed on scientific subjects in the schools (277). The importance of scientific research for economic growth in Ireland has in fact been challenged (280). Economic development had begun without any corresponding increase in scientific effort. The export sector is dominated by foreign companies — and this is the area in which the most significant growth is made — which get their technology from their parent companies. Scientific research and development are almost entirely financed by the State and almost half the money goes to agriculture, although grants for industrial research increased from 15 per cent in 1967 to 25 per cent in 1974 (*276*). The Institute for Industrial Research and Standards, which diffuses technological progress and adapts it to local conditions, is primarily concerned with assisting native industries, the sector that contributes least to industrial growth. In short, the advances of scientific research and its application do not contribute much to economic development in Ireland. In almost all advanced industrial societies, scientific research and development have been closely associated with the State but in Ireland the dominant project of the State does not appear to demand such a close association. Scientific research and development is only a secondary aspect of the State project.

The Minister for Transport and Energy plays a supporting role, in that his task is to establish an efficient and cheap system of transport over the whole country and to ensure a constant supply of energy. Semi-state bodies carry out these tasks on a more or less commercial basis. The Minister has only a rather distant supervisory role to play in relation to these bodies: he appoints the boards, supervises investment and intervenes directly in the more delicate and sensitive political decisions. He is responsible for the administration of the ports, for essential transport services (regulation of transport by sea and air, meteorological service, the issuing of transport licences) most of which are merely technical matters and are governed by international regulations. But this department is not always a neutral organ of support for the project of industrial growth. It is also implicated in a very serious controversy which hits at the whole project of growth. Continuing growth requires an uninterrupted and practically unlimited supply of energy. The authorities in Ireland decided in favour of nuclear energy, to complete or replace energy from petroleum products, which is expensive and destined to run out. This policy has met with serious objections that the State cannot entirely ignore. But in spite of the fact that transport and energy form an important part of the infrastructure without which industrialisation of any consequence cannot develop, the State in Ireland has not developed a coherent policy. It answers needs as they arise and takes care of the most pressing arrangements, but with no clear vision of the future. One can, however, predict that in the near future the energy question will assume an important and indeed a priority position in the deliberations of the State and in the realisation of its project.

A Department of Labour has been established to take charge of a labour policy and the regulation of relations between employers and workers. Economic growth requires a rapid development of techniques and hence of training. It requires constant readjustment and a flexible labour force (*263, 273*). An improvement in the general level of education should increase flexibility. The human cost of industrial progress is reduced if the possibilities of redeployment and of continuing education are improved. The Department of Labour has given the responsibility for industrial training to a semi-state body (AnCO), but this body has not developed a systematic policy of retraining or continuing education. The labour policy is not only not very well thought out but it also has a residual characteristic which has been criticised and denounced. The Department of Labour applies a policy decided elsewhere and centered exclusively on the adaptation of the labour force to present and future needs. It pays no attention to the often severe social problems which accompany such changes and concerns itself only with redundancy payments. The department also tries to regulate the labour market, to facilitate co-ordination of offer and demand for labour. It attempts to predict the structure of future employment, and to identify future imbalances. During the 1960s it financed studies of the labour market in several urban centres (*227*).

The Department of Labour also attempts to harmonise relations between employers and labour. An arbitration court for labour conflicts (The Labour Court) recommends solutions, to which the conflicting parties often agree. The National Employer-Labour Conference brings employers and labour together and negotiates agreements between the two camps. For almost a decade the level of wages was fixed by negotiations between the Irish Congress of Trade Unions, the Federated Union of Employers, and the government. These National Wage Agreements, national contracts concluded at regular intervals, presented considerable advantages for the State project. They moderated the increase in wages, a leitmotiv of all government pronouncements. They subordinated the demands of the more favoured categories to those of the categories that are less well organised or less effective in their actions. They guaranteed a certain stability and limited the number of strikes. They put a brake on salaries, which facilitated the competitiveness of Irish products on export markets and attracted foreign capital. Ireland's relatively low level of strikes and salaries for some time was a feature of the publicity aimed at attracting new productive investment.

Telecommunications are under the responsibility of a Minister for Posts and Telecommunications, who also oversees radio and television. The constant complaints about inadequate telephone services seems to show that the State has not given priority to this aspect of the infrastructure. The Minister for the Environment, formerly Minister for Local Government, is in charge of functions which are essential for economic growth: the maintenance of roads and drainage, water supply, the construction of dwelling-houses, control of pollution of the environment, and local planning (*258*). Although important, these tasks are not matters of priority in the preoccupations of the government or budgetary allocations.

The road network is often not up to standard, the control of pollution is often not effective, the housing policy, apart from local authority housing for the less well-off, is left to the private market, which fluctuates and is subject to speculation. Indeed the budgetary measures taken in this regard are principally concerned with the health of the building industry.

Regional imbalances are also more particularly the responsibility of the Department of the Environment. Since 1950 various governments have tried to correct regional inequalities. Several governmental bodies distribute special grants for industries setting up in the less favoured regions: the IDA, Gaeltarra Eireann, the Shannon Free Airport Development Corporation. The local authorities have been given the role of development agencies and the responsibility of satisfying local infrastructure needs. There has been intense debate on the strategy for regional reform, some proposing a concentration of industrial growth in certain carefully selected urban centres, others calling for a dispersal of growth throughout the community. The government has refused to choose between the two approaches and tries to combine them (262). In fact it is difficult to marry a policy of regional development with one of general economic growth. Special measures of a differential nature have little weight when it is a question of attracting 'at all costs' foreign industry to Ireland. To differentiate between forms of assistance amounts to imposing restrictions on the location of new investments, which is incompatible with, and perhaps fatal to the State project of growth. Whether through inability to make a firm decision or through insuperable difficulties, government policy since the 1950s has been unable to prevent the concentration of industry on the east coast and in the Cork region. Recently, however, the entry of Ireland to the EEC has somewhat redressed regional balance (269). The rise in agricultural prices has brought a certain prosperity to the rural areas, but that occurred 'accidentally', without real effort or intervention on the part of the State.

The dominant aspects of the State project, as we have observed it, correspond quite closely to the project of the bourgeoisie which was examined in a previous chapter: modernisation understood as industrialisation, economic growth under the aegis of private enterprise, confidence in the profit motive as a stimulus for development. The State project is richer and more complex than that of the bourgeoisie, which it embraces as its central element without being smothered by it. The State principally relies on budgetary measures to realise this aspect of its project. Such confidence in economic manipulations pushes the development of the infrastructure into the background, even though it is considered to be the *sine qua non* of progress. The lack of a transport or energy policy has already been noted; the labour policy is marginal to government considerations; and economic growth in Ireland does not necessarily demand considerable investment in scientific research.

That there is close correspondence between the projects does not mean that the State is simply submitting to the project of the bourgeoisie. The initiative for economic modernisation came from the State and not the bourgeoisie, which was on the whole happy to stagnate behind the protection of tariff barriers. Rather was the State project, formulated in the 1950s, imposed in part on the undeveloped and reluctant bourgeoisie. The petite bourgeoisie would probably not have supported this reforming zeal without the pressure of the State apparatus and, in this sense, it can be said that the State made the bourgeoisie, promoted it as a social force, and continues to give it meaning and unity of direction. The dominant role of the bourgeoisie in the State project can quite easily be explained by the determination of the State: far from the bourgeoisie imposing its will on the State, the State may well be manipulating the bourgeoisie to realise its own project.

It may be that originally the dominant position of the bourgeoisie merely reflected the project of the State, but the bourgeoisie has developed, grown in confidence and strength. The national project rests on its shoulders, imposing constraints but also conferring privileges and influence. It takes on a project that suits it, interprets it in its own way and profits from it. It acquires a strong position because its interests coincide with the national interest; its project gives it legitimacy. The tables are turned and the bourgeoisie can now dictate to the State, which created it and now, like the apprentice sorcerer, is dominated by its own creation. Relations between the State and the bourgeoisie cannot be expressed in terms of one becoming the instrument of the other. The fact that the bourgeois project is incorporated into the State project as a key element and that in return the bourgeoisie exerts a very weighty influence on the State for the satisfaction of its interests does not prevent there being conflicts of interest or even open confrontation. Which proves that they have some measure of autonomy one from the other, the source of which is worthy of investigation. The State has to consider needs other than those of the bourgeoisie. It incorporates the particular project of the bourgeoisie into its general project, modifies it, goes beyond it, and links it to other orientations. It assembles its project from the relations between the particular projects, the active forces that have come to its attention. In the process of organising its own project it escapes the control of particular projects but not their influence. That is where its relative autonomy is based. We must look at it more closely.

The Complementary Aspect of the State Project

Although it looks principally to industry to accelerate economic growth the State also considers agriculture as an important contributor. An increase in agricultural production is presented as the aim of all farmers, even though, as we will recall, there is divergence on the spirit and manner of growth. The activity of the Department of Agriculture leaves little room for doubt (*241*) that its concern is to change Irish agriculture, often traditional still, into an efficient and commercial enterprise. Progress in agricultural productivity, more intensive cultivation, and the creation of viable farms are the principal objectives. In order to bring about this modernisation the State has established a variety of measures, incentives and services. It reduces production costs by subsidising products such as chemical fertilisers or by selectively lowering duties. In order to increase agricultural productivity it introduces programmes to improve soil quality, etc. It finances agricultural education, sets up research laboratories and a network of agricultural advisors. It creates agencies to co-ordinate market research and stimulates the export of agricultural produce. More important still, because more controversial, it encourages the reform of land use, eliminating small farms. The Land Commission is charged with the task of restructuring farm holdings, buying or compulsorily acquiring vacant or under-utilised land, and redistributing it. It attempts to carry out this work by giving land to farms that are too small or by putting together farms that are then placed at the disposition of farmers transferred from elsewhere (*257*). Thus it patiently builds up 'viable' agricultural units, capable of supporting a reasonable standard of living for a family. The viability of a farm clearly depends on the quality of the soil but for a long time the size was fixed at about thirty acres, a threshold which gradually rose to its present level of fifty acres. The desire to create viable farms (of medium size and large enough to engage in commercial agriculture) was reinforced by Ireland's entry to the EEC. EEC agricultural policy has, as one of its two principal aims, that of encouraging farm modernisation. The European Community gives special assistance to farmers who have the ability to prosper, and to achieve efficient production and economic viability. It proposes retirement pensions to old farmers, who are often traditional farmers.

In the State project, with its effort to modernise agriculture in Ireland and to help farmers able to grasp opportunities for development and adapt themselves to change, one can recognise the dominant project of the farmers and the kind of society it proposes: the elimination of traditional agriculture and the lifestyle that goes with it through land reform (*241*). Within the overall State project, the principal project of the farmers co-exists without major modification with the project of the bourgeoisie. The State takes up the farmers' project and, on the basis that it is compatible with that of the bourgeoisie, establishes them as complementary projects. Perhaps they are more than complementary, since there is an affinity between their visions of growth, given the new definition of the farm as a business. They support one another, even though tensions can appear when each one wishes to benefit from budgetary favours or alternatively avoid the rigours of the budget.

For a long time price support consumed a large part of State expenditure on agriculture, especially regarding milk prices. More recently in Ireland high farm produce prices has been the second element in the agricultural project of the European Community. But systematic support of agricultural prices enables many small farmers to subsist without modernising, developing or increasing their production. This has often been the subject of comment. High prices for agricultural produce thus work against the effort to modernise farms. It has even been suggested that this policy cannot guarantee an adequate standard of living to small farmers. In spite of itself the European Community is guaranteeing the survival of small Irish farmers, at least for a time. This is due to an ambiguity in the policy of agricultural price support. A disguised form of social assistance, it acts through economic mechanisms and makes it possible for small farmers to survive. In other words, this form of intervention blocks reform of agricultural structures. This is perhaps a contradiction but in hiding social assistance in economic subsidies the State pleases all farmers, for high prices for agricultural produce give greater profits to 'commercialised' farmers than small farmers and thus bring together the two projects associated with farmers: modernisation by the reform of land use and the commercialisation of agriculture; and the preservation of a high number of small farms working the land intensively and retaining a traditional way of life. The State adopts the principal project of the farmers and to some extent neutralises the secondary project. It satisfies certain needs of the small farmers and promotes certain of their interests without adopting their project. Thus one discovers that the State project contains a paradox: it supports particular projects but sometimes opposes the interests which derive from them, and it satisfies interests so as all the better to block the projects that lie behind those interests. The State answers the demand for high agricultural prices, thus neutralising the secondary project of the farmers, not because small farmers are such a formidable force that it hesitates to alienate them, but simply because this neutrality is cheaply bought by the very ambiguous measures of price support for agricultural produce.

A Subordinate Aspect of the State Project

The project of industrial growth directly involves the working class simply because it constitutes the labour force. Included in the State project the working class is the subject of a policy that seeks to adapt it to the changing needs of development. Governments firmly declare their commitment to full employment, which has never been known to exist in Ireland (273). For a long time emigration concealed the underemployment of the Irish labour force; when emigration began to slow down unemployment rose, reaching extremely high levels. But full employment also fits in with the State project, which seeks an expansion of the productive base. So the fulfilling of this need of the working class is in this sense subordinated to the success of the State project. The Department of Labour's policy is also concerned with industrial relations, the search for relative harmony between employers and employees. Frequent and prolonged strikes undermine the confidence of customers, threaten progress in exports, frighten foreign investment and thus weaken the foundations of the State project. Several bodies have been given the task of arbitrating on conflicts, mediating betwen the camps, or negotiating settlements. During the 1970s successive governments took an active part in national wage agreements, acting as guarantors of relative social peace and wage control. Every official economic publication reiterates, like a ritual, an appeal for wage restraint, and the control of wage increases. It is a never-ending task, for increases have to be conceded while holding the general level down. It is endlessly repeated that too high a level of wages will lessen the capacity of Irish manufactured products to penetrate European markets, and that improvements in living standards must wait on increases in productivity. The national wage agreements compel the social partners to consider the situation as a whole, to decide on overall objectives, accept the State project as the framework for their activity and thus to subordinate their interests to it.

It is interesting to note the change of emphasis and of style in the three programmes for economic expansion (*281, 283, 291*) around which the commitment to growth has crystallised. The first programme principally concerned itself with the manipulation of economic variables and with public investment. It insisted on the need to develop the productive base of the economy and to limit non-productive investment, and stated that there is a tension between the economic and the social aspects of growth, aspects which are in fact difficult to distinguish. The second programme reaffirmed the principal economic objectives of the first but it broadened the perspective. Incentives to invest, purely financial measures, are no longer sufficient because the success of the industrial project requires an adequate environment and adequate human material. The third and latest programme takes into account social and cultural objectives, in order to motivate the people, to involve them in this struggle for growth and, on occasions, to justify present sacrifices by holding out future rewards. It invokes the quality of life and the general benefits of material growth. But while these social and cultural objectives are taken into account, the programme subordinates them to the achievement of economic objectives. Yet one should not overemphasise the tension between economic and social goals. The satisfaction of certain social needs, such as education, is required by industrial growth. Other social needs, such as the correction of regional disparities or the defence of the environment, are in fact products of economic growth. For our purposes it is enough to point out that, as it matured, the State project had to take on a social dimension. It solves the problem of competition between economic and social needs by subordinating the social to the economic.

The two projects of the working class push in the direction of industrial-isation as a creator of jobs, an area of possible agreement with the State project. They also demand a certain equalisation of living standards and the wage policy of the State takes this into account in slightly favouring low-paid workers in the national wage agreements. Yet we should not overestimate the importance of this concession, which is most likely ritualistic and of marginal importance when one considers that industrial relations in Ireland display a wide range of wage rates and institutionalised inequalities between wage categories (relativities). The equalisation of living standards is a matter of social policy, and the State here presents itself as redistributing national resources. The activity of the Department of Health and Social Welfare is a crucial test of the commitment of the State to equalisation. The department has two distinct general pro-grammes (253, 264, 271). The first concerns social insurance of employees, giving protection against unemployment, sickness, widowhood, retirement, etc. These benefits are financed by a fund to which employers and employees are obliged to contribute, and also the Exchequer to a certain extent. But this fund is essentially a mutual insurance fund and if there is any equalisation effect it occurs within the group of contributors who invest to protect themselves from the uncertainties of the future. The department also administers a system of social assistance which gives a minimum income to those who are unable to provide for themselves: pensioners, widows, unemployed, blind and handicapped, unmarried mothers, etc. These pensions and assistance payments are indeed a redistribution of national wealth, since they are financed by taxes, but solely to ensure the physical survival of the poorest. More significant are the free medical and hospital care for those holding medical cards, whereas well-to-do families pay for these services (113, 253). Today health policy is slowly heading towards free health care for the population as a whole.

The Minister for the Environment, who supervises the local author-ities, presides over the construction and letting of local authority housing at moderate cost. But in addition to overseeing this kind of housing he encourages families to buy their own houses through building grants and exemptions from stamp duty. He helps even the most well-to-do to buy their houses. As we have seen, taxing does not effect an equalisation of income or wealth; direct taxes fall almost entirely on employees, while the other social categories, often more affluent, escape taxes or manage to reduce their impact considerably. In this sense taxation in Ireland is progressive only within the restricted group from which the State draws its revenue. Finally, primary and secondary education in Ireland is often presented as an example of the commitment of Ireland to equal oppor-tunity. But it is well known that education in Ireland benefits the middle classes above all, and that the less favoured classes are often unable to profit from the opportunities offered. Free secondary education has principally benefitted the children of skilled workers or office workers who would probably not attend secondary school if they had to pay fees. The universities are almost entirely financed by the State and yet they benefit the upper and middle classes more than the so-called lower classes (*26, 160*). Educational policy, far from creating equal opportunities, seems to reinforce the differences between classes and still assist the favoured classes.

The above considerations throw some light on the nature of relations between the State project and the working-class projects in Ireland. These projects agree in their insistence on increased industrialisation as the only way to create jobs; they agree also, but only partly, on the role of the State as the driving force of economic development. They meet, finally, when the State declares its intention of reducing social inequality, even though it is doubtful that it is really part of the State project to carry out this intention. These points of agreement suggest the presence of the working-class project in the State programme of action, although its presence is limited and subordinate to the dominant aspect. Job creation is made conditional on the success of private enterprise and the improvement of living standards depends on industrial success. Rather than equality, the State prefers to speak of equity, because the prosperity it is hoped to create by stimulating private enterprise will enable social needs of a pressing kind to be met without calling for sacrifices, that is to say without moving towards equality. The realisation of the State project, which has as its central element the project of the bourgeoisie, requires the mobilisation of the working class, so as to diminish its resistance. The State involves it in its project by answering some of the needs of the working class and satisfying some of its interests. Better still, the promise that the State will satisfy such interests undermines the working-class project, by threatening the sources of support for it. The State prorgamme tries to establish, through its social policy, a compromise with the working class which includes it in the programme in a subordinate role, because such a compromise is not in conflict with the bourgeois project. Nonetheless the presence in this way of the working class in the State project introduces a social dimension, puts a brake on the bourgeois project of unlimited economic growth, modifying and transforming it without negating its predominance, creating in fact a hiatus between the State project and the bourgeois project.

The Letter and the Spirit of the Nationalist Movement

It is doubtful if one can still credit the nationalist movement with such a social project. Nonetheless it is an important force and one which has had its policy adopted by the State, and partly institutionalised. The Irish language, designated the first official language, taught in all national schools, is still given a position of great importance up to and including university entrance qualifications, and a minimum fluency in the language was required of all civil servants. The regions in which the language survives are protected and given special development grants. In 1956 a Department of the Gaeltacht was established to co-ordinate policy, secure the provision of proper local services, stimulate local industry, stop the exodus of the population by creating new jobs, bring about the restructuring of the farms, which are often too small, and encourage more intensive farming. There is a special radio station which broadcasts in Irish for the scattered Gaeltacht community. Finally, the State encourages the greater presence of Irish in cultural life, giving grants to magazines and films, and putting pressure on the national television corporation to include more Irish programmes. But this language policy has not had the success that the movement hoped for and the language is little used in everyday life. A commission set up to review policy on the restoration of the Irish language in 1963 put forward a series of recommendations which the government accepted (*245, 285, 286*). But these recommendations above all concerned the encouragement of the use of Irish in social life and in institutions where the State has little control or influence. The failure of that institutional policy has led to a call for a reorganisation of the institutions to bring about greater co-ordination of language policy; a department with special responsibility for the language, a state body to shape policy for the Gaeltacht — Bord na Gaeltachta — and another to deal with the promotion of the language — Bord na Gaeilge (*246*). But at the same time, considering the limits of a purely institutional approach, concern is expressed about attitudes to Irish, motivations to speak Irish, and the whole social context in which Irish could prosper (*240, 252*).

While the State has institutionalised this aspect of the nationalist project, it displays no great enthusiasm for it. It fulfils the letter of the project, the better to betray the spirit. Fewer and fewer pretences are being used by the State; unable to force its civil servants to use Irish to communicate with each other, it abolished the requirement of a minimum knowledge of Irish for entry to the civil service. Only a tiny portion of the budget is devoted to the revival of the language, since the State recognises the apathy of the population in this respect and its own inability to change the position of the language. It prefers to use Irish as a sort of symbol of nationality, more or less relegated to a ritualistic and ceremonial role. The same ambiguity can be observed with regard to the demand for the reunification of the country: proclaimed in the constitution, that demand for unification inspires little government activity, since the government accepts partition as a fact and does not intend to intervene directly in Northern Ireland. In short, the nationalist project is quite peripheral to the State project, and the State makes a serious effort only to develop the Gaeltacht regions, which are at the same time the regions where the Irish language survives as the language of daily life and the regions of some of the greatest poverty in Ireland. Aid and assistance of this nature amounts to a social measure and is of little consequence, indeed of no importance in relation to the State project. Yet it can be said that the ambiguity of the State in relation to the nationalist project and the moderation of its commitment to the revival of the Irish language is due perhaps to the possible tension between it and the modernising zeal of the State. The industrial classes are the least well disposed to the language (*252*). The nationalist movement still has a traditionalist image, that of the old rural way of life, even though, as we have seen, the nationalist impetus in its sense of national unity and revival of the language does not appear to be linked to any precise image of society.

So it appears that the State has transformed the nationalist project into a language policy and a policy of national unity to which it does not commit itself. The State, as we have said before, only carries out the letter of the nationalist project and has abandoned the spirit. The dialectic of relations between the State and the forces that support the nationalist project illustrates the ambiguity of the project itself. Accomplices in the partial institutionalisation of the language, they are nonetheless suspicious and occasionally hostile to each other. The nationalist spirit, embodied in various organisations, finds little satisfaction in the letter of State institutions, which it must nonetheless support.

The Church Conciliated

The Catholic Church proclaims a rather vague project of community, equity and greater equality, a model of society still mostly inspired by rural life. It represents an important force, since it has won for itself a place in the State project, not only for a long time as an article of the constitution, but also in the educational system and in the elaboration of social policy. The State partly protects the interests of the Church, tolerates its outlook and sets apart for it a sort of niche where its relevance is limited. Tolerance towards the Church project does not eliminate tension or indeed confrontation between the interests of Church and State. Clerical control of schools channels education into directions that do not always please the State. The State has had to set up technical education entirely on its own and intervene to adjust secondary schools to the needs of the economy by constantly appealing for realism (*243*). The presence of the Church in the social services and the authority it possesses in this area brought about a direct confrontation with the State when the Church forcefully opposed the extension of public medical and social services (*230*). Since then the Church has changed its mind and nowadays stresses the responsibility of the State in this area, calling on the State to meet the needs of the weaker social groups. In this the Church and the State — whose project contains a social dimension — find a common ground, all the more so in that the 'poor' remain a marginal social category (not so much in their numbers as in their lack of collective will).

In short, the fact that the State project respects some of the interests of the Catholic Church does not mean that the State has adopted its project, or even that it is attempting to avoid conflict: it makes use of the Church and neutralises it. First of all, the Church legitimates its form of parliamentary democracy. More important, the predominance of the Catholic outlook may serve to neutralise the socialist project, because the social justice of the Church is not egalitarian and is concerned above all with the extremes, with poverty. In conclusion the Church is included in the State project in a limited form, without guaranteeing harmonious relations between Church and State.

Relations between the State and the Social Forces

We must now bring together all the threads of the network that links the State to the other social forces. First of all, the State takes the bourgeois project as the pivot of its own project. It led this hardly developed class out of its indolence, elaborated and formulated its project and, designating it as the central social force, laid on its shoulders the responsibility of pulling the whole economic machine along. But the bourgeoisie, now developed and strengthened, has acquired specific interests of its own, acts according to its own project and keeps its distance from the State which moulded it and put it into a dominant position. On the other hand the State still continues to carry out the project of the bourgeoisie but has transformed it by placing it in a larger context, a more global perspective. The State cannot ignore the other social forces, and their inclusion in the State project, in various ways, sets the State apart from the bourgeoisie, distances them one from the other. The farmers, in their principal project, see themselves as transformed into a class of small independent entrepreneurs, involved in commercial agriculture. This project completes that of the bourgeoisie, with which it combines well and which it joins up with at the centre of the State project. This is not to say that there are no tensions or conflicts between the two forces — as regards their relative contribution to public finances or the distribution of grants and exemptions. The State also satisfies some of the needs of small farmers, by defending a policy of highly-priced agricultural produce, which is of benefit to all farmers and represents their common interest. But this does not mean that the State also supports the project of the small farmers, far from it, it is simply that the State neutralises it without having to compromise itself. The projects of the working class also show their presence in the State project. First of all the project of the bourgeoisie and that of the working class overlap to some extent in the commitment to industrialisation through private enterprise. The State puts down roots in these points of contact, these areas in which projects overlap, because it is there, more than anywhere else, that it hopes to anchor itself and gain stability. But otherwise the working class is included in the State project in a subordinate role, included

191

only in order to mobilise that group, but always relegated to a secondary position. The State compromises, negotiates, blunts the cutting edge of working-class activity, neutralises its project and contains it. The inclusion of the working class is the result of pressure and its presence is a constant source of tension and therefore of manoeuvrings within the activity of the State. The State also finds a niche for the Catholic Church, a 'reservation' within which it exerts its influence. This limited and controlled presence does not entirely eliminate the risk of conflict. Yet the State tolerates it, all the more so in that it counterbalances the socialist project. The nationalist project has also been institutionalised by the State, which observes its letter rather than its spirit, ritualising it rather than realising it. Ambiguity is the hallmark of its inclusion. Finally, the State goes beyond the organised forces and combines with interests which are necessarily unstable, are attached to no project, and links itself to some groups that have no common will and do not take the form of social forces. Only circumstances dictate the manner of their inclusion. Tolerance, subordination, ambiguity, opportunism, all these forms of insertion of secondary projects contain, at the heart of the State project, elements which go against its dominant aspects. They set a limit and put constraints on the State, preventing it from identifying fully within the bourgeois project.

Thus the State project is rich, broad and more complex than any particular project. It also displays great realism in its outlook, great sobriety, since it daily experiences its limits in the form of particular social forces. Its activity is thus severely limited, bounded by the determination of the projects and the interests which flow from them. The State project contains the rather paradoxical dialectic that we have already noted, between interests and projects. The State has adopted the project of the bourgeoisie but is opposed to some of its interests. It takes into account certain interests of the working class but refuses to adopt its major project and fiercely resists its secondary project. The same is true for the small farmers whose project the State neutralises by satisfying some of their interests. The State proclaims the legitimacy of the Catholic Church but relegates its influence to rather narrow and specialised areas: it tolerates it rather than welcomes it. It has also institutionalised the project of the nationalist movement and ignores its interests. Thus we observe a game of hide and seek between interests and projects which gives a good indication of how the State relates to the other social forces, and of the principle of inclusion of particular projects in the State project.

It is upon this complexity, this diversity of modes of inclusion, that the State bases its autonomy in relation to the particular forces. The relative autonomy of the State does not mean that the social forces it envelops do not determine its orientation, that the activity of the State is not limited by other projects, or that it is not compelled to yield to interests. But it is important to remember that the State project does not integrate

192

the individual projects by fusing them together; it relates them to one another, structures them. The process of articulating the State project is not that of a simple aggregation or even the assembly in coherent form of diverse projects. The unity of the State, its coherence and its autonomy, arises only from placing the various elements in perspective, some aspects dominating and others being relegated to secondary and subordinate positions. The predominance of a particular project in the overall State project is not simply a reflection of the social balance of power. When the State 'agglomerates' the different projects by including them in a coherent perspective, it modifies them all, and adapts them to its needs. While one cannot deny the privileged relationship that exists between the State and the bourgeoisie, the State project does not simply embody that of the dominant social forces in Ireland. They do not coincide because the presence of a complementary project around the central project, of secondary projects overlapping, tolerated, neutralised, relegated, and subordinated changes its nature. The State project is not to be found at the point of balance between social forces, reflecting them. The will of the State draws for strength upon these projects, but the balance of power between social forces only finds expression in the State, that is to say only realises itself through it. There are various ways of organising relations between the social forces, without losing sight of the realities of the global situation. The State, in organising these, enjoys great autonomy, and structures the different projects from the viewpoint of its own perspective. Its will here becomes original and specific, and it situates itself at the hub of the dialectic of liberty and constraint which characterises the nature of the State itself.

We have taken a roundabout route in our efforts to trace the project of the State in Ireland and to analyse its relations with particular social forces. Can one speak of a dominant class in the Republic of Ireland which the State uses as an instrument of domination? Only the study of the different projects to be discerned in Ireland, such as undertaken in this chapter, will allow us to answer the question. The project of the State does not correspond to that of the bourgeoisie, even though the latter coincides with it to a large degree; on the contrary, the opposition which the bourgeoisie offers to the State is proof of the distance separating them both. Neither does the State merely act as a balancing agent between the different social forces. Rather, it organises within itself a complex web by means of which particular projects are drawn into its perspective and structured accordingly. No doubt can be entertained as to the dominant position of the project of the bourgeoisie, in the sense that its needs are given priority and its demands are never ignored – which is not to say that they are invariably satisfied. How shall it be decided whether, at the outset, the dominance of the bourgeoisie determined its privileged position with the project of the State, or whether the State, having chosen the bourgeoisie as its instrument, pushed it forward to the centre of the stage? Whatever the answer, we have at least identified in Ireland a dominant class, in other words a class whose particular project dominates those of the other classes.

19
The State and the
Management of Contradictions

No single formula can account for the intricacy of relations between State and society. The analysis of the complex and often confused web through which the State binds itself to society offers no easy shortcuts or neat answers. One must, at the end of the day, attempt to reassemble the various elements revealed by analysis into a coherent whole. This last chapter undertakes that task, which is always a delicate one, since every synthesis tends to simplify the diversity and complexity of reality by emphasising only its most salient aspects, and to confidently assert what in fact are no more than hypotheses and ways of seeing and thinking whose validity remains to be demonstrated. The itinerary we have taken may have seemed long and often roundabout, but it is now hoped that the result will show each stage as a necessary step in our research.

In the first place, what is being referred to when one uses the term 'Irish society'? In a certain sense the answer to this question is obvious. The Republic of Ireland is a clearly defined territorial entity, even one which many Irish people distinguish from the Irish nation, which is allegedly coterminous with the whole island. The Republic of Ireland also constitutes a society in the sense that its inhabitants are organised, their social relations regulated by laws and customs, and that these are generated from an institutional framework. But this book seeks to discover a deeper level of identity, a 'structure' which adequately describes the most durable characteristics of Irish social reality and the forces acting upon it. This necessarily abstract perspective will allow us to discern the internal social landscape of Ireland as well as the cleavages and hierarchies which have developed within it. The charting of social stratification makes it possible to establish such a structural table, since it reveals the network of material inequalities, and the hierarchies of prestige which play such an important role in Irish society. But this social stratification is less important than the social differentiations which are generated by it; these form the empirical base for the elaboration of the 'social framework' — or, in other words, a simple, durable portrait of what is essential in Irish society. By social differentiation is simply meant the network of lines which separates or brings together individuals and places them in a particular 'social category'. The great diversity of ways in which Irish people act and think is patterned by underlying regularities. The network of such cleavages is what circumscribes social categories, each one distinct from the others and possessing its own special characteristics. The establishing of such a 'social framework' is by no means a simple matter, but if we confine ourselves to its dominant traits a structure of social classes (which corresponds moreover to occupational groupings) clearly manifests itself: bourgeoisie and petite bourgeoisie, the white-collar workers and professions, the working class and the farmers.

This social framework does not, however, reveal the social forces at work on the Irish scene; neither does it tell us which are the collective agents who by their interactions are forging Irish society, both now and for the future. All the social categories which we have designated do not display the same capacity to put their mark on Ireland's future. The capacity of a social group to act collectively cannot be measured by its ability to define its interests and to organise in order to defend them. Collective action here refers to the emergence of a force capable of exerting direct influence on society, and crystallises around what I have called 'a social project', or a coherent orientation on the future. This orientation possesses an objective base, since each social category identifies itself by its place in the system of social relations, and by the needs which it strives to satisfy. It is this striving to satisfy needs that gives impetus to collective action. These needs can of course be satisfied in different ways. Class interests are therefore expressive of a choice and are decided by reference to the projects from which they derive. A project points to a type of society which a particular class sees as the fulfilment of its own needs, and which its collective activity, consciously or not, is committed to attaining. As we have seen, only the bourgeoisie, the farmers and the working class possess such projects.

Projects and Interests

The second part of the book has attempted to chart the orientation behind the main forces in Irish society and to grasp the principles underlying them. Both the working class and the farmers are involved in two projects simultaneously, but the emergence of divergent projects in each category cannot simply be explained by internal differentiations — such as big/small farmers, skilled/unskilled workers — though such differentiations are important. These divisions remind us of the fact that one social force may contain diverse orientations, and that the predominant orientation is that which represents the choice to which the group has collectively committed itself. Other projects, sometimes secondary or marginal, or embryonic, may develop within social groups. The future, therefore, for every social category represents a field of possibilities, so many options from among which to choose the desired society. But to use the word choice, however, does not rule out the existence of external influences and each social class seeks to satisfy its needs (while itself being influenced by the existence of other projects in conflict with it). The project depends on the nature of the social class which contains it. This nature corresponds to the sum of its needs and is finally determined by its place in the system of social relations.

Collective action is usually explained by relating it to the interests of the group which engenders it. For example, everything that the Irish bourgeoisie does or proposes to do would derive from its desire to defend its class interests. Without denying the relevance of interests, the preceding chapters approached the issue from a different perspective. Far from class interests determining the orientation of collective action, it could be said that these interests only come into existence within the project to which they belong, and in the light of the principles which underlie the collective action of a given social class. The interests in question are not determined by the situation, but define themselves in the actual process of the project being realised. They embody the will of a collective agent to satisfy its needs and to overcome opposition. Far, then, from determining the orientations of collective action interests imply the existence of underlying projects.

The idea that there exist different methods of satisfying the same needs leads to the complex interplay of class interests and projects which in effect constitutes the focus of attention of the second part of the book. Not only, as we have shown, does a social class choose the orientation of collective action (in the sense that several possible projects may coexist within it), but the interests defended with reference to the same project may also vary. Let us here summarise the principal points of our empirical analysis.

- The farmers have embraced two projects — which are contradictory in the sense that to realise one would make the realisation of the other impossible: that is to say, agricultural production based on the intensive cultivation of small farms is incompatible with large-scale agricultural production by viable farms. But the interests which these projects embody overlap in part, such as the support of both small and large farmers for high agricultural prices.

- The working class illustrates a comparable situation: two projects compete for predominance, but certain interests are common to both. In fact the two rival and conflicting projects of the working class do not necessarily contradict each other and in a sense the project for a reformed capitalism points towards the project of an embryonic socialism. The tension between the two does not necessarily break down into incompatibility.

- The bourgeoisie embraces only one project, but it involves the defence of very different interests. The carrying out of its project demands very delicate choices among interests: whether to align itself with international capitalism and risk being swallowed up by it or whether to depend upon an ever increasing State intervention and risk engendering a State capitalism which would subordinate it to its

197

interests. It is not difficult to discern the rather large overlap between the project of the bourgeoisie and that of the State, an overlap which does not, however, prevent occasional but serious clashes of interest between the two.

- Finally, the insistence within the dominant project of the working class on economic development, which will lead to the creation of more jobs, coincides with the project of the bourgeoisie. but compatibility, partial or otherwise, between projects does not necessarily mean compatibility of interests, which remain in fundamental conflict.

This is not to say, however, that interests acquire independence from projects, and the intricate criss-cross of class interests would be incomprehensible seen in isolation from the projects which back them up. Nevertheless the passage from projects to interests represents another link in the structure of relative autonomy in which collective action by a given social class takes place. The different social classes, in elaborating their projects by reference to their needs, and subsequently defining their interests in the light of these projects, acutally give concrete expression to the dialectic of freedom and necessity which lies at the heart of social life.

Not all social categories engage in collective actions. Office workers sway between solidarity with the trade union movement and affirmations of their superiority to other wage earners. The liberal professions strive to preserve their autonomy and regulate their own affairs, at the same time seeking optimum remuneration for their services. In doing so they do not succeed in achieving solidarity among themselves. The petite bourgeoisie is no more successful in engaging in collective action, and makes no contribution as a class to the building of Irish society. Nevertheless, while not embracing a project, all these categories strive to advance their interests. Or rather, instead of embracing a project, they strive only to perpetuate the status quo. The satisfaction of needs and their transformation into interests take on a particular character in this context: interests define themselves negatively in the sense that these categories react only to what are perceived as threats and give formulation only to what they reject. Such interests as they espouse concern only the short term and are inevitably unstable as they fluctuate with circumstances. In other words, categories without a project experience serious difficulty in deciding where their interests actually lie.

Despite what is often said, the Catholic Church no longer constitutes an essential social force in Ireland for the reason that it has ceased to lobby for a precise type of society. Its natural affinity for rural society and small-scale capitalism has not prevented it from adapting to the urban industrial society which Ireland is steadily becoming. The Church is not participating in any great way in the building of the new Irish society, but reluctantly coming to terms with it, and limiting itself to piecemeal attempts to modify those aspects of it which it finds most repugnant. Its control over education and the social services, as well as its moral authority, contributes to whatever success it has in this domain. Similarly, and without minimising the extent of its influence, the gaelic movement cannot be regarded as a vital social force in modern Ireland. Irish language and culture have traditionally been associated with rural Ireland, supporting the nationalist project of political and economic independence, all of which were also associated with rural Ireland. Nowadays nationalist sentiments in Ireland may be found over a wide social spectrum, which suggests that by itself nationalism embodies no preference for any particular type of society. Nevertheless the gaelic movement is having more difficulty in divesting itself of its associations with peasant culture and we have previously referred to the great paradox of the movement — that it will fail in its aims if it does not surmount its affinity for rural Ireland and will prosper only to the degree that it penetrates the cities and adapts itself to whatever the future holds for Ireland. In the latter case, it would cease to identify itself with a particular image of society and would cease to exist as a social force. The above remarks do not in the least deny the relevance of the Catholic Church and the gaelic movement for the study of Irish society — both are extremely important. It is possible even to assert that both do embody a social project, but if they do it is rather a matter of inertia than of deliberate intent. Nowadays they no longer occupy a dominant place in society and operate within a social framework that is fashioned by forces beyond their control. The mode of their participation in Irish society becomes clear when one analyses relations between the social forces at work at every level in that society.

Apart from particular projects one can point to another form of collective action, another perspective on the future. The Republic of Ireland affirms itself as a society and acts collectively through the State. It is seemingly here, where a general project becomes linked with particular ones, that relations between the State and society are forged. (All projects are general insofar as they invoke a type of society and crystallise around a principle of totality. But the project of the State is general since, further, it embraces society as a whole whereas other projects merely express the orientation of particular forces in society.)

The State and the Social Dimensions

To chart the table of divisions, hierarchies and aggregations which characterise Irish society is by no means to give an exhaustive account of the country's social landscape. For these cleavages and aggregations differ according to the different economic, ideological and political dimensions in which they occur since social forces are engaged in different relations with each dimension.

The economic dimension is clearly dominated by the project of the bourgeoisie, that is of economic development based on private initiative. The project for agricultural development runs parallel with the latter, but it possesses neither the same importance nor the same scope. In contrast the project of the working class looks towards the State to promote industrial growth. In this dimension the other projects are virtually ignored, or at the very least have marginal economic relevance.

The ideological dimension reveals a totally different picture. Here the projects of the Catholic Church and the nationalist movement are the predominant influences in the production of ideas, beliefs and attitudes. The nationalist project overlaps rather closely that of the small farmers, who present their programme not only as one of survival, but of the defence of a particular life-style, of a culture, of a traditional rural society, and even of Irish national identity. The two projects of the working class, with their demands for greater equality and social justice, also exercise a certain influence in the ideological dimension. The projects of the bourgeoisie and of the large farmers have only limited ideological relevance, rarely given explicit expression.

Political activity in Ireland spans all the projects we have identified. Different political parties have affinities of one kind or another with all the projects and introduce into the political dimension even the most marginal among them. But, focusing our attention on the two main parties, it can be seen that the projects of the bourgeoisie and of the large farmers predominate, that the Catholic Church continues to reserve for itself certain zones of influence and that the nationalist project finds privileged political expression in Fianna Fail.

The three dimensions referred to are not simply reflections of one another. The projects differ considerably and their relative importance, as well as their interrelations, also diverge. Each is activated by a specific network of forces and evolves its own orientation, thrusting in a particular direction according to its own logic. The relative autonomy of each dimension indicates nothing other than its capacity to move in different directions. This permanent threat of dispersal poses a serious problem of coherence and cohesion. How can society have a sense of direction when its economic, ideological and political dimensions pull it in different directions? How does the State operate, given such tensions and disharmonies? In short, an analysis of the State ought to cast light on the manner in which the State deals with the relations between the different social dimensions which, as we have first seen, overlap, criss-cross and mutually determine each other in a complex and asymmetrical network of reciprocal influences.

The State is situated at the centre of economic activity and, moreover, its project defines itself in economic terms. The various competing economic projects thus place the State at the centre of their strategy and expect its actual support and direction, though entertaining different notions as to how it should intervene. In any event, State intervention has for its object the support of the capitalist mode of production and the stimulation of economic growth by private enterprise — and this is the unequivocal pivot of the State project. This insistence by all the social forces, despite regular pronouncements to the contrary, that the State play a central role in economic development and that it animate and direct the economy in ways that would be of benefit to them raises questions. That the working class should demand increased State intervention and even nationalisations at least fits in with its respective projects. But the bourgeoisie itself demands greater State intervention and seems not to fear the presence of the State in certain industrial activities. Moreover, this confidence in the State is not misplaced, in that the State restricts itself to supporting and stimulating the activity of the bourgeoisie, without going beyond certain limits that it has itself defined. What is it that prevents the State from taking complete command of the economy and behaving as a capitalist enterprise itself within the international capitalist system? What obliges the State to respect the limits it imposes upon itself and stops it from advancing into an area where it would certainly be welcome? Is it that the bourgeoisie — which, as a class, it has actually created — imposes its will so strongly on the State that the latter scrupulously respects certain limits that the bourgeoisie does not even have to define? Or on the other hand do there exist certain ideological and political restraints that oblige the State to contain its own economic power? The facts remains that the State does limit the scope of its interventions and only reluctantly competes with private enterprise.

The State, omnipresent in the economic dimension, carefully keeps its distance from ideological debate. It seldom intervenes in ideological production but is not slow to fall back on certain dominant ideological positions when it is convenient to do so. The school without a doubt is an important locus of ideological transmission, but the State rarely intervenes in the educational forum. It frequently makes appeals for realism, expresses the wish that the schools be geared towards the present and future needs of the economy, and regularly invokes the necessity for economy and rationalisation. But it leaves the task of education to other forces — to the Church which controls it, and to the gaelic movement which continues to exert its ideological influence. The place and function of the State in society are the focus of sustained ideological attention and, as we have already said, the individual/State dichotomy occupies a significant place in the ideological structure of Ireland. In a somewhat paradoxical manner the State sees itself charged with the task of regenerating public morality while at the same time it is expected to protect the fundamental civil rights of its citizens. Finally, though the definition of the limits of legitimate State intervention penetrates virtually the whole ideological field, the State pays little attention to an issue which goes to the root of its legitimacy.

The State might not contribute much to ideological production, but it does not hesitate to make use of it. For ideology is not only concerned with norms and with legitimacy but also with equity, which underlies almost all forms of ideological expression. The State constantly evokes the concept of equity, which as a result is to be found at the heart of every social and economic policy. It accepts that the Catholic Church, so influential in the ideological domain, acts as the moral conscience of Ireland and formulates the criteria for equitable behaviour. Promoting a sense of equity agreeable to the State, counterbalancing those forces hostile to the orientation of the State, the Church gains access to the State project. Perhaps in thus conferring upon the Church this ideological task, the State seeks to isolate the dominant conception of equity from the arena of everyday conflicts, to give it stability by anchoring it to an institution of proven caution and which has the ear of the public. The influential presence of nationalism in the ideological field, out of all proportion to its actual contribution to the State project, follows a similar logic. The national movement has for a long time assured the predominance of national over all other questions, thus playing a stabilising role in conflictual relations between the social forces. Through it, ideology turns away from social questions or considers them from a more general, and perhaps more generous, point of view. But the presence of the nationalist project in the ideological field is less effective and less worthy of confidence than that of the Church — especially when it involves marginal groups which take nationalism very seriously and engage in activities radically hostile to the State. The considerable autonomy granted to ideological play and the absence of the State from the field of ideological production can pose serious problems; for not only does ideology fail to adapt to the dominant State project, but it often actually opposes it.

Political life spans three levels of apparently disconnected activity. Local politics in the small towns and constituencies revolves around a system of exchange, the satisfaction of down-to-earth local or personal needs. Local politicians compete with each other to render services for voters which the State in actual fact often grants automatically. National political life is based on competition between political parties which rely heavily on nationalist rhetoric. Votes are distributed to parties whose image is in some degree influenced by their stance on the national question. Also, governmental activity distinguishes itself from the other political levels by a high degree of pragmatism. The lack of homogeneity in political action suggests the existence of activities which are not only differentiated, but are also animated by different, potentially contradictory, logics. Only an effective separation of such activities within their respective spheres keeps them apart and thus avoids bringing their tensions to a head. It is also quite characteristic that each compartment integrate, in a privileged fashion, a particular dimension of society. Party politics tend to give full rein to nationalist ideology, codifying it to the point where it becomes a collection of rhetorical figures. Governmental activity is more particularly geared to economic activity. On the other hand, local politics occupies itself with the events of daily life. The close correspondence between political compartments and social dimensions is not fortuitous since it enables the hostility between ideology and economics to be transferred to the field of politics. Thus political compartmentalisation, while projecting contradictions into the political arena, fails to either resolve or surmount them. Tensions are removed from civil society which as a result acquires greater flexibility. But neither do these contradictions lead to breakdown in political life, which is safeguarded from incoherence by the compartmentalisation already referred to. There is in fact an integrating and unifying principle at work which enables internal differentiation to be contained. This relative unity is a result of the way in which each compartment links up with the State, political focus *par excellence.*

Local political activity enables the State to rally support for State institutions, for the regime and even for the government in office. The State also becomes involved in the game of transactions, exchange of favours: various administrations have not baulked at resorting to 'political machines' as well as to the various intermediaries who channelled requests and arranged a hearing for them in the interests of their individual careers. Moreover, the State needs to keep in touch with the grassroots, and its acceptance of 'transactional logic' is one means of doing this.

Party politics itself affects the functioning of the State in different ways. It constitutes the mechanism by which political personnel are recruited at the highest level, since it is the majority party which forms the government. It confers legitimacy by enabling the State to present itself as the embodiment of the majority will; or again by inviting individuals to participate in a limited way in political life. Also, and perhaps more essentially, parliamentary confrontation provides the State with its own power base. Universal suffrage brings onto the political stage those social categories who lack a real collective will and who, because of their relative passivity, perform a stabilising function. The equality of individual votes gives these groups a certain political leverage, and thus removes them from the margins of political life. At the same time they act as buffer groups between the social forces. Thus party politics facilitates the task of the State in its governing function by introducing outside forces, so to speak, thus diminishing the possibility of direct clashes between the social forces and the State. These categories without a project, because of their very instability and passivity, give the State room to manoeuvre, and a certain freedom in its relations with the social forces. They enable the State to invoke larger considerations and to orchestrate them at will.

Governmental activity, embodying as it does the will of the State apparatus, acts as a binding agent between live social forces and the State. It is this obligation to respond simultaneously to diverse pressures while at the same time elaborating relatively coherent policies that gives State activity its specificity. At the same time direct contacts between government departments and organised pressure groups, while rendering the State more flexible and attentive to demands, increases the possibility of conflict. In which event, as we have seen, party politics acts as a shock-absorber and limits the damaging effects. This illustrates the fact that political levels, despite their compartmentalisation, nevertheless exercise part control over one another, preventing a situation where each level, following only its own logic, functions in a vacuum.

Thus, the Irish State takes advantage of the tension between different social dimensions by anchoring itself in the various political compartments. In the first instance it draws its strength from every compartment. This opens up a range of strategies to the State, since it can simultaneously play on several registers while at the same time remaining the master of ceremonies — as long as it can avoid telescoping the different political logics already described. Moreover, its links with one compartment may reinforce its position in another field. For example, local and especially party politics, by securing support as well as a power base for the State, facilitates the task of governing, either by mediating between opposing social forces or by imposing the government's will.

The contradictions between economics and ideology, by being transferred first from the social to the political level, and finally to the State, are not thereby surmounted, but are rather minimised, attenuated, domesticated, and institutionalised within the State itself. To the latter then falls the task of coming to terms with and managing these contradictions, but in doing so it succeeds only in finding provisional, precarious and approximate solutions. The success of the Irish State then, reflected in the remarkable stability of its political institutions over a sixty-year period, may be measured by the degree to which it has succeeded in domesticating and managing the contradictions which have been passed on to it from the different levels of Irish society. The characteristics of the political elite reflect the role of manager and co-ordinator of the social forces which the State has taken upon itself. The petite bourgeoisie, anxious to preserve a *modus vivendi* between the social forces, provides a significant proportion of this elite, thus binding the State to the grassroots. By contrast, the liberal professions, a major element of the Irish political elite, as well as being cosmopolitan in their outlook, focus the importance of the State on more general considerations. The liberal professions include ideologists and 'experts' who move at ease from political to non-political rhetoric and who involve the State in the political field at the level of party politics. By their lack of a project they are perceived as being above immediate conflicts, and they are sufficiently content with the present situation not to wish to change it radically, without, however, being rigidly committed to it in detail. Their enlightened conservatism and their expertise single them out for the role of political mediators which the State has appropriated for itself: to bring the social forces under its wing, elaborate a social project through them and endeavour to reconcile their conflicting interests.

The State and Social Forces

The State attaches itself to the social forces by the interests which it defends and through projects and interests of the various social forces which exist only by virtue of one another, and whose dialectic the State itself orchestrates. The project of the State, in other words the sum of principles underlying its actions, its orientation on the future, gives it a many-faceted and diversified image. This complexity influences the manner in which it enters into contact with the other social agents, in which it embraces divergent forces, without however compromising either the coherence or the unity of its orientation. It focuses the orientation of its actions on the project of the bourgeoisie (economic growth by private enterprise) and completes it with the project of the large farmers (a modernised agriculture, through land reform and commercialisation of production). In the latter case it opposes the maintenance of traditional land holding structures. The State project also overlaps the dominant project of the working class, when the latter seeks to fulfill its needs by a growth in the industrial capacity of industry and confers this task on private enterprise, though also demanding support and vigorous control by the State. But this project of the working class occupies a very subordinate position within the State project, and is invoked only to demonstrate that the realisation of certain aspects of the working-class project depends on the success of the capitalist project. The State nevertheless uncompromisingly rejects the socialist thrust of the secondary and marginal project of the working class. It also succeeds in rallying to itself the Catholic Church, whose project can be accommodated by confining it to a carefully defined domain, as well as the nationalist project, whose aims it has ritually institutionalised. Particular projects, therefore, are incorporated into the State project in differing, but always precise and rigorous ways, which take account of circumstances and are responsive to the spirit underlying State action. The presence of other projects around it enables the State to maintain its independence, both by keeping a firm rein on the bourgeois project and simultaneously allowing it to play its dominant role. The other projects exert pressure on the State—bourgeoisie relationship, allowing the former to distance itself from the latter, thus escaping its control.

The network of contacts between the State and particular social forces cannot be fully understood unless one studies the criss-cross relationships between projects and interests. Let us repeat: the State backs the project of the bourgeoisie to the hilt but resists, where it deems appropriate, certain demands and certain interests of the bourgeoisie. Similarly, while backing the project of the large farmers, the State often finds itself involved in clashes of interest with representative farming bodies. On the other hand the rejection of the secondary project of the small farmers and working class is accompanied by an acceptance of certain aspects of both. High agricultural prices constitute an essential interest of all farmers and ensures the survival of small farmers in spite of everything. Further, certain working-class interests, such as job creation and improved living conditions, also preoccupy the State. The partial satisfaction, and the promise of full satisfaction, of these interests involve the working class in the effort of capitalist growth, and mobilises its *de facto* co-operation in the project of the State: in doing so it neutralises and undermines its project. The Church's orientation is only included in the State project because it justifies and legitimates a definition of equity which contradicts the socialist project of equality: but this inclusion does not eliminate the possibility of serious differences. The State officially endorses the project of the gaelic movement but conveniently ignores it in practice. Finally, the State takes account of the interests of diverse social categories, the more so as these interests are unstable and contradictory since they flow from no definite project. In conclusion, coincidences between projects do not rule out conflicts of interests while divergence in projects is often compensated for by coinciding interests. Here is to be found the essence of relations between the State and the social forces, and the subtle play by which the State advances its project and involves the social forces in it.

That the pivot of the State project should correspond purely and simply with the project of the bourgeoisie would appear to designate the latter as a dominant class. However, this is not the whole of the relationship between bourgeoisie and State. The State, taking upon itself the capitalist function, makes little distinction between the different elements within Irish capitalism, but in fact relates to the differing elements in different ways. The needs of international capitalism are acknowledged because only through it will the State project be realised. Here it is a simple matter of interests coinciding, one using the other. Relations between the State and the national bourgeoisie are much more dense and organic. In the first place the bourgeoisie does not exist as a collective force except through the State, which in turn unifies it. The State supports the bourgeoisie in the face of international competition not, as before, by erecting tariff barriers but in streamlining and rationalising its structures, by stimulating market research and by ensuring the competitiveness of Irish manufactured products. The national bourgeoisie has not yet confirmed that it is capable of playing the role conferred on it by the State. Unlike international capitalism, which takes advantage of the State while remaining independent of it, the national bourgeoisie runs the risk of disintegrating if it does not integrate itself into the State. But the apparent subordination of the bourgeoisie to the State, at least in the economic dimension, does not prevent the former from exercising a powerful ideological influence over the latter. Both share a past which ensures that they have more in common than they care to fight against.

The designation of the bourgeoisie as a dominant class, in the sense that the State project grants it a privileged role, does not deny the autonomy of the State in relation to all social forces. This relative autonomy of the State manifests itself in particular in the capacity of the State to assimilate different projects and satisfy divergent interests, by the way in which it encompasses the social forces and organises their presence within its own project. For, without ever losing sight of the realities of the situation, relations between projects and interests may structure themselves in different ways, which would indicate that the activity of the State takes place as part of a dialectic of 'determinism and voluntarism', which this book set out to unravel. The State constantly plays on the limits that particular projects impose upon one another, by manipulating these mutual constraints. Its autonomy is guaranteed by the capacity of the social forces to keep each other at bay. Also the ultimate dependence of the dominant class on the State relieves the latter of considerable pressure. It frees it from the control of this class and enables it to enlarge and enrich its own project, to complicate and thus stabilise it, to root itself profoundly in society by attaching diverse groups to itself. The dialectic of projects and interests and their criss-crossing inter-relationships helps the State to affirm its strength and its specific perspective on things. It also looks to the interests of groups with no project, who are relatively easy to manipulate and mobilise when the need arises. And let us not forget that the State only acts through the agency of a political elite and a bureaucracy, which in turn have needs of their own, ways of doing things and orientations which further contribute to its independence.

The State and The Dialectic of Social Functions

The State speaks for society as a whole, and symbolises its unity. It ensures public order and creates coherence out of manifold opposing social forces. In carrying out these tasks it confronts contradictory elements, of whose unstable and problematic existence it is the sole guarantor. It sets in motion a dialectic of conflict and integration, of diversity and unity, of incoherence and coherence. How does the State accommodate these contradictions, how does it go beyond these tensions and does it operate within this dialectic of integration? The Irish State possesses effective means of ensuring social order. Its monopoly of legitimate strength ensures that a minimum of force is necessary; it has privileged access to the communications network, and, to a lesser extent, ideological control through the schools and the media, which exalts the sentiments of solidarity and national cohesion. But all these are not sufficient to explain the survival and the stability of Irish institutions of which they are only the minimum conditions. The State had to learn that it should not try to eliminate the tensions and confrontations which exist within it, but to live with them. It must structure them in such a way as to prevent them from destroying it.

207

The passage from diversity to unity is effected by the project of the State, which structures the social forces by including them in its collective orientation. In doing so, moreover, the State acquires its autonomy – which, again, is always a relative one. When it underestimates the social forces, or fails to appreciate the strength of certain constraints, the State is quickly made to feel the pressure. It then aligns itself with the social forces which, however, pull in different directions, by including them in its project. The complexity of the State project is an index of its success in effecting the passage from unity to diversity. Let us recall the essential methods of inclusion: pivot, complementarity accommodation, partial overlap, ritual institutionalisation and criss-crossing of projects and interests.

The obvious disharmonies between the different dimensions of social reality – the lack of correspondence between ideology and economics – pose a constant threat to social cohesion. The dialectic of coherence and incoherence directly involves the State, since the task of balancing these contradictory movements falls to it. The compartmentalisation of the political field is in great part a reply to this challenge. By dividing political activity into different levels (local, party, governmental), each one joined to the State, diverse tendencies are reconciled and harmonised, without tensions simply being suppressed. Economics (on the governmental level) and ideology (on the party level) affirm their respective presences in the political field, while refusing to adapt to each other. Again it is the State, by its own alchemy, which reduces the incoherence of diverse particular projects to the relative coherence of its own.

As well as its integrating function the State assures the continuity of the society over which it presides. But the desire for continuity does not necessarily lead it on a conservative path, or towards a wish to change nothing. For the State both directs society and builds its future which by definition expresses a wish to transform – a process by which society reproduces itself in the act of changing. Social reproduction, a functional summary of all the dialectics of integration and transformation, cannot be regarded as an automatic, passive process, though it does to some extent depend on the inertia of social structures. It requires great determination and effort – the effort, in effect, of realising the State project. But what ought the State project to produce, what is the cornerstone without which the whole edifice would collapse? In a word, the pivot of the State project is capitalist development, whose predominance must be guarantteed and must subordinate all other considerations. It is not, therefore, a matter of retaining the status quo but of setting in motion a dynamic of change.

The Relations Between State and Society: What Has Been Proved?

The present study has examined the network of links which, in the Republic of Ireland, unite the State and society. What definitive conclusions may be drawn? Does the study, based on close observation of the Irish scene, enable us to choose between rival conceptions of State-society relations? What will test the validity of our choice? At the outset, the chosen perspective, which localised the different forces in Irish society and attempted to reconstruct the logic of their actions, put no emphasis on the State as the expression of a general will, bearer of the common good. It is true that people are in accord as to the legitimacy of parliamentary institutions and the desirability of an Irish nation. But such a vague and general consensus is not much help in understanding the relations between State and society and ignores all the actual activity in which the State is involved. The State succeeds, in one fashion or another, in transforming the diversity of social forces and particular projects into a unified whole. But it does not embody a pre-existent general will: it creates it and imposes it on a society which simultaneously sustains and undermines it.

Another approach, related moreover to the preceding one, perceives in governmental activity (to which it reduces, without any great distortion, the State activity) a sort of apex of the social forces, a somewhat unstable and not necessarily harmonious balance. The structure of domination which is revealed in the way in which different social forces are included in the State project naturally reflects the pressures exercised and the control imposed upon the resources which count. In this sense the State project, sensitive to realities, represents a balance in which a flexible State negotiates and compromises itself in order to bring diverse orientation under its wing: it also rejects other projects and refuses to consider certain interests. If, then an equilibrium exists, it is the State which patiently constructs and defends it. Moreover, the existence of such an equilibrium, which proves no more than the State's sense of realities, does not determine the activities of the State: it merely imposes limits on it within which it operates more or less freely. In other words, several possible State projects exist within the same social parameters.

The notion of the State as an instrument of a ruling class, according to which the State systematically defends the interests of a particular social class, competes with the above perspective. Our analysis of Irish society does not deny that privileged links exist between the bourgeoisie and the State, since the project of the latter pivots around that of the former. The priority accorded to the satisfaction of the needs of the bourgeoisie, the responsiveness of the State to capitalism, does not, however, hide the fact that a gap exists between their respective projects. Our analysis thus does not assert the hypothesis of a ruling class which has appropriated the State to itself, but that of a dominant class which weighs more heavily than any other on State activity. The State thus embodies a structure of domination in which a particular class occupies a dominant place in a consistent and stable manner.

Lastly, a final perspective emphasises the autonomy of the State as an arbitrary power within society, defending its interests, and increasingly exercising its power. This perspective expresses alarm at the increase in State power and suspects the bureaucracy of being the embodiment of this arbitrary power. But in the Republic of Ireland, the alleged arbitrariness of the State surely does not emanate from the bureaucracy, which is relegated to a secondary role. However, without referring to the alleged arbitrariness, our analysis has pointed to the autonomy of the State, its capacity to orchestrate relations between social forces while recognising their influence on it. The State negotiates, co-ordinates, conciliates and, in the end, manages to achieve a relatively coherent orientation of its actions, a unifying vision for the future. On it lies the entire responsibility for the construction of the State project. The task of the State could be defined as the structuring of particular projects, and it is this which constitutes its autonomy. Nobody controls the State, but everyone, in the last analysis, influences and determines it.

Many political analyses, on the particular point of relations between State and society, revolve around these four perspectives. However, these theories do not contradict each other except in their most extreme formulations. Our analysis validates equally the existence of a socio-political equilibrium which the State takes in hand, that of a dominant class and even that of a State enjoying great autonomy in its activities. The question no longer is which of the three theories is borne out by empirical research but how these three aspects of the State can coexist side by side. The third section of this book attempted to answer the question, and suggested that each view merely furnished an impoverished perspective and thus falsified the real relations existing between the State and society. Taken together they provide a valid picture of the facts as they may be observed.

Our analysis depended heavily on the concept of a project since it constitutes the distinguishing mark of social forces and enables us to differentiate between them and mere social categories. A social force pushes in a particular direction; it projects a vision of the future which in turn underlies its activities, and decides where its interests lie by reference to this vision. The concept of project also enabled us to penetrate those somewhat obscure zones where relations between State and society are forged. The contrast between particular projects and that of the State, as well as enabling us to grasp the nature of these relations, helped to ground our analysis on a solid empirical base and make a useful research tool of the project concept. The elaboration of the State project, the structuring of divergent projects and interests into a unified orientation, reveals also the source of the State's autonomy in relation to all the social forces which are content to influence without controlling. The study of social projects loses none of its relevance when it comes to the analysis of relations between social dimensions, whose specificity results from the clash of projects in their midst. The concept of project is also relevant in analysing the social functions of the State. These functions belong in fact to a series of dialectics which the State manages. Its activity, that is to say its project, reveals the ways in which it succeeds in living out these dialectics. The State project crystallises the State's mode of existence, and of doing, as well as its mode of relating to the other social forces. The usefulness of the concept of project as an analytical tool is to be judged by the degree to which it enables us to penetrate the relations which exist between State and society in Ireland.

Bibliography

1. Akenson, D.H., *The Irish Education Experiment*, London: Routledge and Kegan Paul 1970
2. Akenson, D.H., *A Mirror to Kathleen's Face*, Montreal: McGill-Queen's University Press 1975
3. Arensberg, C. and Kimball, T., *Family and Community in Ireland*, Cambridge, Mass: Harvard University Press 1940
4. Barrington, T.J., *The Irish Administrative System*, Dublin: Institute of Public Administration 1980
5. Barron, F. and Egan, D., 'Leaders and Innovators in Irish Management', *Journal of Management Studies*, V (1968)
6. Bart, M., 'Patronage Irish Style: Irish Politicians as Brokers', *Sociologishe Gids*, XVII/3 (1970)
7. Bart, M., 'Integration, Forms of Communication and Development: Centre-Periphery Relations in Ireland, Past and Present', *Sociologische Gids*, XIX/2 (1972)
8. Bart, M., *Harp Strings and Confessions: Machine Style Politics in the Irish Republic*, Amsterdam: Van Gorcum 1977
9. Berresford Ellis, P., *The Irish Working Class*, London: Gollancz 1972
10. Binchy, D.A., 'The Law and the Universities', *Studies*, XXXVIII/3 (1949)
11. Bohlen, J., 'Irish Farmers' Use of Information Sources', *Irish Journal of Agricultural Economics and Rural Sociology*, III/1 (1970)
12. Bolger, P., *The Irish Cooperative Movement*, Dublin: Institute of Public Administration 1977
13. Bristow, J.A. and Tait, A.A., *Economic Policy in Ireland*, Dublin: Institute of Public Administration 1968
14. Brody, H., *Inishkillane*, Harmondsworth: Penguin Books 1974
15. Boyd, A., *The Rise of the Irish Trade Unions*, Tralee: Anvil Books 1972
16. Boyle, J.W., *Leaders and Workers*, Cork: Mercier Press 1965
17. Breatnach, R.A., 'Revival or Survival, An Examination of the Language Policy of the State', *Studies*, VL (Spring 1956)
18. Breatnach, R.A., 'Irish Revival Reconsidered', *Studies*, LIII (Spring 1964)
19. Brennan, M., 'The Restoration of Irish', *Studies*, LIII (Autumn 1964)
20. British and Irish Communist Organisation, Belfast
    Pamphlets
21. Busteed, M.A. and Mason, H., 'Irish Labour in the 1969 Elections', *Political Studies*, XVIII/3 (1970)
22. *Christus Rex*, Maynooth 1947—71

23. Chubb, B., 'Going About Persecuting Civil Servants: The Role of the Irish Parliamentary Representatives', *Political Studies*, XI/3 (1963)
24. Chubb, B., *The Government and Politics of Ireland*, London: Oxford University Press 1970
25. Chubb, B. and Lynch, P., *Economic Development and Planning*, Dublin: Institute of Public Administration 1969
26. Clancy, P. and Benson, C., *Higher Education in Dublin: A Study of Some Emerging Needs*, Dublin: Higher Education Authority 1979
27. Clarkson, J.D., *Labour and Nationalism in Ireland*, New York: Columbia University Press 1925
28. Cohan, A., *The Irish Political Elite*, Dublin: Gill and Macmillan 1972
29. Common Market Study Group, Dublin
    a) Coughlan, A., *The Alternative to Membership*, 1972
    b) Crotty, R., *An Economic Analysis of the Effects of Membership*, 1971
    c) Crotty, R., *Irish Agriculture and the Common Market*
30. Communist Party of Ireland, Dublin
    a) *Ireland in Crisis, a Communist Answer*, 1975
    b) *Irish Socialist Review*, 1970–
31. Communist Party of Ireland, Marxist-Leninist, Dublin
    Red Patriot
32. Confederation of Irish Industry, Dublin
    Newsletter
33. Confederation of Irish Industry, Dublin
    Signpost, Industry in the Seventies, 1971
34. Connell, K., *Irish Peasant Society*, London: Oxford University Press 1968
35. Connolly, J., *Labour, Nationality and Religion*, Dublin: New Books Publications 1972
36. Connolly, J., *Labour in Irish History*, Dublin: New Book Publications 1973
37. Connolly, J., *Selected Writings*, Harmondsworth: Penguin Books 1973
38. Craft, M., 'Economy, Ideology and Educational Development in Ireland', *Administration*, XVIII/4 (1970)
39. Cresswell, R., *Une Communauté Rurale de l'Irlande*, Paris: Institut d'Ethnologie de Paris 1969
40. Cullen, L.M., *An Economic History of Ireland since 1660*, London: Batsford 1972
41. Cullen, L.M., *The Formation of the Irish Economy*, Cork: Mercier Press 1976
42. Curry, J., 'Farmer's Dole, a Lifetime or a Bounty', *Irish Times*, 11 and 18 March 1976
43. Curry, J., 'Part-time Farming: One Solution to the Small Holding Problem, *Irish Times*, 22 April 1976
44. De Burgh, U.H., *The Landowners of Ireland*, Dublin: Hodges Foster and Figgis 1878
45. Dillon-Malone, P.J., 'Research in Management Attitudes and Behaviour', *Journal of the Statistical and Social Inquiry Society of Ireland*, XXII part I (1968–9)

46. Donnelly, J.S., *The Land and the People of Nineteenth-Century Cork*, London: Routledge and Kegan Paul 1975
47. Dooney, S., *The Irish Civil Service*, Dublin: Institute of Public Administration 1976
48. Drudy, S., 'The Occupational Aspirations of Rural School Leavers', *Social Studies*, IV/3 (1975)
49. Farrell, B., 'The New State and Irish Political Culture', *Administration*, XV/3 (1975)
50. Farrell, B., 'Dail Deputies, the 1969 Generation', *Economic and Social Review*, I/3 (1970)
51. Farrell, B., 'Labour and the Irish Political System: A Suggested Analysis', *Economic and Social Review*, I/4 (1970)
52. Farrell, B., *The Irish Parliamentary Tradition*, Dublin: Gill and Macmillan 1973
53. Farrell, B., 'Irish Government Reobserved', *Economic and Social Review*, VI/3 (1975)
54. Faughan, P., 'Social Class, a Study of Subjective Elements', University College Dublin 1970 (unpublished M.A. thesis)
55. Federated Union of Employers, Dublin
    a) *Industrial Democracy*
    b) *Women in Employment, Implications of Equal Pay*
56. Fennel, R., 'Structural Change in Irish Agriculture', *Irish Journal of Agricultural Economics and Rural Sociology*, I/2 (1968)
57. Fennel, R., 'The Agricultural Sector, 1926–1967', *Irish Journal of Agricultural Economics and Rural Sociology*, I/2 (1968)
58. Fennell, D., 'The Irish Cultural Prospect', *Social Studies*, I/6 (1972)
59. Fianna Fail, Dublin
    a) *Iris* (party journal)
    b) *Report of the Ard Fheis*, 1972–7
    c) Brennan, S., *Some Notes*, 1975
60. Fine Gael, Dublin
    a) *Towards a Just Society*, 1965
    b) *Winning Through to a Just Society*
    c) *Fine Gael Policy for a Just Society*
    d) *The National Coalition at Work*
61. Finlay, I., *The Civil Service*, Dublin: Institute of Public Administration 1966
62. FitzGerald, G., *Planning in Ireland*, Dublin: Institute of Public Administration 1968
63. FitzGerald, G., 'Investment in Education', *Studies*, LIV (Winter 1965)
64. Fogarty, M.P., *Irish Entrepreneurs Speak for Themselves*, Dublin: Economic and Social Reserch Institute, broadsheet 8, 1973
65. Frawley, J. *et al.*, 'Scale and Farm Management in Ireland', *Irish Journal of Agricultural Economics and Rural Sociology*, V/1 (1974–5)
66. Frawley, J. *et al.*, 'Personal and Social Factors Related to Farming Performance in Ireland', *Irish Journal of Agricultural Economics and Rural Sociology*, V/1 (1974–5)
67. Garvin, T., 'Political Cleavages, Party Politics and Urbanisation in

Ireland – the Case of the Periphery-Dominated Centre', *European Journal of Political Research*, II/4 (1974)

68. Garvin, T., 'Political Action and Ideology in Dublin', *Social Studies*, VI/1 (1977)

69. Gaughan, J., 'Publication of First Year's Results of Farm Management Survey', *Irish Journal of Agricultural Economics and Rural Sociology*, II/2 (1969)

70. Geary, R.C. and Hughes, J.G., *Internal Migration in Ireland*, Dublin: Economic and Social Research Institute, paper 54, 1970

71. Geary, R.C. and Hughes, J.G., *Certain Aspects of Non-Agricultural Unemployment in Ireland*, Dublin: Economic and Social Research Institute, paper 52, 1970

72. Geary, R.C. and O Muircheartaigh, F.S., *Equalization of Opportunity in Ireland*, Dublin: Economic and Social Research Institute, broadsheet 10, 1974

73. Gibbons, P. and Higgins, M., 'Patronage, Tradition and Modernisation, the Case of the Irish Gombeenman', *Economic and Social Review*, VI/1 (1974)

74. Gilmore, G., *The Irish Republican Congress*, Cork: The Cork Worker's Club 1964

75. Gorman, L. *et al.*, *People, Jobs and Organizations*, Dublin: Irish Productivity Centre 1972

76. Gorman, L. *et al.*, *Managers in Ireland*, Dublin: Irish Management Institute 1974

77. Greaves, C.D., *Liam Mellows and the Irish Revolution*, London: Lawrence and Wishart 1971

78. Greaves, C.D., *Marx and Engels on Ireland*, London: Lawrence Wishart 1971

79. Gwynn, S., *Henry Grattan and His Time*, Dublin: Brown and Nolan 1939

80. Hannan, D., 'Status Inequalities within Families in Relation to their Structural Differences', *Economic and Social Review*, I/2 (1969–70)

81. Hannan, D., *Rural Exodus*, London: Geoffrey Chapman 1970

82. Hannan, D., 'Kinship, Neighbourhood and Social Change in Irish Rural Communities', *Economic and Social Review*, III/2 (1971–2)

83. Hannan, D. and Beegle, A., 'Evaluation of Occupations by Irish Rural Adolescents on the Basis of Prestige and Difficulty of Achievement', *Rural Sociology*, XXXV/3 (1969)

84. Hannan, D. and Katsiaouni, L., *Traditional Families? From Culturally Prescribed to Negotiated Roles in Farm Families*, Dublin: Economic and Social Research Institute, paper 87, 1977

85. Hart, I., 'Public Opinion on Civil Servants and the Roles and Power of the Individual on the Local Community', *Administration*, XVIII/4 (1970)

86. 'Who's Who in Irish Banking', *Hibernia*, Dublin, 15 February 1974

87. Hillery, B. *et al.*, *Trade Union Organisation in Ireland*, Dublin: Irish Productivity Centre 1975

88. Humphreys, A., *The New Dubliners*, London: Routledge and Kegan Paul 1966

89. Hutchinson, B., *Social Status and Intergenerational Mobility in*

Dublin, Dublin: Economic and Social Research Institute, paper 48, 1969

90. Hutchinson, B., 'On the Study of Non-Economic Factors in Irish Economic Development', *Economic and Social Review*, I/4 (1970)
91. Hutchinson, B., *Social Status in Dublin, Marriage, Mobility and First Employment*, Dublin: Economic and Social Research Institute, paper 76, 1973
92. Inglis, B., *West Briton*, London: Faber and Faber 1962
93. International Labour Organisation, Geneva
    Restructuring the Irish Trade Union Movement, 1975
94. Irish Bank Officials' Association, Dublin
    a) *Annual Report*, 1972-4
    b) *Irish Banking Magazine*
95. Irish Congress of Trade Unions, Dublin
    Annual Report
96. Irish Congress of Trade Unions, Dublin
    Trade Union Information
97. Irish Creamery Milk Suppliers' Association, Limerick
    Irish Farming News
98. Irish Creamery Milk Suppliers' Association, Limerick
    Crotty, R., *Agriculture in an Expanding Irish Economy*, 1972
99. Irish Farmers' Association, Dublin
    a) *People and the Land*, 1972
    b) *Irish Agricultural Development*, 1975
    c) *Rural Degeneration*, 1976
100. *Irish Farmers' Journal*, Dublin
    a) Maguire, D., *The Land Commission*
    b) Maguire, D., *A New Tomorrow*
101. *Irish Independent*, Dublin
102. Irish Labour Party, Dublin
    a) *Programme of 1969*
    b) *Northern Policy Statement*, 1972
103. Irish Management Institute, Dublin
    Management
104. Irish Medical Association, Dublin
    Irish Medical Journal
105. *Irish Medical Times*, Dublin
106. *Irish Press*, Dublin
107. Irish Republican Socialist Party, Dublin
    The Starry Plough
108. *Irish Times*, Dublin
109. Jackson, J.A., *The Irish in Britain*, London: Routledge and Kegan Paul 1966
110. Jackson, J.A., *Report on the Skibbereen Survey*, Dublin: Human Science Committee 1967
111. Jackson, J.A., 'Ireland', in M.S. Archer and S. Giner, eds., *Contemporary Europe, Class, Status and Power*, London: Weidenfeld and Nicolson 1971
112. Kane, E., 'Rural Poverty', *Social Studies*, I/4 (1972)
113. Kaim-Caudle, P., *Social Policy in the Irish Republic*, London:

Routledge and Kegan Paul 1967

114. Kellaghan, T. and Greany, V., 'Factors Related to Choice of Post-Primary School in Ireland', *Irish Journal of Education*, IV/2 (1970)

115. Kennedy, G., 'Who Owns Our Lakes and Rivers?', *Irish Times*, 28 August 1974

116. Kennedy, K. and Bruton, R., *The Irish Economy*, Luxembourg: EEC Studies (Economic and Financial Series), 10, 1975

117. Kennedy, K. and Dowling, B., *Economic Growth in Ireland: the Experience since 1947*, Dublin: Gill and Macmillan 1975

118. Kennedy, L. *et al.*, 'Factors Influencing Farmers' Attitudes to Cooperative Amalgamation', *Irish Journal of Agricultural Economics and Rural Sociology*, V/2 (1974-5)

119. Kennedy, R., *The Irish, Emigration, Marriage and Fertility*, Los Angeles: University of California Press 1973

120. Knight, J. and Baxter-Moore, N., *The General Elections of 1969 and 1973*, London: Arthur McDougall Fund 1974

121. Lee, J., *The Modernisation of Irish Society, 1848–1918*, Dublin: Gill and Macmillan 1973

122. Leon, D., *Advisory Bodies in Irish Government*, Dublin: Institute of Public Administration 1963

123. Linehan, T.P., 'The Structure of Irish Industry', *Journal of the Statistical and Social Inquiry Society of Ireland*, XX part V (1961–2)

124. Longford, Earl of, and O'Neill, T.P., *Eamon de Valera*, London: Arrow editions 1974

125. Lucey, D. and Kaldor, D., *Rural Industrialisation*, London: Geoffrey Chapman 1969

126. Lyons, F.S.L., *Ireland Since the Famine*, London: Fontana 1975

127. Lyons, P.M., 'Estate Duty Wealth Estimate and the Mortality Multiplier', *Economic and Social Review*, VI/3 (1975)

128. McAleese, D., *A Profile of Grant-Aided Industry in Ireland*, Dublin: Industrial Development Authority 1977

129. McAuley, D.J., 'Collective Bargaining and Industrial Disputes in Ireland', *Journal of the Statistical and Social Inquiry Society of Ireland*, XXI part VI (1967)

130. McCann, P., 'The Curriculum of the Secondary Schools', *Studies*, LI (Winter 1962)

131. McCarthy, C., *The Distasteful Challenge*, Dublin: Institute of Public Administration 1968

132. McCarthy, C., *A Decade of Upheaval*, Dublin: Institute of Public Administration 1973

133. McCarthy, C., *Trade Unions in Ireland, 1894–1960*, Dublin: Institute of Public Administration 1977

134. McCarthy, E. *et al.*, *Attitudes of Workers to Their New Industrial Environment in Shannon*, London: Tavistock Institute of Human Relations 1967

135. McCashin, T., 'Rural Dole Payments', *Social Studies*, IV/4 (1975)

136. McCluskey, D., 'Leaving School at Intermediate', *Social Studies*, II/1 (1973)

137. McCracken, J.L., *Representative Government in Ireland: A Study of*

Dáil Eireann, London: Oxford University Press 1953

138. McDowell, R.B., *The Church of Ireland, 1869–1969*, London: Routledge and Kegan Paul 1975

139. McGreil, M., 'Religious Beliefs and Practices of Dublin Adults', *Social Studies*, III/2 (1974)

140. McGreil, M., *Educational Opportunity in Dublin*, Dublin: Catholic Communications Institute of Ireland (Research and Development Unit) 1974

141. McGreil, M., *Prejudice and Tolerance in Ireland*, Dublin: College of Industrial Relations 1977

142. McInerney, M., *Peadar O'Donnell, Irish Social Rebel*, Dublin: The O'Brien Press 1974

143. McNabb, P., 'Social Structure', in J. Newman ed., *Limerick Rural Survey*, Tipperary: Muintir na Tire Rural Publications 1964

144. McManus, F., *The Years of the Great Test*, Cork: Mercier Press 1967

145. McNamara, J., 'Report on the Irish Language, Psychological Aspects', *Studies*, LIII (Summer 1964)

146. Macra na Feirme, Dublin
    a) *The Torch*
    b) *Retirement in Agriculture*, 1973
    c) *Farm Inheritance and Succession*, 1973
    d) *Modernising Irish Agriculture, the Real Issues*, 1975
    e) *The Young Irish Farmer, Macra na Feirme Yearbook and Annual Report*, 1976

147. Manning, M., *The Blueshirts*, Dublin: Gill and Macmillan 1970

148. Manning, M., *Irish Political Parties*, Dublin: Gill and Macmillan 1972

149. Meghen, P.J., *A Short History of the Public Service*, Dublin: Institute of Public Administration 1962

150. Messenger, J., *Inis Beag*, New York: Holt Rinehart and Winston 1973

151. Miller, D.W., *Church, State and Nation in Ireland, 1898–1921*, Dublin: Gill and Macmillan 1973

152. Mitchell, A., *Labour in Irish Politics, 1890-1921*, Dublin: Irish University Press 1974

153. Moody, T.W. ed., *The Fenian Movement*, Cork: Mercier Press 1968

154. Muintir na Tire, Tipperary
    a) *Report and Paper of an International Seminar on Western Development*, 1965
    b) *A Plan for Community Development in Ireland*, 1965
    c) *Review Committee Report on Muntir na Tire*, 1973
    d) Roseingrave, R., *Towards an EEC Regional Policy*, 1973
    e) Roseingrave, R. and Talbot, D., *Parish and Community*, 1975

155. Murphy, C., 'Farmers and Their Wives', *Irish Times*, 13 and 16 November 1973

156. Murphy, G., 'Irish in Our Schools, 1922–1945', *Studies*, XXXVII (Winter 1948)

157. Murphy, I., 'Primary Education', in P.J. Corish, ed., *A History of Irish Catholicism*, V/6, Dublin: Gill and Macmillan 1971

158. Nealon, T., *Ireland, a Parliamentary Directory*, Dublin: Institute of Public Administration 1974

159. Nevin, M., 'A Study of the Social Background in UCD', *Journal of the Statistical and Social Inquiry Society of Ireland*, XXI part V (1966–7)
160. Nevin, M., 'A Study of the Social Background in the Irish Universities', *Journal of the Statistical and Social Inquiry Society of Ireland*, XXI part VI (1967-8)
161. Newman, J., *The Limerick Rural Survey*, Tipperary: Muintir na Tire Rural Publications 1964
162. Nic Ghiolla Phadraig, M., 'Religious Practice and Belief in Ireland', *Social Studies*, V/2 (1976)
163. O'Brien, C.C., *States of Ireland*, St Albans: Panther Books 1973
164. O'Broin, N. and Farren, G., *The Working and Living Conditions of Civil Service Typists*, Dublin: Economic and Social Research Institute, paper 93, 1978
165. O'Callaghan, S., 'A Just Society for Mankind', *Irish Theological Quarterly*, XXXIX/1 (1972)
166. O'Cathain, S., 'Education', *Studies*, XL (Winter 1951)
167. O'Cathain, S., 'Secondary Education in Ireland', *Studies*, VIL (Winter 1955); VL (Spring 1956); IVL (Spring 1957)
168. O'Cathain, S., 'The Future of the Irish Language', *Studies*, LXII (Autumn–Winter 1973)
169. Ó Cinneide, S., 'The Extent of Poverty in Ireland', *Social Studies*, I/4 (1972)
170. O'Connor, S., 'Post-Primary Education, Now and in the Future', *Studies*, LVII (Autumn 1968)
171. O'Connor, T. and Wilding, R., 'The Civil Service in the Modern State', *Studies*, LIX (Summer 1970)
172. O'Connor-Lysaght, D.R., *The Republic of Ireland*, Cork: Mercier Press 1970
173. O'Faolain, S., *King of the Beggars*, London: Nelson 1938
174. O'Farrell, P.N., *Regional Industrial Development Trends in Ireland*, Dublin: Industrial Development Authority 1974
175. O'Hagan, J.W., *The Economy of Ireland, Policy and Performance*, Dublin: Irish Management Institute 1975
176. Ó Huiginn, P., *Regional Development and Industrial Location in Ireland*, Dublin: An Foras Forbartha 1972
177. O'Mahony, D., *The Irish Economy*, Cork: Cork University Press 1962
178. O'Malley, P., *Irish Industry, Structure and Performance*, Dublin: Gill and Macmillan 1971
179. Ó Mathuna, S., 'The Christian Brothers and the Civil Service', *Administration*, III/2–3 (1955)
180. Ó Murchu, E., *Culture and Revolution in Ireland*, Dublin: Repsol, pamphlet 2 (1971)
181. O'Neill, J., 'Departments of Education, Church and State', *Studies*, XXXVIII (Winter 1949)
182. Ó Raitefeartaigh, T., 'Changes and Trends in our Educational System since 1922', *Journal of the Statistical and Social Inquiry Society of Ireland*, XX part II (1958–9)
183. Penniman, H.R., *Ireland at the Polls: The Dail Election of 1977*,

Washington D.C.: American Enterprise Institute 1978
184. Pyne, P., 'The Irish Civil Service', *Administration*, XXIII/1 (1974)
185. Rothery, B., *Men of Enterprise*, Dublin: Institute for Industrial Research and Standards 1976
186. Raven, J., 'Some Results from Pilot Surveys on Attitudes, Values and Perceptions of Socio-Institutional Structures in Ireland', *Economic and Social Review*, IV/4 (1973)
187. Raven, J. *et al.*, *Political Culture in Ireland, the Views of Two Generations*, Dublin: Institute of Public Administration 1976
188. Reason, L., 'Estimates of the Distribution of Non-Agricultural Incomes and Incidence of Certain Taxes', *Journal of the Statistical and Social Inquiry Society of Ireland*, XX part IV (1960–61)
189. *Report of the Committee on the Functions, Operation and Development of a Money Market in Ireland*, Dublin: Bank of Ireland 1968
190. Retail, Grocery, Dairy and Allied Trade Association, Dublin
    Retail News
191. Ross, M., *Personal Income by County*, Dublin: Economic and Social Research Institute, paper 49, 1965
192. Rudd, J., 'Survey of National School Terminal Leavers', *Social Studies*, I/1 (1972)
193. Ryan, L., 'University Education and Social Class in Ireland', *Christus Rex*, II/2 (1966)
194. Ryan, L., 'Social Dynamite, a Study of Early School Leavers', *Christus Rex*, XXI/1 (1967)
195. Ryan, L., 'Irish Seminaries Report', *Social Studies*, II/3 (1973)
196. Sacks, P., 'Bailiwicks, Locality and Religion: Three Elements in the Irish Dáil Constituency', *Economic and Social Review*, I/4 (1970)
197. Sacks, P., *The Donegal Mafia, an Irish Political Machine*, New Haven: Yale University Press 1966
198. Schmitt, D.E., 'Aspects of Irish Social Organisation and Administrative Development', *Administration*, XVIII/4 (1970)
199. Schmitt, D.E., *The Irony of Irish Democracy*, Lexington, Mass: Lexington Books, D.C. Heath 1973
200. Secondary Teachers of Ireland, Association of, Dublin
    The Secondary Teacher
201. Sexton, J., 'Retail Trade in Ireland: A Study of its Structure and an Analysis of Trends over the period 1956–1966', *Journal of the Statistical and Social Inquiry Society of Ireland*, XXII part II (1969–70)
202. Sheehan, M., 'Factors in the Choice of Careers', *Social Studies*, III/1 (1974)
203. Sheehy-Skeffington, F., *Michael Davitt*, London: McGibbon and Kee 1967
204. Sinn Fein (Provisional)
    a) *Eire Nua*, 1971
    b) *Ireland, the Facts*, 1971
    c) O'Bradaigh, R., *Our People, Our Future*, 1974
205. Sinn Fein the Workers' Party, Dublin
    The Irish Industrial Revolution, Repsol 1977
206. Smyth, W., 'The Responsibility of the Civil Servants in Ireland', *Administration*, XXIII/4 (1975)

207. Strauss, E., *Irish Nationalism and British Democracy*, London: Methuen 1951
208. Streib, G., 'Migration and Filial Bonds, *Irish Journal of Agricultural Economics and Rural Sociology*, III/1 (1970)
209. Streib, G., 'Social Stratification in the Republic of Ireland: The Horizontal and the Vertical Mosaic, *Ethnology*, XII/3 (1973)
210. Streib, G., 'The Restoration of the Irish Language: Behavioural and Symbolic Aspects', *Ethnicity*, I/1 (1974)
211. 'Survey of Catholic Clergy and Religion', *Social Studies*, I/1 (1972)
212. Sweeny, J., 'Foreign Companies in Ireland', *Studies*, LXII (Autumn–Winter 1973)
213. Tait, A.A. and Bristow, J.A., *Ireland, Some Problems of a Developing Economy*, Dublin: Gill and Macmillan 1972
214. Thornley, D., *Isaac Butt and Home Rule*, London: McGibbon and Kee 1964
215. Tierney, M., 'What did the Gaelic League Accomplish?' *Studies*, LII (Winter 1963)
216. Toner, J., *Rural Ireland, Some of its Problems*, Dublin: Clonmore and Reynolds 1955
217. Tuama, S., *The Gaelic League Idea*, Cork: Mercier Press 1972
218. Vaizey, J., 'Education and the Irish Economy', *The Irish Journal of Education*, I/2 (1967)
219. Viney, M., *Western Alliance (Report on the Western Development Conference, 1972)*, Tralee: Anvil Books 1973
220. Wall, M., 'The Rise of a Catholic Middle Class in the Eighteenth Century in Ireland', *Irish Historical Studies*, XI/42 (1958)
221. Wallace, J., 'Science Teaching in Irish Schools, 1860–1970', *Irish Journal of Education*, VI/1 (1972)
222. Walsh, B., *Some Irish Population Problems Reconsidered*, Dublin: Economic and Social Research Institute, paper 42, 1968
223. Walsh, B., *Religion and Demographic Behaviour in Ireland*, Dublin: Economic and Social Research Institute, paper 55, 1970
224. Walsh, B., 'Economic and Demographic Adjustment of the Agricultural Labour Force 1961–66', *Irish Journal of Agricultural Economics and Rural Sociology*, III/2 (1970–71)
225. Walsh, B., 'Trends in Age at Marriage in Post-War Marriage', *Demography*, IX/2 (1972)
226. Walsh, B., *Religion and Demographic Behaviour in Ireland*, Dublin: Economic and Social Research Institute, paper 77, 1974
227. Ward, C., *Manpower in a Developing Community*, Dublin: An Roinn Saothair 1967
228. White, J., *Minority Report, the Anatomy of the Southern Irish Protestant*, Dublin: Gill and Macmillan 1975
229. Whyte, J., *Dáil Deputies*, Dublin: Tuairim pamphlet 15, 1966
230. Whyte J., *Church and State in Modern Ireland, 1923–1970*, Dublin: Gill and Macmillan 1971
231. Whyte, J., 'Ireland, Politics without Social Bases', in R. Rose, ed., *Political Behaviour, a Comparative Handbook*, London: Collier-Macmillan 1974
232. Wilson-Davis, K., 'Irish Attitudes to Family Planning', *Social Studies*, III/3 (1974)

Central Statistics Office
233. *Census of Distribution and Services*, 1966
234. *Census of Ireland*, London: H.M. Stationery Office 1881, 1891, 1901, 1911
235. *Census of Population*, 1926, 1936, 1946, 1951, 1956, 1961, 1966, 1971
236. *Household Budget Inquiry*, 1966, 1973
237. *Irish Statistical Bulletin*, quarterly
238. *Statistical Abstract*, yearly
239. *Vital Statistics*, yearly
240. Comhairle na Gaelige
    a) *Language and Community*, 1971
    b) *Towards a Language Policy*, 1971
    c) *Local Government and Development Institutions for the Gaeltacht*, 1971
    d) *Implementing a Language Policy*, 1972
    e) *Irish in Education*, 1974
241. Department of Agriculture and Fisheries
    a) *Annual Report of the Minister for Agriculture and Fisheries*
    b) *Agriculture in the Second Programme for Economic Expansion*, 1964
    c) *Report of the Inter-Departmental Committee on the Problems of Small Western Farms*, 1962
    d) *Report on the Committee on the Review of State Expenditure in Relation to Agriculture*, 1970
    e) Scully, J.J., *Agriculture in the West of Ireland*, 1971
242. Department of Industry and Commerce
    a) *General Report of the Committee on Industrial Progress*, 1973
    b) *Report of Studies into Industrial Concentration and Mergers in Ireland*, 1978
243. Department of Education
    a) Council of Education, *The Functions and Curriculum of the Primary Education*, 1954
    b) Council of Education, *The Curriculum of the Secondary School*, 1961
    c) *Investment in Education*, 1965
    d) *Presentation and Summary of Reports of the Commission on Higher Education, 1960–1967*, 1967
Department of Finance
244. *Economic Development* (The Whitaker Report), 1958
245. *Commission on the Restoration of the Irish Language* (summary in English), 1963
246. Devlin, L., *Report of Public Services Organisation Review Group*, 1969
247. *Budget*, yearly
248. *Report of the Commission on the Status of Women*, 1972
249. *Capital Taxation*, 1974

250. *Company Taxation in Ireland*, 1974
251. *Proposals for a Corporation Tax*, 1974
252. *Research Committee Report on Irish Language Attitudes*, 1975
253. Department of Health and Social Welfare
    a) *Report of the Department of Social Welfare*
    b) *Restructuring the Department of Health, the Separation of Policy and Execution*, 1973

Department of Labour
254. Murphy, C., *Dispute between F.U.E. and Maintenance Craft Unions*, 1969
255. Fogarty, M.P., *Final Report of the Committee on Industrial Relations in the E.S.B.*, 1969
256. Fogarty, M.P., *Report on the Banks Inquiry*, 1971

Department of Lands and Forestry
257. *Report of Irish Land Commissioners*
258. Department of Local Government (Department of the Environment)
    a) *Report of the Department of Local Government*, 1972–6
    b) *Report of the Department of the Environment*
    c) *Report on Pollution Control*, 1977

Department of Posts and Telegraphs
259. *Broadcasting Review Committee Report*, 1974
260. Department of Transport and Power
    a) McKinsey and Co., *Defining the Role of Public Transportation in a Changing Environment*, 1971
    b) *Restructuring the Department of Transport and Power, the Separation of Policy and Execution*, 1974

National Economic and Social Council
261. *Comments on Capital Taxation Proposals*, paper 2, 1974
262. *Regional Policy in Ireland*, paper 4, 1975
263. *Comments on the OECD Report on Manpower Policy in Ireland*, paper 6, 1975
264. *An Approach to Social Policy*, paper 8, 1975
265. *Incomes Distribution, a Preliminary Report*, paper 11, 1975
266. *The Taxation of Farming Profits*, paper 15, 1976
267. *Statistics for Social Policy*, paper 17, 1976
268. *Report on Public Expenditure*, paper 21, 1976
269. *Personal Incomes by County in 1973*, paper 30, 1977
270. Llewellyn, G.E.J., *The Potential for Growth in Irish Tax Revenues*, paper 31, 1977
271. *Universality and Selectivity: Social Services in Ireland*, paper 38, 1978
272. *Rural Areas: Change and Development*, paper 41, 1978

National Industrial Economic Council
273. *Report on Manpower Policy*, paper 3, 1964
274. *Comments on the Report of the Inter-Departmental Committee on Administrative Arrangements for Implementing Manpower Policy*, paper 9, 1965
275. *Report on Full Employment*, paper 19, 1967

National Science Council
276. *Research and Development in Ireland*, 1967, 1974

277. *Science Policy Formulation and Resource Allocation*, 1972
278. *Studies in Irish Science Policy*, 1973
279. *Ireland, Background Report on Science and Technology*, 1972
280. Cooper, C. and Whelan, N., *Science, Technology and Industry in Ireland*, 1973

White Papers (and diverse documents)

281. *Programme for Economic Expansion*, 1958
282. *Direct Taxation*, 1963
283. *Second Programme for Economic Expansion*, 1963
284. *Closing the Gap (Incomes and Output)*, 1963
285. *The Restoration of the Irish Language*, 1965
286. *Progress Reports on the Restoration of the Irish Language*, 1966, 1969
287. *The Accession of Ireland to the European Community*, 1972
288. *A National Partnership*, 1974
289. *Economic and Social Development, 1976–80*, 1976
290. *Economic and Social Development*, 1978
291. *Third Programme for Economic and Social Development, 1969–72*

224

Index

AUTHOR INDEX

225

Messenger, J., 15
Miller, D. W., 89
Mitchell, A., 89
Murphy, G., 152

Nevin, M., 16, 28, 29, 188
Newman, J., 40
Nic Ghiolla Phadraig, M., 151

O'Brien, C. C., 90
O'Cathain, S., 100, 151
O'Connor, S., 148
O'Mathuna, S., 174
O'Muircheartaigh, F. S., 38
O'Neill, T. P., 89
O'Tuama, S., 103

Penniman, H. R., 111

Raven, J., *et al*, 122, 174
Ryan, L., 39, 89

Sacks, P., 127, 128, 129
Schmitt, D. E., 123, 124
Sexton, J., 25
Smyth, W., 174
Somerville and Ross, 9
Streib, G., 14, 102
Sweeny, J., 58

Tait, A. A., 158
Tierney, M., 104
Toner, J., 65

Wall, M., 20
Walsh, B., 14, 21, 22, 28, 31, 37, 38
Ward, C., 45, 181
Whelan, N., 179
Whitaker, T. K., 159
Whyte, J., 119, 190
Wilson-Davis, K., 38

SUBJECT INDEX

227